TALES OF AN ANCIENT GO-GO GIRL

JOAN JOBE SMITH

marJo BOOKS

LONG BEACH, CALIFORNIA

ISBN-13: 978-1502898289 / ISBN-10: 1502898284

Cover Design by Marilyn Johnson
Cover Photo & Photos pp 144 & 284 of "Joanie Gentry"
  by "The Silver Fox," 1967

marJo BOOKS
3030 E 2nd Street
Long Beach, California USA
www.pearlmag.com

I Dedicate These Twelve True Tales of
personal history, adventure, experience
& observation
to
My Incomparable Mentors

HENRY CHARLES BUKOWSKI

and

MARVIN MALONE

and to My Indefatigable Father

AVNER RAY JOBE

and to My Benevolent Listener

FRED VOSS

The Author wishes to thank the editors of the following literary journals in which some of these Tales previously appeared:

Prose: "Der Menchen Horigkeit" ("Of Human Bondage"): *L.A. Woman: Literatur von Los Angeles Ladies,* Ariel-Verlac, Frankfurt, Germany (2000); "The Night After I Helped To Kill A Man": *Chiron Review,* USA (2002); "Amalgamated Bricks": *Ambit,* UK (2003); "Went-Went Girl": *Ambit,* UK (2009); "Les Demoiselles de The Fort": *Ambit,* UK (2010); 13enote's *LADYLAND: Anthologie de Litterature Feminine Americaine,* Paris, France (2014); "Beercan in the Garden": Thunder Mouth: *Drinking with Bukowski,* USA (2001); *Beat Scene,* UK: (2004); *Yearbook of the Charles Bukowski Society,* Germany (2011); 13enote's *Charles Bukowski: Shakespeare N'A Jamais Fait Ça:* "Une Canette de Biére Dans Le Jardin" Paris, France (2012); Silver Birch Press, USA: *Charles Bukowski: Epic Glottis: His Art & His Women (& me),* (2012). Poems: *A Common Thread* (Chance Press, USA), *Beside the City of Angels, Bukowski Boulevard, Georgia Review, How Dirty Girls Get Clean, Nerve Cowboy, Outlaw Bible, Picking the Lock on the Door to Paradise* (Liquid Paper Press, USA), *The Pow Wow Café* (The Poetry Business, UK), *Sequin Soul* (Chance Press), *Wormwood Review:* 105 & 133, *The Giant Book of Poetry* (Level 4 Press, 2014), *Quincunx* (UK, 2014)

Photo: John Densmore & Joan Jobe Smith, p. 281, by Fred Voss

Eternal gratitude to Marilyn Johnson and Michael Hathaway for their extraordinary friendship and expertise—and special thanks to "Laura" and "Brother Ward" for their compassionate corroboration. And: to Charlotte Brontë and her picaresque Jane, *Jane Eyre:* for inspiring my own personal Glotessey: a deep, respectful farthingale-wide curtsy.

4

In 1963

In 1963,
I likened myself to Jacqueline Kennedy.
We both had a daughter and a son
the same age, and we both had lost
our husbands: hers to bullets
and mine to vodka and Vegas.

Although I
wasn't even half as pretty as Jacqueline Kennedy
I tried to do the things I thought she would do:
I never blew my nose in public, I wiped
only the edges of my mouth with my napkin while dining
and never put my elbows on the table and I
read good books and kept my hair perfectly coiffed.

I taught
my children to name the parts
of their faces in French,
dressed my daughter in good clothes,
showed my son to salute when sad
and regretted not naming him John.

And then
Jacqueline Kennedy married the Greek magnate,
I married a manic-depressant,
and then that hippie and things
were never again
so nice and neat.

"If you haven't lived it, it won't come out your horn."
— *Charlie Parker*

Chapter 1 | Amalgamated Bricks

Amalgamated bricks, I thought, for no good reason that very last time my father and I rode in his beige company car station wagon over the Golden Gate Bridge on our way October 24, 1966 to his jobbers he sold traveling salesman automotive paint to in the industrial areas of San Francisco, the clackity-clack dark orange steel girders of the Golden Gate Bridge streaking by looking like tall thin strips piled high, high into the sky, of brick as we sped by in the bright noon sunshine bursting through billowy clouds pinked autumn by equinox and burnt fallen leaves.

"Never a goddamned place to park in this city," my father said that day as he drove around looking for a parking place just like he'd said every day he spent in San Francisco during my whole life of 26 years, the first time 21 years ago. No place to park in San Francisco the reason he and my mother and I would move away, go down south to Los Angeles where he'd buy a no-down-payment G.I. tract home in North Grove where there were plenty of parking spaces.

A scrawny, tall young auto-body man just discharged from World War Two in 1945, my father had to go where there were cars, lots of cars, and wide-open L.A. spaces to park the cars. Tear down those orange and lemon groves, plow up those pepper, corn, tomato and strawberry fields and pour down all the hot asphalt you could find and cold concrete slop to make freeways and parking lots, the biggest slabs of black in the whole wide world for all the cars. Cars my father would bang dents out of, paint cream color, battleship gray, Al Capone getaway sedan shiny black, metallic Robin Hood Green, Lake Tahoe Aquamarine, Sierra Sunset Red, Hollywood Boulevard Pink, gold Cadillac

Coupe de Ville, Buick 69, Studebaker rocket ship, Pontiac, Chrysler, Packard streamline, Nash Rambler, Ford Fairlane and "See the U.S.A.!"—sang southern belle Dinah Shore at 6:30 p.m. on Channel 4 in 1950—"In your Chevrolet!" Cars.

Up till my father'd had his back operation and had to become an automotive paint salesman on the road three out four weeks a month because he couldn't stoop anymore to bang and sand and mask up the cars to paint, my father worked on every make of car made in America of the twentieth century, even Model T's and Model A's, Essexes Oaklands, LaSalles, Tuckers, amalgamated bricks of four-doors, two-doors with bumpers, axles, fenders, rumble seats, running boards, wooden-spoke hubcaps and steering wheels and chrome-toothed grills that were born to laugh at gridlock. Cars.

"Ors," says my father to his first jobber of the day because it was the first parking space he could find, Orson Johnson, the owner of Orson's Paint Supply on High Street in the wholesale district, an-A-bomb-was-just-dropped-here dreary-dead part of town with a view of the Oakland Bay Bridge. "Want you to meet my daughter, Janie Gentry."

My father has startled me by calling me by my married name, saying "Gennn-uh-tree" in his growling, baritonal Texas macho-man voice as if he's cursed me while enunciating the syllables to sound a lot like and rhyme with "enemy"—which his ex-son-in-law, my second husband Mr. Reave Gentry Junior, truly is.

"My, my, my, Ray, you never told me you had such a good looking daughter," says Ors, obliged to say this since I am so dressed up wearing off-white leather gloves, I. Magnin pointy-toed high heels, purse to match on a slinging brass chain and an imitation Oleg Cassini white double-breasted cashmere coat with big brass buttons and underneath a sleeveless white cashmere mini dress purchased last winter when I was a rich go-go girl. I look gussied up enough for opening night at the San Francisco Metropolitan Opera where I could sit on the same row with Jackie Kennedy and she might lean over and ask me where I got my groovy getup. This is the most elegant I will ever dress. Times are a'changin'. The hippies are coming. To declare the most bloody generational war of them all and deplore such finery as white cashmere and brass buttons as Establishmentarian white supremacist ostentatious display.

"Doll up," my father had commanded before we left home 90 miles away in Sacramento where he lived in a tract home with my mother, getting me ready for this outing that was supposed to boost my morale. Although he deplored the mini as cloth corruption worn only by Lolitas, he allowed it that day when he saw me dolled up and said, "Snazzy."

Girls my age, 26 in 1966, were the first generation since the 1920s Flappers who didn't want to dress like their mothers. And mothers in 1966 wanted to look like their daughters, us girls brave enough to defy convention and wear the mini, some hemlines stopping peek-a-boo only an inch below the crotch. In Orson's Paint Supply outpost, my father pats my white cashmered shoulder fondly, proud of me for inspiring Ors's compliment. Shyly, beneath my long bangs, I nod to Ors and try to appear flattered, though modest. I am used to men looking at me; I'm a bit hard; I have been a go-go girl at La Pink Pantera, a rocking go-go bar near Whisky's on the Hollywood Strip, for a year and a half.

Until my "car accident." No doubt my father has not disclosed to Ors my tawdry past as a scantily-clad barmaid because my father was appalled to know of it himself when he found out only last July. This is my first outing since my

9

"car accident," our family euphemism for "What *he*—that no good son of a bitch—did to you." My father thinks this trip to see this beautiful city by the bay will cheer me up, help me "pull" myself "together" as my father's commanded me to do now for nine weeks ever since *he* did what he did to me.

"Ha-ha-ha," my father chuckles to Ors, regarding the "good looking" bit, says with his Texas drawl, "Yep, takes after her ol' pappy," at which Ors and my father have a chuckle duet over the impossibility of me bearing any resemblance whatsoever—though I do, a lot—to my father aged 47 jowly and high fore-headed and sunken-chested from his recent heart attack of September 2nd, Labor Day when, after getting word of what had happened to me, he keeled into my mother's arms and was driven by her to the hospital. Merely a "mild heart problem," my father euphemized "coronary occlusion" to his regional manager lest Bob Shelldrake reassign permanently my father's California Northwest territory to one of the new, younger, stout-hearted men recently hired by the company.

After the chuckles subside, while Ors looks in his enormous storeroom for what he needs to buy from my father this time, my father eyes me warily, inspecting me again to see if there really are any traces of good-lookingness left of me after what I've been through, what that Mr. Gentry, that Amalgamated Bricks did to my face and as he does so I know from the white stark look on his face, can hear him thinking this again: "You should've seen her, Ors, nine weeks ago after that son of a bitch got through with her" and then he lights up an unfiltered cigarette, his second one since giving them up after his heart attack, doctor's orders.

When Ors returns with his order sheet scribbled in many squares that will mean a lucrative month-end

10

commission for my father, my father offers him the camaraderie of an unfiltered cigarette. Ors accepts with the affirmative and fond redeclaration of the old advertising slogan of the 1940s that got my father smoking Luckies to begin with: "Lucky Strike means fine tobacco!" My father chuckles approvingly and, with unanimous acquiescence, they blow smoke into each other's faces while they discuss automotive paint: how good, how much, what color and curse the proliferation of the goddamned Volkswagen Bug which means less paint needed these days by the auto-body shops for my father to sell to Ors to sell to them.

"They should burn every one of those goddamned Nazi foot lockers," growls my father about those "little shit cars that only need half as much paint to cover their pipsqueak asses." My father, in order to heal his heart, should be living life mellow right now wearing his paisley pajamas instead of a brown business suit, white shirt and bow tie. He should be sitting in an easy chair listening to Strauss waltzes with his feet propped up and slippered in his "Romeos," his shiny oxblood soft leather house shoes his mother bought him for Christmas at Sears.

"I'll smoke to that!" says Ors. "In fact, I'll drink to that—" He pulls a brown bottle of whisky from out of his beat-up desk drawer that was once blonde oak and offers some to my father who at first shakes his head then says oh what the hell though he's not supposed to touch liquor, doctor's orders, plus he's losing his breath a little, this first week back on the job making him tired, shoulders bent over, at only 49 minutes past noon.

Shaky from my own feebleness, the strain of this outing and the tight toes of these designer shoes I call my Andy Warhol shoes because he draws the ads for them in all the fashion magazines, I sit down in a beat-up armchair that had been covered with posh, un-torn white Naugahyde in its long-ago prime, probably 1955, and thumb through a 10-year-old *Playboy* magazine showing semi-nude beauties du jour inside wearing spit-curled pixie haircuts like my mother wore back then, thick, dark Audrey Hepburn eyebrows and purplish-red Cutex's "Cherries in the Snow" lipstick like I wore. These glossy old pages showing breasts, little half-moons peek-a-boo white-puff from behind a just-so-placed towel or scarf or umbrella, are as quaintly old-fashioned now as a Flapper's garter-belted kneecap was then when compared to the tough-cookie topless dancers shaking their G-stringed tail feathers that very moment in San Francisco North Beach bistros and smoky dives. How I wished I were one of those simple, sweet sexpots of 1956.

Mr. Amalgamated Bricks, AKA S.O.B., now a fugitive-at-large someplace in Los Angeles, tried to kill me slowly starting with my eyeballs. He quit at my rib cage when he heard the police sirens and ran away into the Echo Park dark night. My face was healing oddly: surprisingly my shattered nose actually smaller than before, my purple-plum-fat eyes still swollen, but the purple-green eyelids rather flattering, giving me a silent film femme fatale look.

An expensive dentist in Beverly Hills had made me big, new front teeth whiter than my own that give me a bimbo-bunny look and the long, blonde wig with the nose-length bangs I now wore to cover bald spots made when *he* dragged me across my living room floor, make me look eyeless, unemotional and vapid. Like Nancy Sinatra Jr., I resembled, said the hairdresser who sold the wig to me for as much as half a used Volkswagen Bug cost in 1966 while she sang, "These boots are made for walkin'."

I won't realize for 35 years what I didn't see that 1966 day because I was only seeing so much of myself, how my father watched me out of the corner of his sunglasses as he wrote down quantities and colors of paint at each jobber we went to, my father smoking Lucky Strike after Lucky Strike as he watched me when his eyes weren't on the road as we drove the streets and hills of San Francisco. He drove me through Haight-Ashbury for laughs. He laughed, I didn't, at the freaky weirdly-dressed hippies wearing ragamuffin and tatterdemalion feathers and flowers, who—cowards that they were—according to my father, were ruining the world as we knew it with their scofflaw and pot and protests. He went to war, goddamn it, why shouldn't those little shits?

"Times are a'changin', Daddy," said I.

"Change, my foot. Excuses, that's what. They're a bunch of spoiled brats those hippies. They didn't have to starve in a Great Depression like I did; they got plenty of jobs. Your generation, little girl, doesn't know how good it's got to be in this prosperous time and place of this old world, how damned lucky." Then my father went quiet, remembering my recent bad luck.

Then my father watched me at lunch of prime rib au jus I barely nibbled at that great steakhouse near Van Ness in downtown San Francisco where, with his fellow sales reps and his district sales manager, Bob Sheldrake, he feasted on greasy and creamy food his doctor told him not to eat—ever again. My father had seen me all broken as cracked china nine weeks ago and that day, all day, he searched for new cracks, wondering, I am sure, the way I would've wondered too when I reached his age the same about my daughter had it happened to her: Would the cracks ever go away?

Five lollygagging sales reps plus one district manager, six-or-seven-martini-stuffed lunchmen, all of them pushing 50 like my father, interjected often between talk of automotive paint their opinions of my appearance: my youth, my health, my opportunities, comparing mine to theirs, prefacing past tense and present with, "When I was your age—" "When you are my age—" That day I thought

13

them a bunch of old fools for not noticing how white, false-blonde and bruised like a low-priced hooker I looked that day or at least the knocked-down ghost of me looked.

During that endless three-hour lunch, while a piano bar played "I Left My Heart In San Francisco" every 10th song and 1940s love songs like "Stardust" the rest of the time, the men got increasingly, happily drunk except for my father who was restless to get back to Sacramento before dark and he got too tired. He was supposed to remain bedridden, doctor's orders for at least three months instead of only the eight weeks he submitted to as miserably and reluctantly as a hot-to-trot racehorse harnessed to a one-horse stall. Slowly, all afternoon, my father sipped one martini, watered down with ice and water to fool his cronies, think him keeping up with them. When the empty, red-circled packs of Lucky Strikes my father and the men had smoked began to polka-dot Daisy Mae peasant top the tablecloth, I excused myself from the smoke, men and "martoonies" — as they'd begun to nickname them fondly, and went outside to walk around the hilly block, glad to breathe in deeply the San Francisco fog I'd loved so much as a little girl, had missed leaving to live in dusty Southern California, just so my father could find a place to park his cars.

Outside, I noticed that nearly every other car that passed by was a Volkswagen Bug, my father's newest nemesis. World War One had deprived my father of a father, the Measles Epidemic of 1919 deprived him of his 20-20 eyesight, then came the Dust Bowl drought of the 1930s that ruined his life, then the Great Depression, World War Two and now, in 1966, the VW Bug, along with the cowardly hippies and my psychopathic ex-husband, were ruining forever my harried father's peace of mind.

I sat on the corner ledge of a bank building where I

could see the sunset orange glowing arches of the Golden Gate Bridge becoming engulfed—as it did nearly every day at this time of day—in lathering eddies of fog swirling in from the Pacific Ocean. Pigeons began to mob me, cooing, as if they knew my name, had a letter for me tucked beneath their wings. I fed them crumbs of my dinner roll, made of that good sourdough San Francisco is so famous for I'd put in my purse because I couldn't bite into it with my big, new front teeth and didn't want my father, nor the other men to see me gnaw on it with my canines like an animal.

More pigeons came waddling, then a hundred of them, making me the most popular human being on the corner of Lombard and Van Ness. With my Nancy Sinatra wig flowing down to my nose and around my shoulders, my face disappearing into the shadows of hair that did not grow from my scalp, if I stood mannequin-still I could pass for a mannequin, a brainless, pose-and-put-where-you-want-her piece of plastic Nowhere Woman. While the rainbow horde of pigeons gobbled and cooed and pooped on the sidewalk, their little minds filled with only thoughts of aviation and sourdough bread crumbs, I wished I were one of them. When I turned to return to the steakhouse, there stood my father on the sidewalk, watching me, his hands limp at his sides, smoke from his burned-down Lucky blowing south by the foggy 'Frisco wind toward L.A. My father tossed the butt into the gutter where he did not notice a pipsqueak VW Bug was parked, its compacted space economy opening up San Francisco streets for others to park, economic epidemic.

That night as soon as we got home to Sacramento my father called long distance, person to-person to the City of Los Angeles California's Chief of Police, at his home. For nine weeks, eight of which he'd been on sick leave from his automotive paint company, my father'd talked, bellowed, actually, two, three, sometimes four times a day to the Chief

15

of Police whom he'd begun to call by his first name: "PETE!"
I heard him bellow for the thousandth time:

"HAVE YOU LOCATED THAT SON OF A BITCH
YET!" my father badgering as only a man's man with a
Texas baritone voice can get away with, then, blowing Lucky
Strike cigarette smoke into the receiver and the police chief's
hypothetical face, my father salved his verbal assault, like
always, with one of his sales rep dirty jokes which the L.A.
City Police Chief had begun to look forward to, actually
made person-to-person calls to my father now friendly-like
just to hear a new one, that night, this not-dirty one: "Hey
Pete, know what the definition of Eternity is?" No. What's
the definition of eternity, Ray? "Two people and a ham."
Police Chief Pete roared with laughter from my father's
conference speaker so I guess Police Chief Pete hated ham as
much as my father did.

After he hung up, my father came to me where I
holed up in his bedroom waiting for bedtime, reading
slowly for nine weeks to make it last that old, 1920-
copyrighted yellowed and musty and rather creepy Darby
and Joan's *Our Unseen Guest* I'd found stuffed behind my
father's book-of-the-month bestsellers on the bottom shelf of
the book case where he kept his sales records and mileage
reports. "Jane, you've GOT to pull yourself together!" my
father demanded. The word "pull" made me feel like a batch
of blobby taffy, that if pulled, would get good and sweet and
palpable.

"Goddamn it, Jane —" my father muttered helplessly.

"Daddy, please leave him alone. Please. If he goes to
prison he'll just get madder at me, get crazier and want to
get even, finish the job. Revenge —"

"Revenge is mine," blasphemed my atheist father
who believed in nothing, not God or Buddha, Jesus nor
anything except self-reliance and hard work.

16

"Karma—" I whimpered.

"Oh, don't go talking that ridiculous hippie crap."

"He'll never leave me alone. He's crazy. He's so unstoppable, so big—"

"The bigger they are, the harder they fall," he said. Then, with fingers with fingernails gnawed to the quick like mine, nervously he combed through his gray-blonde hair (curly like mine beneath my long blonde Nancy Sinatra wig) and sat down on his own bed where I'd lain for nine weeks all day every day with the drapes shut. Nights, he slept there, my mother sleeping in the room across the hall because of his snoring, my three children in the third bedroom while I slept on the beige sofa bed in my parents' beige-walled living room. I took off my wig and threw it on the floor. I could see in the mirror next to his desk the new growth of hair coming in, little wispy fingers on fuzzy hands reaching for the sky. I covered my eyes not to see how silly I looked.

"Jane. Jane. Do you hear me, little girl? You've just GOT to pull yourself together."

When my own hair grew back in clumps of fists, brown and mousy like it'd always been and I could throw away my Nancy Sinatra long, blonde wig that had become quite shoddy from use, I sort of pulled myself together. But not the way my father would have liked me to have done. Of course, his dying of a second heart attack 12 weeks after his first one and only two weeks after the Los Angeles City Police Department found him: Mr. Amalgamated Bricks AKA S.O.B. (hiding in his mother's closet) and incarcerated him didn't help any to make my taffy good.

Nor, on our way to bury my father in San Francisco, driving over the Golden Gate Bridge where he and I had driven only four weeks earlier when, not trying to and for no good reason, I thought: Amalgamated Bricks. That second

17

time adding, unable to stop myself, you know how the mind can play dirty tricks on you, make you think utter nonsense, put stupid words in your mouth at the wrong place and time:

"Lucky Strike means fine tobacco."

Whisky a Go-Go Slo Mo With Jim Morrison

Whisky a Go-Go in 1965 packed in the sin- and in-crowd:
Brando, Warhol, Frank and Mia, me, high in the corner cage
smoke in my eyes as I auditioned to the new band The Doors.
Stupid name said another go-go girl, lead singer named
Jim Morrison always stoned, she said, throat LSD-corroded
croaking "Light my FIE-YARRR!" over and over till blisters
on our dancing feet began to bleed and we got so tired
we had to dance Boogaloo slow motion so I turned down
the Whisky go-go dancer job, walked out the door to my car
dodged my way down Sunset Strip through Sonny and Cher
look-alike wannabes, runaway teen-aged girls, panhandling
hippies, stalled traffic and worried cops, turned right on a
dark street to find my VW Bug parked up a Hollywood hill
a mile away. I cared not about this hipster counterculture,
the yeah-yeah generation outa sight cool cats and chicks
screaming Bummer, man! when narcs busted them for
possession and vagrancy or worse. Went to work at The Fort
a beer bottle's throw from the L.A. Harbor and oil refineries
packed with the working-stiff sin- and in-crowd stevedores,
crazy bikers, sailors, machinists who dive-bombed into
beer pitchers 8 days a week and left greasy screws on my
tip trays instead of dollars that meant the obvious: Screw you,
Babe and on the August night of the 1965 Watts Riots I stood
on the rooftop of The Fort, a tarpaper flat the size of 100
pool tables where guys in the band partied during breaks, I
watched the L.A. sky glow orange neon FIE-YARRR, black
smoke cringe crow-slap moustaches and pierce the sunset
a vanGogh last earthdream. As gunshots cracked and sirens
screamed, I knew right then as I read another indelible page
of an unfolding starry, scary night, that the Book of My Life
would never be titled The Good Old Days. But at least I'd

have slo-mo shadow memories of dancing upon the Whisky
a Go-Go stage with Jim Morrison; and though a dirty dive,
The Fort was close to home–and the parking space was Free.

Chapter 2 | Les Demoiselles de The Fort

At first, after my husband left me July 4, 1965, his own personal Independence Day, for a Playboy Bunny, the rent due, no milk in the refrigerator and I got lucky and got a job at the hottest, rockingest go-go bar in Hollywood, California, I tried to imagine that I was an old-timey ooo-la-la Folies Bergere can-can girl, transformed through time abra-ca-da-bra and voila: my black lace-up boots and lacy pantaloons magic-wanded into black fishnet stockings and shocking pink high heel shoes and leotard. A leotard because I was a deracinated go-go girl in the raw too shy and skinny to wear a shocking pink-fringed bikini like the other go-go girls wore. I'd only worked three weeks and one day (Tuesdays off) and just started wearing a pink-fringed bikini when La Pink Pantera a Go-Go, a beer bottle's throw from Whisky on the Sunset Strip, got shut down by the Alcohol Beverage Commission for 30 days after Cher (not the real one) served beer to a minor who was really an LAPD undercover cop. Owner Sammy Glassman, rumored to have Mafia ties, got all the go-go girls who wanted one a job as a showgirl in Las Vegas. No peripatetic, I had 3 kids, hated the desert, so Sammy got me, lucky me, a job at The Fort.

The Fort. Oh, dear God. As if I hadn't already felt like I'd been dancing in the frying pan, suddenly I was thrown into the fire — wearing shocking pink to match what more of me might get burned. At The Fort I'd find out what a hard day's night really meant. What a dirty dump. The Fort was built to look like one. It had to be. The Fort needed its particular iniquitous den and din fortressed and self-contained to ward off the onslaught inclemencies of the fate of geography surrounding it. Situated on the skuzzy seaside edge of the armpit middle of L.A. County's erewhon no-man's-land, a beer bottle's throw from the wrong side of the Southern Pacific Railroad tracks, foghorn-listening distance from the harbor, naval station and shipyards, a piled-mile-high auto wreckage yard to the west of it, a marine salvage yard crammed full of scuttled olde rust buckets and deep sea diving gear to the east and, to the north, not getting any prettier, five square miles of stinking Boynt Oil Refinery and its Jupiter oil tanks containing inflammables capable of burning all of Los Angeles, California USA alive with only one careless wrist-flick of one lit Bic cigarette lighter. Nope. The Fort was no French concert hall, no matter how hard I closed my eyes, clenched my teeth and tried to imagine the nearby Boynt Oil derrick an Eiffel Tower.

Sitting in the middle of an ocean moat of gravel and dirt they called a parking lot packed with pickups, semis, cement mixers, choppers, rattletraps and other junk heaps used by working men to get them on the job on time, The Fort was fortressed by huge pier pilings that looked like a gone-mad Goliath had grunted sledgehammer into the terra firma non grata. Propped next door above The Fort's roof stood a dry-rotting, rip-faced billboard showing half a giant smiling toothy-mouth toothpaste ad while the other half showed the un-tanned butt of the cutie-pie Coppertone sun tan lotion girl getting—oh my—her bathing suit bottoms tugged down to her knees by her pet puppy. Rephrasing Charles Shultz's Good ol' Charlie Brown motto "Happiness is a warm puppy" was the graffit'd: "Happynis is a warn pussie" [sic].

There at The Fort there would be Norwegian wharf rats the size of wild dogs that would watch me undress in the beer keg and beer glasses storage room doubling as a dressing room, glare at me soundlessly, mute, hunkering, hairy Peeping Toms with their glowing rats' eyes as I removed my street clothes to put on my Pink Pantera-issue shocking pink fringed bikini. And on the bar after I served the men, there would be left instead of tips on my tip trays painted "Janie Gentry" screws that meant the obvious. No, The Fort would not be the Moulin Rouge. No Manet there to paint me forlorn as I stood behind the horseshoe bar sloshing beer, wearing my ratted mousey-blah flip, shocking pink-fringed bikini and black fishnet stockings asking "May I serve you, sir?" to which a quick retort was always: "Cut the crap, kid, and bring me a beer. And make it snappy."

No Toulouse either to capture me Jane Avril while I squealed and kicked up my heels. At The Fort there would be no le cancan or Concert Bal Tous Les Soirs. Not even a twist 'n' shout. A Funky Chicken, a wa-wa-wa-Watusi, Popcorn, Swim or a Temptation Walk; nor a Pony, a James Brown. Only Carlita with her teen-age-made Mexican gang tattoos on her slender brown shoulders, hands and ankles up on the stage in the middle of the one horseshoe bar doing The Dog, the dirtiest dance there'd ever be, a dance outlawed at La Pink Pantera, a dance if a girl caught doing it would get her fired by Sammy Glassman on the spot, arrested, too, for obscenity if a vice officer was in the place. But at The Fort, no vice dared come into the place to see Carlita on her hands and knees swinging her beer-stained purple-fringed bikini'd rump emulating perfectly a rutting dog so close to the grunting drunken guys they could reach out to cop a feel of her tawny skin. True "odious vermin" if I ever saw them, composed of the exact spit and bones and fermentation of the ones Jonathan Swift had in mind when he wrote about them.

And there at The Fort there would be a drunken German sailor who'd twist my wrist thinking I stole his

23

dollar instead of taking it to pay for his beer and the two seven-foot-tall twin dragon bouncers, the Samoan Brothers, wearing hornets'-nest collars of pure meanness who'd grab the drunken German sailor for twisting my wrist and hit him on the head and shoulders with their sawed-off pool sticks and throw him out onto the gravel parking lot shredding his white skin while he hollered to me: "Du verfluchte Hure du!" He'd get even with me—WHORE!—he screamed in English, for stealing his last dollar. And there would be gunshots every night I'd hear as I drove home from The Fort down the dark street. And lumps on the sides of the road I was sure were dead bodies. And worst of all a carload of Mexican boys who waited for me every night six nights in a row at 2:30 a.m. after my night shift and sang "La-la-la-la-la Bamba!" while they followed me in their waddling low-rider Chevy car to my freeway on-ramp and then waved and shouted to me ADIOS PUTA! The Fort was the kind of place you didn't have to call in sick to or tell them you quit. Because when you never came back again or walked out, like I did, the seventh night, in the middle of a shift, they knew exactly WHY.

"Wait! Wait, babe! Whoa, Nellie!" yelled The Fort manager Mick Jakson at me as I tried not to stumble, watched my high-heeled step through the gravel and dirt to my car, ready and set to go home to my kids. Mick grabbed my arm, gently, affectionately. "Baby, please don't go," he begged, a croak of desperation in his throat, as if I were his woman, leaving him with nothing but a fine toothed comb. "The Fort's not as bad as it looks, really."

"Carlita stole all my tips."

"How much? How much? I'll pay you myself. Ten bucks?" He reached into his shiny mustard-colored sharkskin pants and pulled out a wad of money, peeled off a twenty. "Here. Take what you want, need. I really need you.

Take it all." He shoved the wad into my straw tote bag, looked to be about $50. He was a rich kid, had plenty of money, I'd heard, only worked as manager here for fun. Mikhail Jakovitz his real name, scion son and precious spoiled brat only child of the man who owned all the Jak's Muffler Shops all over Los Angeles, now spreading out to Ventura and Orange County. Next to my faded blue VW Bug was parked Mick's shiny silver Porsche his adoring daddy'd bought him. Mick also, I heard, worked here instead of one of the muffler shops to drive his father crazy. I didn't know why people wanted to drive their parents crazy. My father certainly was going to have a tizzy when he found out what I was doing. His face was going to turn red as sunburn next July eleven months from then when he finds out what I am doing for a living and he'll nearly die young of a heart attack right then instead of four months later. But I wasn't doing this to hurt him. Honest, Daddy. The rent was due when my husband left me 4th of July, his personal Independence Day, for his Playboy Bunny. No milk in the refrigerator either.

"The Fort's gonna be packed tonight, baby," Mick told me, all enthused. "The Rivingtons're gonna be here tonight. Booked them myself. You know who they are, don't you? You know that song of theirs 'The Bird'? And their papa oom mow mow—" he imitated, did a little Twist in front of me. He was a very good dancer, like he could play Broadway, had had lessons from Bob Fosse himself. "Pa-pa-pow-pow-pow— Everybody loves those Rivingtons, man. And the place'll be packed. All those rowdy guys, those thugs, man, they leave when the band comes on and the Chicano couples start to dance. Things mellow out when the groovy shit happens, all the cool sounds and swinging around. You know that, how those dudes don't like to cough up when we raise the beer prices when the band comes on."

25

"They don't all leave. The drunk guys, the horseshoe bar regulars stay to watch Carlita. And they don't tip. They just get meaner." So mean they made me cry sometimes at home alone in bed when I got to remembering them.

"Hey, babe, I know The Fort out here in the boondocks doesn't attract the same high-class clientele La Pink Pantera does out there on The Strip, all those aerospace execs and movie moguls and all but they're a bunch of good drinkers, man."

True. They drank from the pitcher at The Fort, day and night from 6 a.m. opening time till 2 a.m. closing time. The Fort crammed with them, stevedores, merchant marines, sailors from every port of the world except Russia, along with bikers, oil field riggers, ditch diggers, construction workers and foremen, machinists, mechanics and any other blue-collared man worked stiff enough to turn mean as sin, all of them in unison as if one big well-oiled stinking army congregated there to drink, drink, drink. Forget about today and yesterday. Get ready for tomorrow to begin again another mean, long, hard sweaty day's night on the face of this mean earth. The Fort was the kind of dive you saw in B movies and film noirs where the bad guys go to hire an assassin. The kind of dirty place where even Genghis and his horde would've been too good for all this and brushed off first with a hanky the wobbly barstools and chairs before they sat down on the sticky. With their backs against the walls. Deracinated, I was an Alice in a weird Wonderland.

"True. They drink from the pitcher."

"Hey, they're just thirsty. They work like dogs."

True. Of all the juke and gin joints from The Lei'd Inn, Daisy Mae's in Gustin, The Playgal Club in Raptures Gardens, Joe's Bar and Grill in downtown Pomona to La Pink Pantera and Whisky a GoGo in Hollywood where I will work as a go-go girl/barmaid/bartender/cocktail waitress for seven years, the length of bad luck for breaking a mirror, the habitues at The Fort of all the seven thousand men I will know all those seven years, will be the most thirsty, miserable, over-worked dogs I will ever know with their stink and drinking justifiers, such as W. C. Fields' old saw: "T'was a woman who drove me to drink and I forgot to thank her." Or the one I heard just an hour ago when Jolly Joe (who was mean as sin) said to Curly (who was bald as a knee): "Curly you're gonna drink yourself to death" and Curly said: "Gotta drink while I'm still alive Jolly Joe cause I can't drink when I'm dead."

"And last night that German sailor twisted my wrist—" I showed Mick my bruised wrist the purple and black of it visible in the last bit of August dog-day sun going down.

"Yeah, yeah, I know. Heard about that Nazi nut. If he comes in again the Samoan Brothers are gonna knock him on his ass." Mick lifted my arm and kissed my bruise. "There, I've made your boo-boo all well. So come on back to work now. Those guys aren't all that bad, not once you get used to them—"

"I don't want to get used to them. I quit. Odious vermin, that's what they are."

"Odious what? What's that?"

"Odious vermin. What Jonathan Swift called guys like them."

"Who's Jonathan Swift?" Mick asked, frowned, looked around, like he had something to hide and somebody was watching. Mick did a lot of drugs, I'd heard, from my go-go girlfriend at Pink Pantera, Linda Alura, in case I really was a narc (Sammy suspected I might be a narc, I was so square) and wanted to bust Mick; she wasn't especially fond of Mick, told me to arrest his ass first, he'd sold her some stinky marijuana recently. He was into speed, in fact sold it

27

if you needed any, the only kindly advice Carlita had given me. I was just learning about "speed." I couldn't figure out why anyone wanted to go any faster than their bodies could carry them. Mick jerked when he moved, so speeded up was he. He looked up nervously at the billboard as if the little Coppertone girl and her puppy there knew all about the evil that lurked within him. He was paranoid. Speed makes you paranoid, I'd been told by Linda Alura. "Hey now, babe. Whoa. What does this Jonathan Swift know about The Fort?"

"Jonathan Swift wrote *Gulliver's Travels*."

"Aw, never saw that movie. Come on, come on back inside—" He shivered with jitters, took my hand in his shaking one, his hand not much bigger than mine and a lot softer because his wasn't covered with calluses like mine from serving hundreds of pitchers of beer to hundreds of men. Mick rubbed his bony knee covered with mustard-colored sharkskin against my bony knee wrapped in fishnet stockings. Joe DiMaggio will touch that very same spot in 1969 when I am a cocktail waitress at a swanky hotel and he orders a cappuccino and I will "x" marks the spot with a dab of pink nail polish. "Come on, you'll make lots of money tonight. Honest. I promise." Mick crossed his heart that beat inside his scrawny, accordion-boned ribcage I could see because his brown linen shirt was unbuttoned and flapped like a flag when he jerked around, posing self-aware as a fashion model to look cute. Mick's blown-dry black shiny pompadour reached for the sky four inches from his scalp and he kept poofing it with his hands to make it higher. I'd never seen before anyone, especially a man, who thought so much of himself, so pleased with himself, so much in love with himself.

I pulled away. "No. I can't work with Carlita. She hates me. She said she was going to kill me. She has a switchblade in her beehive hairdo. She showed it to me."

"Carlita just talks tough. Doesn't mean it, baby. She's just lived a tough life. From East L.A. Thinks that's the way you gotta talk to new girls, keep them from stealing her tips."

"She stole mine."

"She's just bummed. She's got five kids. Her old man's in prison three-to-ten. Soledad, man. That's a bad-ass place, y'know. For something he didn't do. Carlita just gets needy. And she's just pissed off how easy you white chicks got it. You can work any go-go bar you wanna."

I looked at The Fort. The Fort built to look like one. Cigarette and cigar smoke wafted out its front door like steam from a mouth of Hell and swirled up past the billboard's "warn pussie" graffiti into the smoggy Los Angeles August dusky sunset sky to mingle with the pollution that huffed and puffed out the priapic smoke stacks beyond of the stinky Boynt Oil refinery. "Yeah. White chick, me. Aren't I lucky, though?"

"Come on, come on, come on back in." He tugged on the mini skirt of my yellow faux Rudy Gernreich, smiled at me with his perfect, orthodontia'd teeth, finely reliably smooth as ivory piano keys. "Cool duds, babe. I saw Natalie Wood at Pansy's in Hollywood last week wearing an orange Rudy just like this one twistin' the night away with Warren Beatty. You get this at Saks? This made of poplin or polyester? Cool. Groovy get-up. Come on back in, we'll go into my office and smoke a joint, mellow out." He winked at me with a beautiful brown eye with such extraordinarily long lashes that they looked false and looking closer I could see that they were. Then he wrinkled his teeny bobbed nose-jobbed nose at me. He was quite beautiful. Like a woman. "Smoke a joint. How bout it? You and me? Please? Please?" He did the James Brown step across the gravel, scraping white the toes of his shiny oxblood penny loafers he wore without socks. He was like a man on a fuzzy tree, all itchy,

29

couldn't stand still for a moment, shook up. "Puh-leeeeeez?" Then he got down on his knees, held up his hands and imitated James Brown some more and said please, please, please—

I didn't know what a joint was but presumed it was a drug so I said, "I don't do drugs."

"Okay, okay," he got up, tried to stand still, couldn't, began to snap his fingers in time to the jukebox music inside The Fort playing full blast the Stones' "Can't Get No Satisfaction." "And I tried, and I tried—" he sang as he jerked around making me dizzy from his locomotive motion and then said, "Sammy told me you were a square. A nice girl, I mean." Needing something more to do with his hands, Mick pulled me close to him, pushed his pelvis into mine and kissed my cheek. He swiveled his hips, dancerly. "How bout a quickie, then, on my desk in the office?" His office was a musty cubbyhole behind the storage room. His "desk" that held only a telephone and an ashtray was one of the broken cocktail tables with only three legs he sat in front of on a wooden orange crate.

"No. I don't do quickies." I really wasn't sure what a quickie was. I was really a stupid girl. Then.

"Don't do sex. Don't smoke. Don't drink. Don't do drugs. What do you do for fun, babe?" He looked deep into my eyes to find and capture light so's to reflect his own image, see his own self in my irises. He puckered to kiss me.

"No," I said, moving toward my faded blue VW Bug, "I'm going home."

"Come on, babe. I'll pay you 50 cents more an hour. Out of my own pocket. With the Rivingtons here tonight, The Fort's gonna be one rockin' good time. And it's gonna get even better. Next week we got Junior Welles, then Otis Spann's coming, Buddy Guy, Jimmy Smith. Remember his 'High Heel Sneakers'? 'Put on your high heel sneakers—' "

Mick sang in falsetto pretty as any young girl's and dance-stepped on his toes as if he wore stilettos. "Booked them myself, all those Chicago Blues guys. Come on—"

I took out my car key. "No—"

"I'll pay you a dollar more an hour."

"Okay," I said, sold, and went back to work.

And by the time the rockin' good night was over, by the time Mick Jakson called the cops on that German sailor who came back in to get me and they'd hauled him away dragging his feet in the gravel and by the time the Samoan Brothers, a bone ballet, shoved and shouted the crowds out at closing time so we could clean up the mess the hundreds of rockin' good timers had made, Mick Jakson helping by washing all the beer glasses and pitchers, easy for him so speeded up and antsy on amphetamines, by the time the smoke and beer stench had cleared, Carlita Mariaelena Estrada Consuelos and I had discovered that neither of us smoked marijuana nor unfiltered cigarettes, were born on the same day, January 25, 1940. Also, our mothers were both dark-haired beauties and neat and tidy Capricorns and we both had five-year-old sons named "John," hers a Latino "Juan," mine a blue-eyed Irish "Sean."

And around midnight, in the eye of our hurry-cane. she confessed to me, guiltily, those Mexican boys who followed me to the freeway each night were her brothers and cousins she'd told to scare the shit out of me so I'd quit, so afraid she'd been I'd take her job. So sorry. So she would tell them to stop. And, by the end of our night shift, after laughingly nicknaming each other "Warned Pussies," the only girls working at The Fort that totaled record-breaking beer sales that rockin' good time night, Carlita and I would make so much tip money I'd be able in August to pay the rent early for the month of September, and she'd have enough money to retain a new lawyer for an appeal for her

31

innocent husband in Soledad Prison, incarcerated for something he didn't do.

Carlita's and my biological essentials, maternal imperatives, done, done to, and done in. Not to the riotous ooo-la-la-la-la of an Offenbach *Gaîêté parisienne* but to the rockin' good tune of the Rivingtons' "Papa oom mow mow — papa oom mow mow — dit-dit-dit — baba-baba-baba —

"WHOOOO — "

Chapter 3 | A Ticket To Ride

"Damn her, lewd minx! O, damn her!"
— Othello to Desdemona

Getting used to dancing in the fire at The Fort, that stinky hellhole, the next week, on August 12, 1965, unaware that the Los Angeles Watts Riots had begun in the night as I lay sleeping, not knowing that it was an Apocalypse Now, not subscribing to a newspaper, my kids not home watching TV, away on a camping trip in Big Bear with my neighbor Madge and her kids, I went to The Fort to work the night shift as usual. So I had no idea why the freeway was barren of cars, only my faded blue VW Bug put-putting along, did not know why the parking lot of The Fort was empty except for Mick Jakson's silver gray Porsche. At first I thought they'd been shut down too for some alcoholic crime, looked around for a Notice to Close sign tacked up by the Alcohol Beverage Commission Board like the one I'd seen on the door of La Pink Pantera. Nothing. The Fort's door closed but only half-locked, I saw, when I jiggled the handle. Music inside, I heard. Yanking the doorknob, kicking on the door, I finally got it to open, sunset light pouring into the place turning the black empty to sparkling orange-dust glitz. Without the sweaty musky drunken men reeking inside the dank and dark I could smell how awful The Fort stunk all by itself of mildew, dry-rot, urine, beer mold, decomposing murdered corpses maybe — and a Doberman pinscher-sized Norwegian wharf rat in its pear tree.

On the stage in the middle of the horseshoe bar dancing away instead of Carlita Mariaelena Estrada Consuelos was Mick Jakson, the Rolling Stones' "Satisfaction" turned up so loud he'd obviously not heard my commotion outside the door.

33

"And I tried, and I tried—" Mick Jakson sang along with Mick Jagger, huffing and puffing as he danced jerky back-and-forth pelvic thrusts like hippies will do naked in a couple years at love-ins. Smiling, Mick stared at his reflection in the ceiling-to-floor streaky mirrors on the walls facing him, pleased with what he saw, then turned to the right and left to catch sight of more of himself in the mirrors that The Fort's twin bouncers, those goal-post-shouldered seven-foot-tall Samoan Brothers guarded with their canyon-wide bods from barstools being slung into them during barroom brawls, the mirrors us barmaids (no one wasted their breath calling us go-go girls at The Fort) Windexed and scrubbed smoke and spit and beer and bugs off of every night after the bar closed, mirrors on three walls that doubled the size of the place, doubled the maelstromed-amount of miserable men. Seeing The Fort empty of them was a strange surprise, like looking into an empty coffin you've dug up out of its grave. Mick was such a good dancer and I was enjoying his show so, I must've been smiling when he turned and saw me standing there below him watching.

"What the fuck are YOU doing here? And WHY ARE YOU LAUGHING?" he screamed, covering the front of himself as if he were naked. Then, flinging his arms upward like a Nureyev who might fly away, he jumped, landed softly on his feet, a thump barely audible, like that of a cat's from a hot tin roof. He'd had some dancing lessons, that's for sure. And a lot of mirror-watching practice, too, because he craned quickly his chin to look over his shoulder at his backside, see how it looked in the mirror bent like that. Looked great. He had cute, round, firm buttocks like perfect twin angel food cakes. Gracefully, but manly like one of the Jets or Sharks in the movie *West Side Story*, he ran to the jukebox and unplugged the Rolling Stones—BRRRT!—to shriek at me one more time: "What the fuck are YOU doing here?"

"Ta-da. I work here. Remember? Have you hit your head bang on something and suffered amnesia? Why's the door closed and almost locked? Where's the odious vermin? The clientele? All those workingstiff thirsty men? You take some drug and forget to open up today?"

"There's a riot going on. Don't you know? A RIOT, man! In Watts! L.A.'s on fire! They've called out the National Guard!" Mick shook his head in disbelief, all shook up from the enormity of it all, and my stupidity of it. Trembling, he looked like one of those cowards or patsies or innocent men on Death Row going to the electric chair you see in the movies. His pupils were dilated too and sweat glistened all over him as if he were wrapped in cellophane. He'd taken some drug, all right.

"A riot? And you've taken some drug?"

He smiled. "Yeah. You sound like my mother." He said mother to sound like "muh-thuh." I hated how people were pronouncing "mother" in those days. I loved my mother. "What you going to do about it? Call the cops? Give me a spanking?" He was really a spoiled little brat, all right. He bent over, stuck out at me his cute derriere encased in black pants tight as a bullfighter's, then trotted haughtily to the bar and poured himself a beer from the tap, drank half thirstily then said, breathlessly, "Or are you really a narcotics police officer like Sammy Glassman and Linda Alura think you are? Wanna arrest me? Got handcuffs?" He held out his wrists. "For your information, narc, if you are one, LSD is not a drug. It's a legal mind expander." Mick stared up at the dirty ceiling as if his mind expanded up there someplace amongst the cobwebs and rain stains.

"That's why Carlita wants to kill you, you know. Her old man got set up for a bust by a fucking narc."

35

"I wish I were a narcotics officer." I really did. I longed for an ordinary, law-abiding life. A respectable uniform to wear instead of all this fringed bikini garb.

"Well, just in case you are a narc—" Mick reached under the cash register into the dark cubbyhole shelf where cockroaches the size of brass knuckles lived. I knew, because one had crawled up my arm when I looked in there for a flashlight night before last and saw a gun. Mick grabbed that same gun and pointed it at me. "Just don't try anything if you're a narc—Let this be a warning to you if you are—" He bared his teeth like Bogart in *The Maltese Falcon*, then shoved the pistol into the front pocket of his tight black pants, looking like the hard you-know-what he wanted it to resemble. After chugging the rest of the beer, he said to me, sweetly: "You really don't know about the Watts riots?"

"No."

"You stupid or something? How could anyone not know about the riots?"

"I slept all day. I don't subscribe to a newspaper. My kids are gone with a neighbor on a camping trip so I didn't turn on the TV. And I didn't listen to the radio in my car on the way to work because I want some peace and quiet before I get here to this noisy place." I was really getting tired of jukebox music. All those Rolling Stones and rock and roll songs playing over and over for my 9-hour shifts were starting to mind-bust me. And even though the blues guys Mick booked for The Fort were real cool cats and all, they were beginning to get me down, too, with all their songs of sorrow and loss, so much like my own pathetic life I was living in 1965. And The Rivingtons' pa-pa-pow-pow-pow every night now for a whole week was sounding like pie-pan pounding cacophony and reverberated at night when I tried to fall asleep.

"Guess you're not really a narc. A narc would know

about the riots. Come on, I'll show you the riots—" He took my hand. "Fuck, man, the whole fucking world is coming to a fucking end! Wait'll you see—" Mick took my hand, yanking me to lead me across the bar through the askew tables and chairs, across the sticky dance floor, onto the scuffed stage where the Rivingtons had played last night, into the door that led to the hallway that led to the cubbyhole office to the door to a secret staircase that led to the flat, greasy, black-tarred roof of The Fort where guys in the band, the in-crowd, as they called themselves (the "sin crowd" what I called them to myself) hid out to do drugs and drink whisky during breaks and after hours while they sat pow-wow on broken-down old furniture, up-on-the-rooftop flop house decor.

Up there on the roof, "The Penthouse," they called it, the size of 100 pool tables set side by side, a battered old coffee table in the middle of it, strewn with overflowing ashtrays and glasses of half-drunk beer gone black with mold, Mick and I could see for miles north-east-west-south the whole of Los Angeles beyond the southwest wasteland where all the dirty business of a big city took place. This was the pits, the janitorial business, the sludge scrapings off the sewage of all the odious vermin in the county, the mountain-high piles of manure, trash, ash, smashed automobiles, trucks, buses, dead refrigerators, stoves, television sets, railroad cars, maybe some puke and blood and toe jam, too.

The armpits and crotch of Los Angeles, California, USA. And dancing beyond this wild pooh yonder was the fiery fringe of Watts ten miles away, as the buzzards flew, in the distance, burning. Beyond that at Los Angeles's sprawling horizon stood the San Bernardino and San Gabriel Mountains turning purple in the twilight, in front of them a swish-stripe of riotous black smoke like that of a hundred-mile-wide bold and angry Van Gogh brush stroke across the amazingly blue and innocent sky. Over those faraway northeast mountains sprawled the Mojave Desert that gave Los Angeles its sun-shone backlit glow. In the middle of the Mojave basin sprawled Death Valley, that big platter promising mirage of blue water that was really full of dust where, trudging west, countless worn-out god-fearing pioneers couldn't believe their eyes when they saw it, reckoning they'd reached a hell on earth. And for sure they had. To the northwest behind the foothills en route to Pasadena was where I lived four years with my first husband Terence Larrigan, father of Leah and Sean, in Tujunga Canyon. Now, to the southeast in North Grove where I lived as a teenager, permanently disabled from drink, Terence lived a useless, sad life with his mother and stepfather, and would for 25 years.

Thirty years later I will see Jane Fonda on Johnny Carson's Show say how she flew in a jet plane over all this en route to Las Vegas to marry the French movie director Roger Vadim and right then where Mick and I stood on the roof of The Fort, I did see a jet plane crossing overhead in a flight path from LAX, the get-away jet plane glowing mercury from the setting sun as a full moon appeared. A full moon rising like no other, just like every moon ever born is like no other before. That particular full moon, though, the L.A. Watts Riots Moon, and it stared down at us with grand magnificent indifference and self-satisfaction for being as free as a just-let-go helium-puffed balloon, faraway from the maddening, pyromaniacal crowd that was riot-making man.

"Wow! Wow! Just like the burning of Atlanta in *Gone with the Wind!* And this is real! Real! It'd cost a movie studio billions of dollars to set this up! Isn't that something? Isn't that the most beautiful thing you've ever seen? And hear the sound effects? Isn't this FUN?"

Shotguns and rifles and pistols and police and fire and ambulance sirens banged and whined and screamed in the distance as some men, and women too, who weren't really rioting, had nothing to riot about, play-acted rioting, getting in on the "fun," a city running amok the excuse for them to let loose, let it all hang out and do a little or a whole lotta shakin' mayhem.

"Wow—" said Mick, patting his heart to calm its beating, as the hot August 12, 1965, sun finally dropped behind the Pacific Palisades to the west of us and the sky turned royal blue, the horizon turned magenta then blood red, the smoke contributing to one of the most spectacular sunsets I'd ever see. Los Angeles can be so beautiful when it wants to be. Gazing at it there from the roof of The Fort, I couldn't control, though I tried to, the giggle of amazement that rose up in my throat that told me, a part of me I did not yet know, a spark of delinquency latent inside my Goof Girl self, that yes, indeed: Wow, this really IS some kind of FUN.

"Wow—" said Mick, moved by it too just before he turned to me and kissed me on the mouth, the first kiss on the lips I'd had from a man since my gone-away husband, left me on the Fourth of July for his Playboy Bunny. Actually, right then, I couldn't recall him ever kissing me on the lips, though he'd known me since we were 14. I pulled away from Mick. His touching me so much without asking me if he could was starting to get on my nerves.

"Aw, come on. Stop playing hard to get. I know you dig me. I see how you look at me." He pulled my skinny bod close to his skinny bod. He only out-weighed me by about five pounds, if that, and I only weighed 98 pounds. We could've passed for brother and sister except that his nose was smaller than mine and he was prettier than me, the prettiest man in fact I'd ever seen and looking tres French instead of Jewish in a black and white striped boat-neck t-shirt, the kind you could only buy on the French Riviera

39

where he'd obviously been, rich spoiled brat that he was, his rich daddy owning all those Jak's Muffler Shops all over Southern California.

"How about a quickie on my desk? Or on a pool table? We can watch ourselves fuck in the mirror. We'll be the last people on earth to fuck while the world comes to a fucking end." Then he whispered into my ear with the tenderness of a Shakespearean sonnet: "I'm a great fuck, baby. Best you'll ever know. Total sat-is-fack-shun. Fun, fun, fun. I guarantee it."

Again, I pushed him away. Mick staggered a bit. Shook his head. That mind-expanding legal LSD he'd taken was coming on quickly now. "No, thanks, Mick," I said again. "A pool table doesn't sound fun to me. Sorry. I better get home. I didn't know there was a riot going on. I better go home to see if my apartment building's on fire." I walked down the hidden staircase and back into the stinky bar.

"Party pooper," Mick mumbled just as The Fort door rattled, then flung open, flashing sunset through the dank barroom. "Oh, shit!" Mick squeaked like a girl when he saw two huge black men nearly the size of the Samoan Brothers walk in. While they rubbed their eyes to get used to the dark, Mick pulled the pistol out of his pants pocket. "The Fort's closed dudes!" he shrieked. "Get the fuck outa here dudes! Before I shoot your motherfucker asses!"

"'What? What's happening, man?" said one of the black men, huskily fine and mellow. He sounded Texan, like my father. When he finally saw the pistol Mick brandished, he raised his hands over his head. "Hey, man. We cool. We cool. Honest, man. Cool it, man."

"GET OUT A HERE I SAID! NOW!" Mick twirled the pistol in the air like it was a lariat — or a G-string.

"Okay, man. We just come to see the Rivingtons, man. Okay? Put the gun away, okay?"

"LOOTERS! LOOTING MOTHERFUCKERS!"

"Looters? No, man. We paying customers. We just came to see the Rivingtons, man. Pa-pa-pow-pow-pow, man, you know — " He did a little Twist, smiled, friendly.

"The Fort's closed, gentlemen," I said. "There's a riot going on." I pointed in the direction of Los Angeles Watts, California, USA.

"There's a riot going on! And the whole world's coming to a fucking end!" Mick screamed, pointing the gun at one poor confused black man and then the other.

"Riot? We don't know nothing about no riot. We come from Riverside, to see the Rivingtons." Both of them picked up a barstool to shield themselves from possible gunfire.

I walked to the door and held it open for them, strips of sunlight shining in making a path for them. "Come back, gentlemen, when the riots are over," I said calmly. Quickly they backed out through the door, keeping eyes on Mick's gun. Outside: fast shoe tracks on the gravel. Engine of their car roared, gone. Mick laughed, ha, ha, ha. Clicked the gun. It wasn't loaded.

"Oh, ha-ha. Real funny." Somehow I knew he was too puny to be so pushy and brave and unafraid of bullets.

"Ack-shun! Just a little ack-shun. The Fort is a rockin' place!" As soon as he'd tucked the pistol back into the black hole beneath the cash register, its home amongst the demonic cockroaches, Mick started seeing tarantulas crawling on the mirror. Blubbering, he crawled on top of a pool table as if into a baby's crib where he curled into a fetal position and began to scream, his mind expanding, I surmised.

"I'm on fire!" Mick shrieked, writhing in his drug-induced agony, kicking billiard balls that bounced against the green felt rails. I thought briefly about calling for an ambulance to take him away, save his life, but he looked so

41

stupid wallowing there, so willful, so skillful with his choice, and not in any real danger, I left, slammed The Fort door hard, causing it to lock solid, then made fast tracks too on the gravel.

On the barren freeway as I drove home I heard sniper fire ping here and there, one bullet hitting and blowing off the turn-off sign for the street where I lived. Home. Alone. Wow. What do you do on the night a city riots? I watched all the smoke in the sky outside my window for a while, listened to the faraway gunshots. On my hi-fi played my favorite Frank Sinatra LP "... put your head on your pillow, what a lucky pillow," Sinatra sang, making me sleepy enough to get my pillow off my bed, lie down on the aquamarine Naugahyde sofa Terence bought when I was his 18-year-old bride. Now, seven years later, the sofa reeked of old foam rubber stuffing and had holes punched in it caused by the pointy warehouseman's work tally pencils Terence forgot to remove from his back pants pocket when he took long naps there, always depressed, always drunk, always sleepy. Poor Terence, I thought, as I listened to Frank Sinatra croon to me how much he loved me, missed me, had the world on a string, needed one for the road because of me as I lay my head on a lucky pillow.

After midnight, when the rioting noises had subsided somewhat, I was nodding off to sleep when a rattling at the door woke me: A burglar? A Looter? No. Worse: HIM! Jerking his key in the keyhole, seeming to rip it apart: HE entered, a huge black figure, and slammed the door so hard the windows rattled. If my kids'd been home, this would've woken them up in terror. Broad shoulders slung back so his chest stuck out like a barrel, his head jerking side to side, suspicious, as if he searched for enemies, he tilted his aquiline nose, as if to sniff the air for the malodor of phantom assailants. His nose had been broken when he was

42

only six years old, by his father, just home from WW2, Iwo Jima survivor and angry, ever-ready for a fight, who cold-cocked his little son, then punched him in the chest when he cried in pain. "Shut up! Only babies cry! Be a man!" his father roared. When mother Marie tried to comfort her young son, Reave Senior broke her nose, too. His son, Reave Junior, told me this when we were sweet sixteen. Suddenly, I felt sick. Clutching my stomach, I prayed not to vomit.

Blackened by shadows, former high school and junior college varsity football star quarterback, still a graceful athlete, though 30 pounds overweight, resembling a well-fed panther standing erect on its haunches, biped smooth stalker, cat burglar, he walked in like he owned the place. Didn't he realize it was I who paid the rent now? What was he doing here? I'd thought he'd left me for good, for that Playboy Bunny. I'd been so relieved when he left me, glad he was finally done with me, bored with me, disappointed with me for not making him happy. Moonlight illuminating the place, he found his way easily through the kitchen into the living room where I lay on the aquamarine sofa, but, because he was colorblind, he did not see me, the moonlight washing over my salmon-pink pajamas, a color he could not distinguish from white, made me ghostly and invisible, a 5-foot-4 reclining splash of mere illumination. Peanut shells falling off his shoe tops and soles onto the floor, he walked on over them, not caring a bit that he crunched them into messy gravel as he went. Inside the pockets of his baggy red and white Hawaiian shirt were more peanuts, two little lumps of them looking like budding breasts of a pre-teen girl. He stood huge, legs spread apart, human amalgamated bricks, always seeming four inches taller than the six-foot-two he really was because of his thick, black Cherokee hair that stood straight up out of his scalp, reaching for the sky, sometimes two, three hairs rioting out of one follicle.

Standing there in the hot August moonlight, tall and handsome as a movie star, he swung his arms gracefully as if dancing, but aggressively like I'd seen him do when he played football, warding off and forearming offensive opponents on the gridiron; then he swiveled his hips as he twitched around, as if searching for protective teammates but this emulative quarterback squirming made him look just like Elvis Presley in the movie *Viva Las Vegas* doing his Elvis the Pelvis dance, "bright city lights making his soul on fire" this night of the Los Angeles Watts Riots. But he did not smile and act happy like Elvis, he glowered, the moonlight chiaroscuro'ing him ancient light-dark and mythical, making him a mean Elvis, a Jailhouse Rock Elvis about to sing to me "Don't Be Cruel," accuse me of love crimes, too malevolent to be Elvis as he transformed, morphed before my eyes from abused little boy, screwed up teenager, angry young man and now: his eyes rolling so, he was fatal and I feared him: a monster, a Bête Noire and *uxoricidal* and he made me think this, the very first time I'd thought it: Othello. Othello! A Malice in my weird Wonderland, my Deracination Blunderland, Stunnerland, jukebox-noisy Thunderland.

Slurping Pepsi from a king-sized bottle, seeing me at last lying on the sofa, he walked toward me, sat down in his favorite chair, a cavernous dark green swivel rocker next to the aquamarine sofa, chomped more peanuts while he stared up at the ceiling, that same look on his face he wore on our wedding night, that black wolf look, remote but ready to pounce, his eyes dark and fixed on something as faraway as another galaxy beyond our Milky Way. Same bad mood that made me realize that he was an uninhabitable planet when we were only sweet sixteen after he beat up his father, called me from a pay phone to tell me what he'd done, coldly, he told me, a high-pitch tone to his voice, how he'd broken his father's nose.

"S'marvelous," Frank Sinatra had just sung about him: "Too marvelous for words, too very-very to ever be in Webster's dictionary." This man will marvel me for the rest of my life as I try to figure out why he wanted to marry me, made me marry him when I didn't want to, then leave me only 14 months later. My thoughts of him over the decades could fill ten Bibles; what I write about him in woebegotten journals will become rugged Old Testaments.

Rolling his eyes, looking at me, but not looking at me, seeing right through me, his eyes searing my skin, flesh, blood, bones and soul as he leaned so terrifyingly close that I could feel his breath, hot, his head tilted to one side, one-eyed, one-dimensional and strange, he reeked sickeningly of perfume, not his Playboy Bunny's good perfume but a cheap perfume, the same his mother Marie wore that came in a green bottle. At the edge of his lips was a lipstick kiss stain the color of plums, Cutex's "Brandy in the Snow," the color his mother Marie wore. Oh, no, I thought, getting sicker, he knows. He knows all about me, though Marie had promised not to tell him because she knew it would make him mad that I'd done what I'd done. Got a job at that notorious, tawdry go-go bar La Pink Pantera because he'd left me and the rent was due. Slowly, as he turned to face me, looking but not looking at me, with so much hate, my entire torso cramped with pains sharp and deathly as childbirth.

Needing a shave and a haircut, his peanuts all gone, shells all over the beige carpet, exiting his big-man uninhabitable planet made of amalgamated bricks, he said, the first thing he'd said to me since he said "See you later alligator" on 4th of July, 1965, his personal Independence Day, when he walked out with his shaving kit to go to his Playboy Bunny, stuck peanut skins whistling in his craw, Othello growled: "Whore." When I jerked myself out of the moonlight into a sitting position on the sofa, he big-man cold-cocked me, lewd minx, his powerful blow knocking my head back—as easily as it might've a six-year-old child's—onto my pillow propped on the armrest of my worn-out aquamarine sofa. Blood spouted out my nose as he smiled wide and vapid, at the ceiling. Then he looked at me, and demanded to know:

"What's this crap about you working at the Pink Pantera?" Spit from his alliterative "p's" flew into my face. He squeezed hard on my upper arm. "What kind of mother are you?" Muh-thuh, he pronounced it. "Who do you think you are working in a whorehouse like that? Fucking whore!" He grabbed the whole side of my flip hairdo and shook my head till my teeth clacked; fists full of my brown hair fell all around me, and I couldn't think anymore.

Yes, his mother Marie, obviously, had finked on me, though she'd said she'd keep it a secret from her wayward son when she saw him again. She understood. He'd left me. Rent due. No milk in the fridge. Said I had spunk to get a job there at that awful La Pink Pantera. Good girl. Us mothers got to do what we got to do, she cheered on, then wished me good luck. Reave Jr.'ll be back, she promised me just like Reave Sr. came back to her after he left for awhile back in 1946, shell-shocked from World War Two where he got two Purple Hearts, one for surviving Iwo Jima. Another woman, too. Hat check girl. And when Reave Sr. came back and Marie quit her job as a truck stop waitress, they had two more sons and lived happily ever after till he died August, 1963, and they buried him with his two Purple Hearts. Happily ever after, that is, except for those nights Reave Sr. was crazy drunk on beer, vodka and psychosis from thinking about the War and beat her up: fist-blackened her eyes, broke her nose four times, her jaw once.

46

I didn't want Reave Jr. back. I didn't want to marry him in the first place. Blah-blah-blah, he blabbed on and on in an unemotional drone, weird, wired, plugged in, automatic, as if he read this off a script written just for him and this scene. Blah-blah, just like he did on our wedding night. How I'd hoped, en route through the Mojave Desert's eerie and gray sprawl sage that winter, he'd grow bored with the idea of getting married; how I hoped his mania would die down and he'd turn around before we got to Las Vegas. This elopement was his sudden idea when I'd asked him to go away, leave me alone. I was sort of in love with and engaged to be engaged to my real high school sweetheart who wanted to be a cop, a Good Cop. But Reave Jr. would not take No for an answer. He believed what he believed: that we were "meant to be" and that I "belonged to him."

"Tears of joy!" he shouted to the heavens when he saw tears streaming down my face during our wedding ceremony at the Unitarian Church across the street from the Las Vegas City Hall; the minister of the Lord, startled by rave, fell against a basket of plastic gladioli. The Polaroid someone took of us showed how my face glistened as if I wore a cellophane mask but was really wet with tears. Later in the lounge of the Thunderbird Hotel, Reave Jr. gave Fats Domino a dollar to sing "Don't Be Cruel" — "Our Song." I didn't know we had one. Fats Domino wouldn't sing it, said in the microphone, real loud, rather snide, very cool, "Some cat out there wants me to do Elvis. But Elvis don't do ol' Fats and ol' Fats don't do Elvis." Fats Domino sang "Blueberry Hill" instead, had a waiter take the dollar back to Reave Jr. And it was all my fault. Blah-blah-blah, he went on and on, sipping a scotch and water while saying things I willed my ears to not hear. If I didn't hear them, I would never repeat them to anyone. And if you don't think of it, it'll go away. No one would ever want to hear re-runs of his blah-blah-blah, pa-pa-pow-pow-pow thrills on Blueberry Hill as he shoved me, shook me, shouting at me till sunrise of February 15, 1964, Wedding Night over, done, done in, done to. And now it was August 13, 1965, post-midnight of the Los Angeles Watts Riots and he was doing it again. Pa-pow:

"Where's Maureen? Where's my daughter?" he wanted to know as he stomped off toward our bedroom where she normally slept in her bassinette, still small enough at eight months old to do so since she'd been a preemie, now barely weighing ten pounds. He'd not seen her since he'd left, seven weeks ago. She could walk now, sweet little bitty thing that she was. Dear God, he was really going to be angry when he saw her gone. I tiptoed to the door in the kitchen, was just reaching for my straw tote bag containing my car keys when he jerked the back of my hair and threw me across the kitchen to the living room to land upon the aquamarine sofa paid for by my first husband.

"Where's my daughter!" my second husband yelled, furiously.

"On a camping trip in Big Bear with my friend Madge and her husband Marty and their kids—" My kids and theirs loved each other. Little Maureen adored Madge who babysat while I worked in notorious, tawdry, and awful places: La Pink Pantera and now The Fort.

"Got her pawned off on some neighbor, huh, so you can fuck around?" He looked at me, the August 13 full moon shining on me helping him see me, moonlighting me so he could zero right in on the bruise on my arm and wrist the German sailor had caused two nights ago when he twisted it. Othello yanked up my arm to show me the big purple and green bloody blob of it, as if I didn't know the secret of it. Just like the blob he'd put there on our 1964 Valentine's wedding night when he twisted my wrists, grabbing me so I couldn't get away, catch a taxi, then a plane, go home, get our awful

48

marriage annulled. I *never* felt that I belonged to him.

"What's this? Bruises, huh? You got a boyfriend already, huh? I'm gone a month and you're already fucking around, shop-worn whore. Damaged goods. Bruised as an old banana."

Many times during the years of my life when people say cigarettes are bad for you I will say, seriously, meaning it: "A cigarette once saved my life."

Oh, yeah? How's that? they'll ask, thinking I'm kidding. And I will tell this:

When Othello said to me, the night of the 1965 Los Angeles Watts Riots: "You don't deserve to live anymore, whore. I am the hammer and you are the little nail—" I interrupted him to ask him for a cigarette.

"Huh? You don't smoke," he said.

And I said, lying: "I do now, now that I'm a go-go girl. And I could really use a cigarette," I said. When I showed him hands, shaking from terror, feigning them instead to be nicotine-needy, Othello smiled the first smile he'd given me in months and tossed me one of his cigarettes from a pack in his pocket next to the last peanut, gladly, glad to have me on board the Lung Cancer Express, then put one in his own mouth to light up. (You know how people with vices like it when you share their vices with them.) A flash of August 13, 1965, full moon reflecting through my living room drapes turned his aquiline-nosed Cherokee face, black silhouette, handsome fearsome, as he took his first long puff and I stood up, said, blithely: "Thanks," and put the smelly cig he'd given me in the corner of my mouth, tough chick, then walked cool and calm toward the kitchen where next to the front door on Maureen's high chair lay my straw tote bag containing my car keys for me to go-go-GO, miles to go: *Now.*

"Where the hell do you think you're going?" Othello demanded to know.

"To light my cigarette on the stove."

Perfectly okay to Othello who wouldn't've lit a woman's cigarette in a million years with the cheap lighter he'd just tucked back into his red and white Hawaiian shirt pocket. Had Othello been a polite gent, I could not have gotten away with my great escape, barefoot, wearing my salmon pink pajamas, zip quick as a little brown fox down the apartment complex's stone stairs, out to the alley and garage where my getaway car awaited. Because I caught him unaware, because Othello was 30 pounds overweight, lazy and out of shape, when he ran after me, he stopped, wheezing and out of breath. My getaway was as bad as anything would ever get, I thought, as my heart beat lucky me, lucky me, as I backed my car out screeching and drove fast to the only phone booth I could find at the only gas station still open five miles away where I called the police, told them breathlessly, my heart pounding, my nose bleeding all over my pajamas, what happened. But, because Othello was not a real danger to me because he was merely a white man that Watts Riots night and of "no foreseeable threat" to society at large, merely a jealous husband, the police wouldn't come.

"Kiss and make up, ma'am," was the sergeant's curt advice before he hung up.

So I slept in the backseat of my faded blue VW Bug parked in an alley a few blocks from where I lived. Just before sunrise the morning after the Riots, smoke clearing, ash falling black rain upon the streets and sidewalks of Los Angeles and the windshield of my car, a group of white boys woke me up when one of them thumped a baseball bat against the rear tire, loosening the hubcap, clang, as I hovered, pretending to be a heap of nothing beneath a patchwork quilt I kept in the back of the car for trips to the beach.

50

"Let's break the window, see what's underneath that blanket—"

"Naw," said the wiser of the vandals, the ringleader perhaps. "It'll make too much noise and besides, owners of these little Nazi foot lockers don't ever own anything worth anything. Hey, over there, a Cadillac—" They shuffled away, crunching gravel alley debris as I peeked out to see them steal much better hubcaps than I owned. I waited for the sun to rise on the dirty post-Watts Riots Los Angeles, California USA, so I could sneak back home and see if Othello was gone for good.

As dawn's early light painted gray-scape on what would be another scorched-blue August day, I planned another great escape: That afternoon I'd quit The Fort, go back to the Sunset Strip and La Pink Pantera where the men weren't so crazy, pack up all our stuff, call Big Don Maraschino, La Pink Pantera's biggest bouncer and his surfing buddy, bushy-blonde Sonny Buoy, and give them each $10 to move me to some place Othello wouldn't know about.

When new day dawned its pale yellow-bright, I thought again how lucky I was to've gotten away, unharmed except for a bloody nose that wasn't broken; luckier, though, not to have known that that night had just been the first time. Worst times were ahead. A year and four days from then, on August 16, 1966, I would run the wrong way and Othello would get me. Right then, however, still becoming, still crystallizing my latent knowledge, buoyed with hope that all would be okay as I folded up neatly the patchwork quilt my grandmother made me when I was eight, I thought, blithely, about time and place. How crazy it all was what Los Angeles was doing to itself in this time and place.

And I thought about Fate of Geography, how we're dumped in places we don't ask to be to ride on chronological trains taking us to destinations we often do not choose. A

51

pleasure trip for some, a rough road for others where some of us along the way must dance in frying pans and fire.

At least the ticket to ride was free.

Lucky me.

Sergeant Pepper's Lonely Hearts Club Band

It's hard to believe today how bellybuttons
once drove men crazy in 1965, bellybuttons
the raison d'etre, original sin of go-go bars
when French bikinis were still banned on
California state beaches and American TV
and I wouldn't wear a bikini at first,
wore leotards or costumes showing just a
bit of midriff, the go-go beer bar bosses not caring,
a shy new girl give the place class, but it
drove the guys crazy, one guy one day offering me
$20 to show him my bellybutton and I told him
no, I don't have one, but he didn't believe me.
I'm a Martian, I told him, but he didn't believe
that either, he just got drunker and drunker
and yelled at me all afternoon, Hey, baby,
lemme see yer bellybutton, but I kept saying No.
It's all so silly nowadays.
I sure could've used that $20 then.
I still could.

Chapter 4 | Of Human Bondage

"Though I've a chorus of beaux/Stockings are porous
with hole at the toes/I'm here till closing time/
Dance and be merry, it's only a dime ..."
— "Ten Cents a Dance" by
Richard Rodgers & Lorenz Hart, 1932

Big Don Maraschino, La Pink Pantera's hot stuff six-foot-five, 200-pound bouncer, the only man I think I will ever love and the prettiest man I've ever seen, though he knows I desperately need him to be my bodyguard, is leaving this very moment, 3:16 p.m., June 6, 1966, for the 30th Annual Radish Festival in Wahoo, Texas. Wahoo, Texas! A zillion miles away from California and La Pink Pantera, a go-go joint on the Sunset Strip a Styrofoam cup's throw from Whisky a Go-Go where I've worked for nearly a year, no longer a go-go girl in the raw, and now stand in the parking lot in the warm California sunshine. What a tart I am, half-naked, en costume, out in public like that wearing my shocking pink-fringed go-go girl bikini, fishnet stockings, and shocking pink stiletto high heels sinking, stuck, in the sticky parking lot's asphalt ooze. Impaled poor butterfly, I'm shocked pink with fluster as Va-room! Big Don revs his 1959 aquamarine Chevy Impala's souped-up engine to go, GO. A zillion miles to GO. Now!

So upset was I when Big Don suddenly announced to me his unexpected departure from Hollywood for Texas, said Goodbye and walked out of the Pink Pantera as I stood at the front bar pouring pitchers of beer into glasses for Stew and his four aerospace exec cronies, I couldn't help myself for chasing after him, just plopped down the pitchers, splashing foam all over the vest of Stew's Richard Nixon navy blue pin-striped suit, and ran out of the place, not caring if I was half-naked wearing that bellybutton-baring bikini still, in 1966, outlawed on California state beaches and a crime of obscenity if seen on Sunset Strip like this in broad daylight. If I didn't have three kids at home waiting me for, I'd jump into the front seat of Big Don's car and demand he take me with him to Wahoo, Texas, and the 30th Annual Radish Festival. I don't care where he's headed, if Wahoo, Texas's really where he's going, that is, I love him (at least I think I do in 1966).

Most of all: I need him to be my bodyguard: he's the only man I know bigger than Othello. I have a sneaking suspicion Big Don's a lying coward and running out on me and his promise to be my bodyguard, protect me against Othello who's found where I live again (his mother telling him after she'd promised to keep my whereabouts secret), started spying on me, threatening me since March after his Playboy Bunny kicked him out.

"Gotta go, now, Baby Jane, the radishes of Wahoo, Texas await! Gimme a kiss—" Big Don revs his engine again, smoke from his exhaust pipes cloud up the parking lot first row rainbow harem of all the day shift Pink Pantera go-go girls' multi-colored new 1966 Mustangs: the purple Mustang of Cher (not the real one), Suzi Q's white Mustang, Robin's yellow one, Linda Alura's avocado green, Patti's orange, and Brandi Blue's is aquamarine and white like Big Don's 1959 Chevy Impala with its twin marlin-finned fenders and grinning stainless steel grill, a 15-foot-long leering sultan where La Pink Pantera's owner Sammy Glassman's shocking pink Cadillac Coupe de Ville would be parked if he wasn't in Las Vegas trying to get Linda Alura, my best go-go girlfriend, to marry him.

I am the only go-go girl in the whole world who doesn't own a new '66 Mustang. Though I've been "rich" since I've been a go-go girl, make three times what a secretary or schoolteacher makes in 1966 (and twice what a Playboy Bunny does serving cocktails at the Playboy Club a mile down the street because Sammy Glassman, though a get-rich-quick businessman, isn't greedy, doesn't tax our tips or deduct ten percent from our minimum wage to pay "The House" like Hugh Hefner does), I can't afford a new Mustang because I've got the most kids, three, of any go-go girl I know. You dirty rat, I want to say to Big Don but say instead: "I'll miss you—" and lean to kiss his soft, dark lips. "I, I—" I almost tell him I love him but don't.

Every go-go girl that summer of 1966 within a five-mile radius of the Strip's girlie bars and topless joints Big Don frequents day and night loves him. And not just for the usual reasons young silly women love young silly men like Big Don because he is tall, dark and handsome, a good dancer and buffed from lifting beer kegs and doing other go-fer/bouncer stuff at La Pink Pantera. But also because Big Don is kind. Neat. And clean. And most important: Big Don smiles big white teeth he brushes three times a day, and all the time holds out his big arms, gesticulating gusto Italian and proclaims: "I LOVE WOMEN!"

These young women, my honkytonk sisters: the avaricious sexpot topless dancers and the beer-drenched shocking pink-fringed serving-wench wind-up dancing dolls like me, eight-days-a-week go-go girls who love him back, do so in spite of his honest dislike of honest work, his fondness for illicit drugs, viz marijuana and "Mother's Little Helpers" the Rolling Stones sing about. "Yellows" they're also called in 1966, and, called "Dolls" by writer Jacqueline Susann in her book *Valley of the Dolls*. "Nembutol" the pharmacist types on the bottle if you have a doctor's prescription for them and just about everybody does. Eight to ten of Yellows a day are what give Big Don that dreamy, eyelid-droopy, slow-motion ballerino dreamboat look and also what give Big Don the inability and lack of desire to initiate and complete the act of sexual intercourse with even the cutest, most voluptuous of go-go girls which does not include 98-pound Me. I've only heard rumor of this from the other go-go girls. I've been celibate for 11 months, ever since Fourth of July, 1965, Othello's personal Independence Day when he packed his shaving gear and his favorite red Hawaiian shirt and left me after only 17 months of marriage for a Playboy Bunny.

I touch Big Don's big hand, his opal birthstone ring he often twists around to look like a wedding band so girls he doesn't think cute will think he's married. Tenderly he pushes aside my long brown bangs and kisses my forehead as I whine: "Please don't go, Big Don. I need you so. To be my bodyguard."

"Sorry baby, gotta go—" Va-room goes Big Don's big car as he reaches inside the glove compartment for eyeglasses he needs for driving, ones like Malcolm X's, puts them on, looks s o intelligent in them I ask him:

"Are you a poet?" I hope to marry a poet one day.

"As a matter of fact I am a poet. Wrote a poem in high school that even got published in the school paper. And I still remember it: 'Roses are red, violets are blue. If your feet stink, wash your tennis shoes.'" Ha-ha, ha-ha he laughs, showing handsome teeth that smell of peppermint toothpaste.

I've slept with Big Don, though no one knows, not even my best go-go girlfriend Linda Alura. And sleeping with Big Don is plenty. Far more comforting than mere sexual satisfaction that sweet-smelling bod of his next to me. The nights he agrees to be my bodyguard for ten dollars a night, is like owning my own Hawaiian Island for the night after first—he makes a point of doing this, but it never gets old the five times he's done this to me—he lifts me like Scarlett O'Hara into his big arms like he's my Rhett Butler.

57

Yes, it's corny. Big Don is very corny, but I don't know this yet. Or, if I do, I don't care. Thus, a Sequoia morphed into man he carries you off to bed. Your own bed. Because Big Don still lives at home with his parents who spoil the hell out of him. They like the looks and smell of him too, I suppose.

The Beach Boys's "California Girls" plays full blast on Big Don's radio. Their falsettos boom in my ears as I lean one more time into the window to kiss Big Don goodbye and smell his good, Saks Fifth Avenue lemony aftershave one more time. Texas. The only man I'll ever love's going to Texas, so he says. My silly young lips quiver against the smooth skin silk of his close, clean shave. The Beach Boys don't sing about Texas Girls. Doesn't Big Don realize, doesn't he believe the Beach Boys? That every young man in 1966 wishes ALL girls could be California Girls? Like me? (I was born in Paris, Texas feet first during a Norther but Big Don doesn't know that. After all, I've been a California girl since I was six weeks old.) Brian Wilson has even said that "all teenagers want to go to California when they die. For the surf and the girls."

Look at me, Big Don! I want to say. I'm one of the girls you love! A California Girl in the flesh who just came running to kiss him goodbye en costume out of La Pink Pantera where I work the day shift eight days a week half-naked. Half-naked tarty girls like me in broad daylight like this in 1966 when even mini-skirts are banned in Los Angeles eateries—just last week Ann-Margret denied entry to the Brown Derby—I'm defying not just city, county and state ordinances but Alcoholic Beverage Commission regulations and La Pink Pantera house rules to boot. Owner Sammy Glassman thinks I'm a nice girl, have "class" because I'm a square, don't do drugs or use dirty words, but he'd fire me in a minute if he saw me out here in broad daylight breaking the law because the city's looking for any reason they can to close down this place ever since The Shooting.

Big Don pulls away from my pitiful kiss and fluffs the stiff hair-sprayed flip of my big hairdo, one of the biggest next to Ann-Margret's or Natalie Wood's in town. "What a change, huh?" he asks. "When I first met you last July you were such a little square wearing that housewife frump bubble hairdo like Doris Day wears."

"You carried me over the threshold—" He actually did; something neither of my two husbands even did. Big Don saw me confused, wandering around unable to see in the neon-uterine miasma inside La Pink Pantera, It takes a long time for your eyes coming in from daylight to get used to first the darth of the dark and then the shock of the bright shocking pink inside.

"Need a job, babe?" Big Don asked, knowing from experience that I did because no woman alone, unless desperate for a job, willing to do anything for a job, had nerve to walk into this notorious place of taint. Then he heroically rescued me, picked me up in his arms and carried me through the stinking shocking pink barroom packed with about 200 noisy drinking men, through the grease-gray kitchen, down the black cobwebbed hallway in the back to the posh royal blue carpeted office where owner Sammy Glassman sat wearing a star sapphire pinky ring that matched his shimmering blue Italian-made silk suit. Sammy counted piles of money, getting richer every day off this go-go girl thing. Twenty years from then men like him will think of how to make even more money off the boobs and buns of young cuties when they invent mud wrestling, cream and oil wrestling, Gentlemen's Clubs, pole dancing and lap dancing and make the pretty women pay THEM to work for them—odious vermin.

"Don't go. I need you—" I say again, in 1966, drearily.

"Sorry, babe, about not being your bodyguard like I

said I would, hanging you up like this but I gotta go. Meeting with some important dudes at that radish festival who're gonna make me a rich man. Know what I mean?" He winks; letting me in on the dangerous criminality, bound to be drug-related, of his mission. "Sonny Buoy said he'd stay with you a couple nights while I'm away."

Sonny Buoy. Ha. That little jerk. I don't say this aloud, though, because Sonny Buoy and Big Don are very good friends. In fact, Sonny Buoy's looking out the back door at us right now, a look on his face so sad, it looks like he's weeping. He'll miss Big Don as much as me. What good would that scrawny surfer boy do to protect me if Othello came around again? Othello's threatened to kill me with his bare hands. With Big Don leaving town, I'm as good as dead.

"I'm the Big Hammer—" Othello informed me again, growling his words, on the telephone last week at two a.m., "—and you, Jane, you're the Little Nail."

When I told Marie I was afraid of Othello, how he'd actually threatened to kill me, I thought she'd remember how it'd once been with her and Reave Sr. before Reave died just three years ago. Maybe she'd had to run for her life, too, once or twice the 26 years they were married. But all she said about my plight was: "Oh, Reave Jr. just loves you, sweetie."

"How can someone love you when he wants to kill you?" I asked my mother-in-law.

"Oh, that's just how some men are. If he didn't love you, he wouldn't've married you, would he? And you had two kids already, already been married before. See how much he loved you? And you loved him too."

No, I didn't.

"If you'd stop working in those nasty go-go places, you know, Reave Jr. wouldn't be so mad at you."

"But I can't get any other job. I can't type."

60

Even the police department didn't care when I tried to file a complaint for assault after that night Othello chased me: "A woman, a dog and a walnut tree—" said the old balding cop in Homicide, then, his startling punch line: "the more you beat 'em the better they be." Ha-ha, he laughed, along with another cop leaning against the wall.

"But he's spying on me, following me, calls me at two in the morning."

"If he's following you, stop streetwalking."

"He's threatened to kill me. With his bare hands."

"Maybe he's got a good reason—" the leaning one said, then tapped my complaint form where the other cop had written in my Place of Employment: La Pink Pantera. Go-go bars, even the ones that weren't topless, didn't have a very good reputation in 1966. And neither did us go-go girls. All because of bellybuttons. That would be the first time I'd realize the importance, if not necessity, of a damsel-in-distress being "nice." Respectable and respected. And that the priority of her rescue, the IF of it, was determined by her place in polite society.

Everyone had advice for me. Sammy offered to get me a gun. Linda Alura gave me $50 to hire Big Don for my bodyguard. Couldn't ask my father for help; he and my mother moved to Sacramento 500 miles away for my father to take a new job as a regional manager of an automotive paint company. Plus I was too ashamed to tell them Othello left me nearly a year ago, that I've failed again to make a husband happy. Worse: I was too ashamed to tell them that now I was a harlot, a half-naked go-go girl.

"I'm good as dead if you go," I whine to Big Don.

"Aw, I'll be back before you know it. Gotta split!" Big Don shouts to be heard over the Beach Boys's conclusion: "Wish they all could be California gur-rrrrrrllllllzzzz": "Bye-bye, baby!" he shouts. "Bye-bye!"

61

"You'll write me, won't you?" I beg of Big Don.

"Yeah, sure. Would you believe three times a day?" Gently he pinches my chin into a dimple I didn't have there, letting me know he thought I'd look cuter if I had one. "Aw, baby, don't look so sad. Cheer up. It'll all come out in the wash, you'll see. You cute chicks becoming go-go girls drives your boyfriends and exes crazy. You go-go girls know where it's at, man, you're the action here on the Strip, man, and all the guys know it, man, and they gotta have you. Shit, man, I wish I could be a go-go girl for a day, man, I'd be rich. I wouldn't have to go to Wahoo, Texas. You go-go girls are the groovingest."

I wasn't groovy. I was terrified. Nothing but an Eek Girl in constant peril, as well as an eke girl constantly in need of rent money like they told me when I was a little girl I'd always be, an Olive Oyl or Lois Lane, unable to get myself out of a jam — and there'd be lots of jams — without the help of Popeye gulping spinach to come gallop to my rescue, or Superman. Where were my rescuers they promised me when I was a little girl? Is that Man of Steel still inside his phone booth, straightening his cape?

"Look how groovy you are—" He points at a bunch of women, the H.A.D.I.T.S., they'd valiantly acronym'd their movement: the had-it-up-to-here Housewives of Los Angeles County: "Housewives Against Decadence In This Society." Across the other side of Sunset Boulevard, a vigilante gaggle of twenty of them wearing freshly-ironed full-skirted house dresses and 2-inch high heels picketed a new topless go-go bar, trying to close them down like they were trying to do La Pink Pantera a year ago till Sammy Glassman paid the proper graft to the right city officials. How I wished I were one of them, a housewife housed safely, *sans* decadence, in polite suburban society. Married to a cop. A Good Cop, maybe that nice guy I was once engaged to be engaged to.

"See?" says Big Don, pointing at the put-out, pouting housewives. "People can't keep their eyes off you—" The irate women all point en tandem their picket signs at me for baring my bellybutton like this in broad daylight. One woman screaming in a phone booth outside a Boynt Oil gas station is probably calling the police to have me arrested for indecency and obscenity.

"Those women want to stone me, they think me a harlot," I say, telling the truth.

"Yeah, babe, because they can't BE you."

"If they only knew that being a go-go girl wasn't as much fun as it looks." I think about waving a friendly Hello to them, a peace sign of truce, but don't.

"Well, baby, it's a dirty job, all right, but somebody's gotta do it—" Big Don laughs at his own cliché go-go girl joke, a dumb joke you can hear just about every night on TV. He pats my hand clinging to his shirtsleeve, pats it away, swats it, in fact, as if it's a pesky wasp. "Your old man just loves you. He isn't really gonna harm you. Guys talk bad shit when they're crazy with jealousy. See what that one crazy dude did?" He points to the bullet hole that's never been fixed in La Pink Pantera's door. The reason for the bullet hole, the love triangle scandal that led subsequently to The Shooting, is what's made the place so infamously tawdry. Sammy Glassman has never had the hole caulked up and painted because he likes the notoriety.

"After that dude a year ago shot at the dude his old lady was letting it all hang out for yacking over the front bar, she came running back home and they had another kid. Happy ever after. The same'll happen to you, Baby Jane. Lemme prove it—"

He gets out of his car, the engine running, and takes my hand to eyeball my palm. "My great grandmother

63

Sophia taught me to read palms. See this long life-line you got?" A deep-etched wrinkle stretches all the way across my palm like the California San Andreas Fault that might break any minute: plop: half my hand gone: pinky finger: San Diego; ring finger: L.A.; middle Santa Barbara, index San Francisco, thumb Eureka and plop all of California into the Pacific Ocean of La Pink Pantera's parking lot right there in the hot June asphalt next to my shocking pink high heel shoes stuck in black tar ooze.

"Look at that incredible lifeline, baby, longest one I ever saw. I knew you'd have one like that. You gotta small nose. Small noses live a long time. Hell, you're gonna live to be 300! The oldest woman alive! News reporters will come around to ask how you got to be so old and ancient and when they do, you can just show them this long-long lifeline you got!" But Big Don frowns. "Uh oh—You gotta lotta cross-lines through it, though." He tickles my palm with his well-manicured fingernail to show me where: they look like little scars from a toothpick switchblade. "You're gonna have a few rough patches, a few knocks on the old noggin, cracks on the cranium—" Big Don tosses my cross-lined palm back to me.

"Wow, aren't I lucky?" I say sarcastically, glowering at my pitiful palm foreboding Doom.

"Aw, but you'll pull through. You're a tough cookie, baby. A go-go girl! Shake it for me one more time, baby—" Big Don puts his hands on my hips and wiggles them a hula, backs off and does a solo wa-wa-Watusi, showing me what a better go-go girl he is than me. This is the closest I will ever get to partaking in an orgy. Smiling at me smiling at him, loving to be looked at, appreciated for being so pretty, Big Don takes me into his big strong arms and swings me around like a bundle of family dog.

"I LOVE YA!" he exclaims, making my hair stand on end, my face pink with pleasure to be touched by him. "God,

I LOVE WOMEN!" he declares. Then he jumps back into his Chevy, zooms away, and with the San Diego of my pinky finger I wipe away a tear from my eye. Pat it dry before my tarantula false eyelash comes unglued. Just as a police siren screams in the distance, I hear Stew scream:

"Mildred! You should be ashamed of yourself!"

James Stewart Ferguson, the aerospace exec, indignant, still wiping sloshed beer off his vest with a hanky made of the red-white-green-blue tartan of his Stewart Scottish clan he proudly wears in his pocket every day frowns at me while he holds open the shocking pink bullet-pocked front door of stinky, smoky La Pink Pantera where he's been standing on the shocking pink porch the whole time watching, his hands on the hips of his Richard Nixon navy blue pin-striped suit, his chubby cheeks as shocked pink as the shocking pink walls, shag carpet, barstools and jukebox of the shocking pink den of iniquity innards of La Pink Pantera. I was never so sick of anything in my life as I was the color shocking pink. Except men. Especially Stew.

"Prima facie misdemeanor indecent exposure if I ever saw one! Hundred-dollar fine and six months' probation, Mildred," Stew snidely admonishes. He should know because he is an attorney, works in the Contracts Department of the aerospace place near LAX. "Is Don Maraschino worth THAT, Mildred? Getting arrested for and FINED, Mildred?" Nolo contendre, I shrug as I enter the door he holds open for me to return to work amongst the shocking pink just as the police car speeds past La Pink Pantera, chasing something much more despicable than 98-pound Me.

Mildred is not my name. Stew calls me Mildred after that illiterate slattern Mildred in his favorite novel, that tiresome old-fashioned tome *Of Human Bondage* by Somerset Maugham. I'd just seen that old movie on TV last week starring Leslie Howard as the poor sap protagonist Philip who was dumped and double-dumped by the misanthropic avaricious sexpot slattern Mildred played by Bette Davis. Stew wants me to call him Philip. I don't want to. It's such a silly game. I hate the silly games the drunks and drinking men like to play with us go-go girls, us floozies as they like to perceive us go-go girls as being. Only 11 months working here and I am so sick and tired of the noise, the jukebox rumble and silliness of it all, the men, men, men, their stink and lies and smoke and lies, the drunkards, the perverts, the down-and-outs, daydream and delirium tremens believers, the unloved, unwashed and the crazy ones:

Crazy Ted who always carries a gun inside his Navy pea coat, Stingy Rick who tips me a dime per beer when the other men tip a dollar, Whitey with his profanities and stupid jokes, all the Bobs. Seems like every other man is named Bob in 1966: Bearded Bob, Fat Bob, Skinny Bob, Mexican Bob, Little Bob, Big Bob, Bus Driver Bob, Drunk Bob, Stupid Bob, Swordfisherman Bob, Milkman Bob, Egg Man Bob, Taxman Bob who helps us go-go girls with our taxes for free so's to be alone with each of us over coffee or a daiquiri and prime rib at Lawry's on La Cienega for a while even if it is discussing deductions, me the longest with the most dependents, a mother pre-The Pill. And there's Mailman Bob who brings us free stamps and Cowboy Bob who says he owns a horse ranch in the Pacific Palisades but we don't believe him because his hands are so soft. Baseball Bob who comes in every Saturday with his softball team, German Bob who plays soccer Sundays, Biker Bob the only one of the Red Snakes who still comes in after they all got busted for holding a whole town hostage for a whole weekend.

So sick and tired am I of men, men, men and only 26 years old and getting so shop-worn and worn out in 1966, I could spit. And if I did spit, inside La Pink Pantera's shocking pink universe of go-go-go, my saliva would glow bubble gum shocking pink.

After the two pitchers are drunk empty like they always are at exactly 5:15 p.m., Stew's four exec cronies, Walter, Hal, Jim and of course a Bob, Executive Bob, wave goodbye to me, to go home to their fine wives waiting wearing their neat aprons in up-scale suburbia with their waiting dry martinis and steaming casseroles.

"Alone at last," Stew says, sighs, and bats his eyes at me. He has pretty eyes with black eyelashes as thick as mine except that mine are false. Stew, though he is happily married with two pre-teen daughters he adores, is madly in love with me. So he says. Has been since the first day he came in six months ago, two weeks before Christmas, and laid eyes on me, dancing an awkward, laboriously slow-motion Pony and Jerk to the Beach Boys' "Jolly St. Nick," a go-go girl in the raw. That was Then. Last Christmas.

Amazing how quickly we go-go girls in the raw got so hard. A sink or swim thing. It was the first time Stew'd ever been in the place, "this dump," as he calls it, though the walls and bars and the Pink Panther cut-outs leaning in the corners were strewn jolly with multi-colored lights and strings of holly. No looky-loo, no accidental interloper like most of the executives who come into the go-go bars to see "how the other half live" — meaning us tarty go-go girls — Stew proclaims himself "a self-styled funster," who, if he doesn't have a ticket to ride — this is me talking now — full-speed on the merry-go-round of 1966's sexy Sexual Liberation, he at least wants to hop on for a brief dizzying spin now and then for the thrill of the whirl: Me. Mildred. A mousy-brown-maned trick pony. And I'm getting so sick of it I want to spit shocking pink.

"I forgive you, Mildred," Stew says, priggishly,

taking my beer-soaked hand to kiss it. The beer-soak why I stopped biting my fingernails for the first time in my life. "I forgive you Mildred. Your in flagrante obscentia. Your dalliance with that uncouth brute. That troglodyte."

"Lycanthrope" Stew'd called him the two months Big Don'd donned a thick, black beard, looking good, Mr. Hot Stuff, fabulous as a poet who knows it, a Roman god. Puppy dog Stew, his big brown eyes open wide, pretty eyelashes flapping, begging forgiveness as he imagines me a Bette Davis shrew dominatrix, whimpers: "Mildred, tell me: Do you still love me?" Pleasured by his corny contrived scenario, Stew smiles little perfect pearl teeth, the product of expensive childhood orthodontia. Really, really, I am sick and tired of all this. It's starting to drive me crazy. I feel my knees go weak from the responsibility of being amicable. Dizzy, too, from jukebox noise and lonesomeness, missing my kids. Plus I've got a hole in my fishnet stockings making my big toe ache.

I bend over the bar that separates our bodies: my shocking pink fringe from his navy blue serge, to whisper, sick and tired, in his ear to tell him: Go away: "Stew —"

"PHILIP!" he bellows. "Name's PHILIP!" he bellows again causing nearby drinking, smoking, talking men to look around, look over their shoulders, look over each others' heads, even look up at the rain-stained ceiling for a Philip. "WHEN, my darling Mildred, will you ever learn to call me by my real name? Philip!" He yanks on my hand I've allowed him to kiss, jerking me so hard off balance that I land thud on the bar upon my elbows. Touching me like this is prohibited by the management and California State law and if Big Don were on duty as bouncer instead of that scrawny cowardly, almost-girlie Sonny Buoy who's in the corner shooting pool, Stew'd be thrown out into the parking lot.

Loudly, he says again: "TELL ME MILDRED! DO YOU STILL LOVE ME?"

This time even the pool hustlers clacking sticks and balls in the pool room fifty feet away can hear. Bearded Bob, the tallest, meanest one, who is also a dope dealer, La Pink Pantera's main purveyor of all kinds of ill-got goods from dope to purloined fur coats, frowns at us for interrupting his concentration. When "Wooly Booly" begins to play, much louder than Stew's shouts, Bearded Bob shrugs, goes back to his dubious business.

"Stew, please don't embarrass me like this."

"You must love me, Mildred. After all I've given you—"

He means The Gifts. Cheap stuff. Stew is a tightwad supreme. So every dollop of got goods he's given me, to him, is like a squeezed-out pint of his own blood: That stinky green-bottled cologne you can buy at corner drug stores that costs as much as a bottle of Pepto-Bismol. The box it came in still had dust on it from 1958 when they'd stocked it. And he means the beige polyester cardigan with the big sticky plastic buttons he bought me at his aerospace company store with the label "Made in Taiwan," the first clothing I'd ever seen made in China and it makes me feel funny to wear Chinese polyester in 1966 in Hollywood, California, USA, especially after Stew told me it looks exactly like the cashmere sweater his ancient Scottish grandmother Fiona Mary Ferguson knitted herself and always wore. A Chinese Scots woman is what I think of when he mentions her which he does often because he's so proud of being Scottish on both sides, the American Ideal to Be Something whatever it is on Both Sides, a sign of Purity and Superiority. And since he asks about that cheap beige polyester sweater every day he comes in I make a point of bringing it to work with me, drape it over my big straw bag that carries my go-go girl accouterment of make-up, street clothes to wear home, an extra pair of fishnet stockings, pictures of my kids to look at on my break I keep in the corner near the cash register. The sweater comes in handy to keep cockroaches that crawl around amongst cigarette ashes and empty beer boxes on the dark barroom floor from flying into my straw bag to go home with me.

"These customers, all these guys in here, they'll think me a courtesan or a call girl or something worse if they think I love you." Stew winks at me, liking it that I'd said courtesan and call girl, becoming in his mind more slatternly like the Real Mildred he imagines me, wants me to be. Now I am playing the Game Right. "They can't think *you* love *me* either. That'll make it worse."

"But I do, Mildred! I LOVE YOU!" he shouts.

Every man sitting at the front bar stares at us, wondering why I'm bent over in his grip when they know it's against city statute and house rules to touch any of the girls or the girls touch them in any way to suggest anything more suggestive than utter friendliness and servitude. Sexual fantasy, secret lust may be the raison d'etre of these men coming in this place to pay a high price for beer, but "having a good time" is what it's cracked up to be. One of those customers just might be a vice officer looking for cause to cite me — and the owner Sammy Glassman — for obscenity, worse: pandering. My bellybutton indecently exposed in public hanging out of a bikini is bad enough. I do not wish to be arrested for attempted prostitution.

But as I look around for the plainclothes belonging to an undercover cop, I see something much, much worse. There, hiding in the only dark spot in the whole shocking pink-blasted place stands Othello wearing the red Hawaiian shirt with big white hibiscus all over it he took away with him last July and I last saw him wear the night of the Watts

Riots last August. He's gained another ten pounds, at least, since I last saw him a month ago when he began stalking me. Black lycanthrope fur on his forearms looks to be on fire from the glow of the shocking pink lights as he bends them to smoke a huge cigar and chug a glass of Pepsi he holds tight in a fist as if it's a Molotov cocktail he's about to toss. Only working now and then as a bouncer in a poker parlor in Gardena, living mostly off his Playboy Bunny, he doesn't spend much time in the sun anymore and his Cherokee skin has paled to cinnamon cream.

Too good for me, or pretending I do not exist, Othello looks not at me but at a rain stain up on the ceiling when he mimes: "Whore" as he blows one huge cavernous "O" smoke ring from a cigar cloud puff. The shocking pink lights overhead reflect the two wolf glints of his eyes hiding in the caverns beneath his thick, black overhanging eyebrows. Quickly, I lower my head for my long brown bangs to cover my eyes so Othello won't know I see him standing there. I tremble with such terror, I feel so weightless, lifeless, I fear I might float away if I don't stab my stiletto heels firmly into the beer-slick asbestos bar floor. I wouldn't be as afraid of a real wolf as much as I was afraid of him. I'd have a better chance with a real wolf motivated by mere wild fear and hunger. What primal force of nature motivated Othello, a human being, to torment me, want to devour me? Why doesn't he just go away and leave me alone?

"Whore," Othello mimes again in another smoky "O," then another. He looks miserable, on the skids, down on his luck and blaming it all on me, always. I could have loved him had he let me. I did love, for awhile, his graceful walk, his wide shoulders arched back, chest out when he was sweet sixteen. I loved his Cherokee milk chocolate skin. I loved his blood, agreed to be his Blood Wife one night he brought a kitchen knife from home on our date to see

71

Marilyn Monroe in *Bus Stop* at the Sundown Drive-in. He sliced our wrists, too deep, though, till it hurt and we bled all over the aquamarine upholstery of his father's 1955 Ford Fairlane. He pressed our bloody wrists together, again too hard, till, luckily, it made a kind of tourniquet to stop the bleeding as our blood dried to brown mud against each other in the hot August night lit by a full moon and Marilyn Monroe's toothy smiles and moonglow a go-go blonde hair.

"You'll always love me best," he commanded in 1956. "Always."

For a long time he continued slicing his own wrists, I noticed. I supposed he had other girlfriends someplace, other "blood wives." And he did. His many football groupies.

"O, O, O," he blows the smoke letters while saying the wide long "O" of h-OH-errr: whore: this last letter O at Robin as she wiggles through a group of 20 men, then passes by him as she carries a tray holding two pitchers of beer and six glasses. Beardless wolf man, Othello chugs down his Pepsi, eyes her up, top to bottom, her shocking pink-fringed bikini'd bod. Othello frowns at her, disgustedly, and slams his empty glass on to her tray, knocking it out of her hands, all the beer and glass crashing onto the floor a calamity louder than "'Wooly Booly" a-roar on the jukebox.

"WHORE!" he shouts. Brandi Blue dancing up on the stage in the middle of the place jerks, startled, nearly falls, but a quick-thinking aerospace exec gladly holds out his hand to her to grab so's to steady her.

"You son of a bitch!" Robin screams at Othello, but there's no Big Don to throw him out, he's gone to that stupid radish festival. Scrawny Sonny Buoy just glowers, trying to look tough as he checks out the scene. The fear of confrontation with Othello, standing nearly a head taller than him. makes him tremble, twist nervously the ends of his bushy-bushy blonde surfer hairdo. Bearded Bob, though, happens to be sleeping with Robin at the time, is her Pusher Man, dreamy-eyed Robin seriously strung out on Yellows and amphetamines and a little heroin now and then, so he steps forward, brandishing his pool stick, yells, "Hey Asshole! Who you callin' a whore?" So Othello quickly goes, on his own volition. Out the bullet-pocked front door. Gone.

But not for long. Not for long. Tomorrow I'll move again, take that job near LAX Nick the Greek offered me, hide out at his new go-go bar the Lei'd Inn. But Othello will find me again, in 2-½ months, on August 16, 1966, for the last time.

"Mildred, Mildred," Stew is still saying. "Didn't you hear me say I love you?"

I feel sick to my stomach. I feel like I'm going to fall down onto my knees because all my bones have turned to dust. I sigh. "You do NOT love me," I say, utterly certain, and yank my hand away from his grip. "You love your wife Shirley and your two daughters. Remember? Who are at home as we speak waiting for you to come eat your dinner keeping warm in a chafing dish."

"Oh! My stomach!" Stew exclaims and clutches his midriff right below his belt, reaches into his vest pocket for a white tablet. He has chronic colitis and is not supposed to drink beer. That he does twice a week now, comes in here to drink it to see me, is all my fault. Mea culpa. Chewing the white tablet that makes his lips all talcum-powdery, when he grimaces from pain he looks like a pitiful white grease-painted circus clown. "Ohh—Ow, ow, ow," he croaks, massaging his midriff.

"That new high carbohydrate diet the doctor put me on isn't working." It has made him fat, though. His stomach so paunchy now his white shirts can't stay stuffed in his trousers; they poof out his vest like wadded laundry.

"Guess I better go now—" Stew smiles, feebly but bravely. "Give me a kiss, Mildred—"

Which is this: I kiss my palm and wave goodbye. This way there are no lipstick stains upon his chubby chipmunk cheeks or shirt collar for Sweet Good Wife Shirley to see. He catches my "kiss" in his hand and "kisses" it, then tucks it into his vest pocket, next to his box of antacids and his heart. It is now that I will finally play The Game of *Of Human Bondage*, at 5:30 p.m. when I say to him in a tarty Cockney accent, acting out at last the avaricious sexpot illiterate slattern he perceives me to be, co-star antagonist with his Philip the do-good noble upper crust: "Gay-noyt, Fay-leep!"

When "What's New Pussycat" plays, La Pink Pantera's theme song, as it does every half hour and on the hour, all us go-go girls sing along "wohh, wohh, wohh, wohh, wohh, wohh-wohhh—" in chorus one time as Sammy Glassman's insisted that we do, liven up the place, because it makes the guys want to drink more and it does, all this pretense of having a good time, us happy-to-be-there go-go girls. But what it makes me think of each time, every hour on the hour and every half hour is how much that refrain sounds like the word Woe that so many of us go-go girls have a'plenty. Cher (not the real one) with her cerebral palsied little boy; Robin with her drug cravings; Patti with her no-good husband; Cherri Lee whose old man has a gambling habit, takes all her tip money to play the ponies. And if my best girlfriend, Miss California runner-up of 1962 Linda Alura were here working beside me like she usually is, she'd say sourly, because she is in love with another man she won't tell me who and does not want to marry Sammy: "Woe, woe, woe, woe, woe is me."

Stew does a little dance, like he always does and mimes Tom Jones singing "What's New Pussycat" in Las Vegas or on tv: Stew swings around his chubby hips; he's so square I'd

74

blush if I blushed easily like I used to before I became a go-go girl. Stew wiggles his index finger like the teen-aged jitterbugger he was when I was a little girl in World War Two. Then Stew dances The Twist, the dance that started this go-go thing, but stops because it hurts his stomach, jiggles the gastric juices a-boil in there. He motions for me to bend over so he can whisper, "Stay groovy, baby—Do your own thing. But remember: Don't do anything I wouldn't do." I shake my head in disbelief that he can be so square and so unaware of the impertinence of his unimportance to my life. But I laugh at his parting joke. Because he wants me to.

Pleased with how his whole day has gone as highly-paid contracts chief at the aerospace place where he just maneuvered that very day a big Air Force deal for a bunch of military planes that will aid and abet future plans to escalate American aggression in Vietnam, and self-satisfied with his successful manipulation of me in his play-act of *Of Human Bondage*, Stew finally goes home. At last. I'm rid of him. All he's left behind, the tightwad supreme that he is, is that one sticky quarter a day on my tip tray. Stuck in the muck of dried beer and ashes he and his cronies have splashed or dumped in it, I must pick it out with my fingernails this coin that can buy, in 1966, one quart of milk or one pork chop, 25 whole cents for one and a half hours of my undivided attention he demands of me the Tuesday and Thursday afternoons he comes in the place. I figure my indentured servitude of friendship with Stew costs me about $40 in tips twice a week. So I thank God Stingy Stew plays bridge Monday nights, goes to Family Bible Study Wednesdays, takes his good wife Shirley to the movies Fridays and can only stand the noise and sleaze of La Pink Pantera twice a week. Otherwise my children would starve.

And then at 5:45 p.m.: in comes Crazy Ted with a scraggly black beard, six-feet-five-inches tall, weighing 150 pounds, if that, flapping hands the size of elephant ears. He looks like an Abraham Lincoln on a stick. Sloshed from drinking Cutty Sark at One for the Road, the cocktail lounge across the street, he comes in here every day, even Sundays, to "dry out" on six or seven beers so he can go home to his one-bedroom apartment next door to drink more Cutty Sark. An engineer at the aerospace place where Stew and his cronies run things, Crazy Ted will discuss Theory of Relativity with me while I pretend to understand, Crazy Ted liking me best of all the other go-go girls because I remind him of his concert pianist sister because I am skinny like her. Plus I am the only go-go girl who can spell Einstein and, most importantly, the only one who will serve him because he tips only a dollar a day no matter how much he drinks. Craziest of all: Crazy Ted carries in the breast pocket of his Navy pea coat he wears even in California heat wave: That Gun.

With That Gun in just two weeks, after seeing him twist my wrist, Crazy Ted will shoot at Othello in La Pink Pantera's parking lot. Crazy Ted, luckily or unluckily so, will miss. Othello never knowing what almost hit him—Othello thinking the gunfire backfire, his big white 1964 Chevy he calls Moby Dick, the only character from American literature Othello remembers, needing a tune-up. And when Crazy Ted gets out of jail for disturbing the peace he'll use the gun again. Crazy Ted won't miss what he aims at that time: his own head.

Ah, but finally, back at La Pink Pantera on that day Big Don left me, the day shift over at 7 p.m., June 6, 1966, I get to go home to my three kids who wait for me at home with their nanny Peggy while they watch in innocent rapture "Gilligan's Island." How good it is to come home to them, hug them; I miss them so much. How lucky I was to have Peggy, a polite British war bride, now age 60something

76

and divorced, her husband leaving her for a cocktail waitress at the Stardust Ballroom. Peggy didn't think I was decadent bad girl or an avaricious sexpot for working in a go-go bar wearing a shocking pink fringed bikini. Perhaps the fact that I paid her twice as much as she'd make elsewhere helped her think kindly of me.

Six months later after I fell out of love with Big Don Maraschino because he'd only pretended to go to Texas, lied about a Radish Festival awaiting him in Wahoo so's to lay low from some chick, not me, who wouldn't leave him alone, he swore it wasn't me, he'd really wanted to be, honest, my bodyguard, and after Othello tried to murder me with his bare hands and I almost died and I had to leave Hollywood and La Pink Pantera to go to Sacramento to hide out and get well at my parents' house, and then my father died, Stew, so he said, worried himself so sick over me and what I was going through, he had to be hospitalized for three weeks with severe colitis and bleeding ulcers and kidney problems.

"I almost died, too, my Mildred," he croaked from his bed at the City of Merciful Angels Hospital in Los Angeles calling me long distance at my newly widowed mother's home in Sacramento. Stew was very ill, I could tell. "Nearly bled to death. Desanguinated, Darling. Needed three pints of blood. The awfulness of your life caused me to have a nervous breakdown. Made me non compos mentis. That's how much I love you." His voice was small, fearful and faraway as if he were stranded on the moon in a space suit that had a hole in it. And, mea culpa. All my fault. That damned strumpet Mildred.

"Also, I may need dialysis."

"What's dialysis?"

Stew explained in detail. Malfunctioning kidney. And

that was all my fault, too. Dialysis in my Dunderland.

Okay. Though I didn't want to play, I put on my Mildred suit, sighed, and Got Into the Game. To make him feel better: "Philip, my poor Philip. I'm so sorry."

"Mildred. Do you still love me?" Oh, Stew, you silly man, I thought but did not say it.

"Mildred, I love you so. My illness proves to you how much. I nearly died for you, Mildred. I must see you. Come see me. I may die, you know, and if I do, it'll be your fault. I'm still not out of the woods. Lost a lot of weight. Severe anemia. Hemoglobin count of seven. That's a car crash victim's hemoglobin who's thrown through a car windshield and nearly bled to death, the doctor told me. Please say you'll come see me. I get out of here tomorrow."

I had to fly down to Los Angeles next week anyway to testify in Los Angeles Superior Court against Othello for what he'd done to me. I was very nervous about it. Othello'd said if I testified, he'd finish the job. Othello didn't know where I was hiding, but he could find out if he tried. But Big Don promised me, promised on the aquamarine hood of his 1959 Chevy Impala and the soul of his dead grandmother Sophia that he would, for sure this time, be my bodyguard. Escort me to court. I told Stew he could meet my plane.

"Groovy," Stew croaked, pseudo-hip, self-styled funster sounding so corny I cringed in shame for his innocent idiocy. Then he compounded his squareness when he said, "Let's do our own thing, Mildred. Let's spend the night together. I need you more than ever," his voice so close to the hospital telephone receiver so that this wondrous, revolutionary salacity would not to be heard by anyone else. This Rolling Stones' song quote that had been banned on the State of California's rock and roll radio stations, Stew's up-close sotto voce, made a painful roar in my ear, still tender from what Othello'd done to it.

The next week, at LAX terminal, shoving a bouquet of red roses in my face, Stew shouted for the whole world of airline passengers to hear: "Mildred! My Darling! DO YOU STILL LOVE ME?" Everyone looked at us, giving us dirty looks, no one ever having heard anything this disruptive and loud before in this otherwise busy, serious place. Stew pulled me into his arms, squeezed me hard and planted a big sloppy kiss on my lips, smearing my pink lipstick all over my chin while accidentally-on-purpose brushing my breasts with his hands, copping his first feel of Me.

"Tell me! DO YOU STILL LOVE ME?!" he roared operatic, his voice echoing off the giant skyward windows of the airport terminal, basso profundo. A security guard and two stern male ticket-takers glowered and stepped forward. When I did not shriek from my mauling, pushed Stew away, they backed off.

I hated red roses. I preferred pink. Or yellow. I couldn't remember which. I slapped them away, out of his hands, onto the terminal floor. I don't know why I did it. You do things like that when you're stoned, screwed up and melancholy on drugs. A crowd of Japanese tourists stepped on the red bouquet like it was a red carpet spread out just for them, squishing the roses and I felt so suddenly sorry for the poor red ragged roses I began to shed copious tears and sob uncontrollably. The security guard glowered again. This time at ME for disturbing the peace.

"Shush, my Mildred," Stew cooed and shoved a Stewart dress-plaid handkerchief in my wet face. It was made of wool and made my nose itch. Stew reeked of milk of magnesia so strongly I gagged from the stink of it. He looked awful. He'd lost at least 50 pounds. His dreary Richard Nixon navy blue pin-striped suit bagged potato sack on him as did his chipmunk flesh once solid flab around his eyes and jowls. He'd aged a year for every pound he'd shed. He made me sick to look at him and I was so sorry. He was glad, though, how I looked, looking me up and down, then saying: "Hardly recognized you with all your clothes on."

That crummy cliché, again. What squares say in 1966 to hoochy-coochy go-go girls out of costume. Two old ladies wearing Jackie Kennedy pillbox hats next to us heard, moved away. Now they knew I was a tart even though I dressed like a square in my faux Oleg Cassini white cashmere coat and matching dress with big brass buttons like Doris Day wore in *Pillow Talk*.

I was jittery. Felt terrible. Nauseous too. Not just from the smell of Stew but from wine and "Mother's Little Helpers," Yellows, Jacqueline Susann's "Dolls" I'd consumed on the airplane. Ten terrifying inches of rain had fallen within three hours all over the state of California. I know that's not much rainfall for Rangoon but it is for California. Flight 303 down from Sacramento had survived a historically and hysterically frightening seesaw bumpy ride while jackhammer lightning bolts blasted all around the sky jet plane zooming doom during which a couple women and one man yelled "WE'RE GONNA DIE!" And all children on board, about 200 it seemed, wailed all the way: "MOMMY! DADDY!" till I got tears in my eyes, too, wanting my own Mother and Daddy. But my poor Daddy was dead. And my poor mother grieved for him. And day after tomorrow I had to testify against Othello.

So shook up was I as the jet plane rattled through the gigantic Niagara veils of dark sky, I looked shakily into my compact mirror to see if my mousy brown hair had turned white — being stoned on drugs makes you think like this — and then gulped all four splits of pinot noir the stewardess had given me right after take-off before the turbulence began. With the wine, within the hour flight — undelayed because the storm had thrown us to the wind—I washed down four, five, maybe six yellow dolls. So I was not in a very good mood. I was new at this drug-using, did not approve of it and was not very good at it, keeping count or holding my mug—and ashamed and lugubrious.

Staggering, groggy from the yellow dolls, I leaned against Stew to keep from falling over and he embraced me again, copped another feel of my breasts. I hated him. In spite of how I elbowed him to get away from me, somehow he led me out of the terminal, down the escalator where the heels of my off-white shoes got stuck in a vent for a moment and I screamed HELP! I was sure I was going to be sucked flat and ripped to shreds by the steel-toothed gears of the escalating machinery. Yet somehow Stew got me placed only a little bit wet in the front seat of his new Porsche. I hated Porsches. I hated all those little sports cars spoiled brats like Mick Jakson and middle-aged guys like Stew were starting to drive. I hated Stew and was about to tell him so, tell him how stupid he was for being so square, so corny for pretending to be a poor sap character from some tiresome old novel. I didn't know of ANYone who'd read *Of Human Bondage*.

Only my father who had an old tattered copy of it behind his sales reports in his bookcase so I read it while my face healed up in Sacramento. But he was dead, my father, reader of Maugham. And how ridiculous Stew was for trying to turn ordinary me into a dominatrix Bette Davis slattern. Me, a scared rabbit who'd had to run for a second time up the stairs of my apartment to try to get away from black-wolf Othello after he'd Defenestrated. Came in through the living room windows to do to me what he did to me, shattering glass and splattering my blood all over the place, turning the place into an abattoir, while my three terrified kids stood watching and weeping at the top of the stairs.

I guess I was having a nervous breakdown and that's why I decided to punch Stew in his guts as close to his colon as I could. Hard, with my fist, really BE Mildred. I'd show him. Since square old Stew liked Rolling Stones' songs so much I'd sing this one to him: HEY! YOU! GET OFF MY CLOUD! Then pa-pow-pow-pow-ma-mow-mow-mow, I'd watch the excrement inside him explode brown all over the tan leather upholstery of his Porsche. But instead, I let Stew take my fist in his hand, kiss it, pull it apart to place in the middle of my palm amidst my incredibly long lifeline crosshatched with noggin conks Big Don said I had: A Key.

"My darling Mildred, look at this: the key to the door to our paradise. The key to the bridal suite at the Grande Valencia Hotel on Sunset. Beverly Hills's finest. You and me. Spending the night together. At last. Needing each other more than ever." When Stew gazed into my raging messed-up pale blue eyes with his own colitis-recuperating brown-brown eyes, I was amazed by how much they looked full of poop, real poop. "Sex, Mildred. At last we will have sex." Sex? At my age? With all that white hair I felt sprouting out of my scalp I felt old and ancient as yesterday's popcorn. He closed my fingers around the key and kissed the back of my hand and off he went in the Porsche driving 70 miles an hour through the Los Angeles streets filled with puddles and flood caused by the worst rainstorm to hit California since 1938.

Ten minutes later, some of the screwy effects of the yellows and red wine wearing off, right around Wilshire and La Cienega I finally came to my normal senses and had a sane idea: My sweater! I remembered. "My favorite sweater! The one you gave me, Stew, that beautiful beige polyester sweater made in Taiwan. You know what, Stew? I left it at Big Don's." I hadn't. I'd thrown it away, with pleasure after my father died. "Without that beige polyester sweater made in China, Stew, I am nothing."

My smarminess made Stew smile, say, "Groovy."

"And cold, Stew. Brrr—I am so cold from this terrible storm. You know how warm and sweaty polyester makes you. You've got to take me by Big Don's to get my warm beige sweaty polyester sweater. Furthermore, Big Don owes me a bunch of money. And I need it." A tightwad supreme, Stew bit on that. If he thought I needed money, he sure wouldn't want me asking him for any. Better help me get money elsewhere before I hit him up for some.

"And in which cave in Griffith Park does that troglodyte Big Don live?"

Turn there, I said, and there and there and finally we arrived on the flooded street where the only man I'd ever loved lived, finally moving out of his parents' tract home in suburbia to share a two-bedroom bachelor pad with Sonny Buoy in one of those new, huge 100-unit complexes starting to sprout all over Los Angeles. Dutifully, snootily, not wishing to lay eyes upon that uncouth brute, Stew waited willingly for me in his Porsche when I suggested amicably how there was no need for us to both get wet in the downpour. Stew parked his Porsche on a street lined with skyscraper-tall palm trees that go-go danced a hurricane hula in their dark-green fringe bikinis while I disappeared into the dark stormy night, ran splashing through puddles and flood to apartment number 44-B. And, finally becoming the illiterate, misanthropic slattern that Stew wanted, incessantly insisted, I be, I left Stew waiting for me in the dark and dire of his rain-slopped Porsche. And waiting.

And waiting.

Because I never came back.

Hadn't even said first: "Gay-noyt, Fay-leep."

Stew, I would later hear, got so worried, so stressed as he searched the flooded, muddy acreage of the Santa Marina Gardens for me, calling my name (Mildred? Or my real name?), and got so drenched, falling palm fronds and lightning bolts almost striking him, he got so sick again with a new colitis attack, plus bronchitis to boot, he'd have to drive himself to an emergency hospital where he was kept six days. Why didn't he check into the bridal suite at that fine hotel? I'd left the key on the front seat of his sports car.

Meanwhile, as I mulled over, guiltily, what I'd done to Stew, hanging him up like that, I sat in Big Don's and Sonny Buoy's cozy-and dry-bachelor pad, the three of us warm and abreast, Big Don in the middle, all of us on the floor on a plump shag throw rug in front of a roaring electric fireplace listening to Sonny Buoy's new Beach Boys album, *Pet Sounds*. While Big Don and I dropped four more yellows—making my day's total eleven or twelve—my last ever—and the pills would depress me so I'd sob for a solid hour—Big Don and Sonny Buoy smoked a Thai stick of Viet Nam-grown marijuana of which I did not partake.

When "Sloop John B" played, we all three began to weep. Me, because I missed my dead father. Sonny Buoy— whose real name was Sondringham Boynton Junior, only son of the Boynt Oil tycoon who practically owned California— because Sonny Buoy'd just that day been disowned by his father for being a beach bum and a go-go girlie bar go-fer. Big Don, I don't know why he cried. When it was over, Sonny Buoy played the Beach Boys again and we began to sing:

"This is the worst trip I've ever been on—" we sang. And it truly was. Day after tomorrow I had to testify against Othello. "I feel so broke up, I wanna go home," we sang, the three of us shedding lonesome, homesick self-pitying tears as we tried to harmonize barbershop quartet to sound like the Beach Boys but we didn't, we sounded stupid as we

84

croaked: "I wanna go home, please let me go home, I wanna go hohhmm — "

After Sonny Buoy played "Sloop John B" ten times and I finally finished my crying jag, exhausted and dried up, Big Don, dried up too, did his Rhett Butler thing and picked me up in his arms and carried me to his bed where, beside him, his pristine baby sister unharmed in the lemon groves of his big arms and mesa ferns of his big chest, I slept. For 13 hours straight.

Nine years later, after the assassinations of Martin Luther King Jr. and Robert Kennedy, the near-extinction of the peregrine falcon, swordfish, the Viceroy butterfly, the panda bear, the tiger, and abalone, and after the Manson Murders thousands of Love-ins and Be-ins, protest marches and various liberations and Vietnam War's end, times a-changing while they were changing, and after La Pink Pantera became a topless bar named La Pink Pant and bottomless bars replaced the topless bars, bragging "we top the topless," and Linda Lovelace made *Deep Throat* the most watched movie since *The Sound of Music* and even the H.A.D.I.T.S. (Housewives Against Decadence In This Society), some of them now grandmothers, wore bikinis on California state beaches and mini-skirts to church, and I'd given up being a go-go girl for good and was going to college for the knowledge and to literally clean up my act, major in secretarial science, then try nursing school, drop out because I was allergic to formaldehyde, and then go to law school, I ran into Big Don and Stew, amazingly, on the same day, August 16, 1976, but at different places. L.A. is such a big, sprawling megalopolis that sometimes can be such a Small World.

Big Don, all dressed up at 3:00 in the afternoon in a tuxedo, driving a new black Mercedes Benz on Wilshire

Boulevard not far from the Miracle Mile, smiled and pulled over when I honked at him as I drove a white Volkswagen Bug—the one I bought after I bought a beige one. Big Don jumped out of his groovy car and pulled me out of my bitty one and swung me around in the air like he might the family dog—lovingly flopping me. He'd married a rich woman who owned a Malibu beach house and a chain of fabric stores that sold batik, patchwork quilt and tie-dyed cloth to industrious former hippie chick seamstresses who'd later become prosperous fashion boutique-owning yuppies on Melrose. All he did all day was go from store to store to collect the day's profits and deposit it all in the bank after first smoking a joint of marijuana with the girls working there, many of them his former go-go girlfriends who'd gotten too fat to dance anymore. Still a droopy-eyed tall, dark and handsome and buffed dreamboat after all those years, still best buds with Sonny Buoy who lived in the attic in Big Don's rich wife's beach house, Big Don still smelled lusciously of expensive lemony aftershave. "I LOVE WOMEN!" he said just before he drove away, once the only man, in 1966, I thought I'd ever love.

And why on earth, I'll always wonder, was he wearing a tuxedo at 3:00 in the afternoon? So thrilled to see him again, I'd forgotten to ask.

Stew I ran into at the Cavern Club, a sleazy Beatles revivalist bottomless beer bar on Lankershim in the Valley where go-go girls wore tiger print bikinis—before they took them off to show their bottomlessness. Hadn't been in a go-go bar in years and went with Cher (not the real Cher—getting rich on commercial real estate) and Suzi Q (getting her Ph.D. in Psychology) to see how the Other Half lived, see how cute the girls were these days and what the guys looked like and lo and behold: there was Stew: waxed twirls of a big black Snidely Whiplash handlebar moustache meticulously curlicued like two huge question marks around Stew's pink chipmunk cheeks. Reeking of antacid and ancient aerospace exec, an ostentatious display of super-square, Funster Stew wore a Grateful Dead t-shirt tucked into neat, ironed-with-a-crease, blue jeans. And: an incredibly ironic oddity considering the fact how hard Stew'd worked in the 1960s to aid and abet the aerospace industry and the American Air Force accelerate the Vietnam War: Stew wore a peace sign belt buckle the size of a saucer upon which rested his enormous twenty teacupsful-sized belly. Stew stood straight as an arrow next to his barstool and a nearly-full pitcher of drippy beer—and on the sticky bar beside it a 25-cent tip (a quart of milk or one pork chop cost 55 cents in 1976).

With grave, intense tenderness, Stew gazed up, a lonesome dog, at the naked bottom of a young blonde dancer named Michelle (tattooed on her thigh) who did a slo-mo bump and grind to George Harrison's "Something In the Way She Moves—attracts me like no other lover—"

"FAY-LEEP! DARLING!" I proclaimed, incongruous Cockney, startling Stew so that he knocked over his half-drunk pitcher of beer onto his lap, pseudo-strains of urination streaming down his blue jeans darkening to black yuck.

And then, as Stew jerked around to look at me, his puppy dog brown eyes blurring to focus at the sight of me and the Who and What-the-hell of Me, I shouted, for the whole thirsty, jukebox-Beatles's bottomless world to hear:

"DO YOU STILL LOVE ME?!"

Chapter 5 | Lettuce

After his wife Lois kicked him out January 25, 1966, with nothing but a fine-toothed comb because, according to her, he was an alcoholic sex maniac, Les Church went to the girlie go-go bars along Sunset Strip looking for True Love. Instead, poor thing, Les Church found Me, accidental dancer, shocking pink-fringed floozie working the back bar at La Pink Pantera pretending to have a good ol' time as I sloshed beer and more beer on the day shift for the men, men, men and more men, the never-ending maelstrom of men. Sucking beer, watching the bellybutton-baring bikini'd ain't-we-got-fun go-go girls, lonely, lugubrious Les Church, like so many guys like him at the time, with no place else to go, was happy to be there amongst the funseekers, crotchwatchers and dipsomaniacs as he descended side by side with them into the shocking pink passion vortex of 1966's sexual liberation and revolutionary desire.

For the first two weeks after first finding me, his True Love, Les Church did not speak to me. Solemnly sipping imported bottled beer Cher (not the real Cher) always served him, three max (evidence he was not the alcoholic ex-wife Lois proclaimed), the two hours max he stayed weekday afternoons, gentlemanly he eyeballed me as I served Crazy Ted, other assorted crazy ones, and the many and boundless Bobs. Les Church arrived on the dot at 5:45 Monday through Friday, noon on Saturday and Sunday, days I worked too. Arbitrarily, for there was no handy, accurate abacus by which to keep count, I numbered him #777 — for good luck — of the nearly thousand men I'd met so far, out of the 7,000 men I didn't know yet I'd meet the years I'd endure go-go servitude and dance in frying pans I didn't know would amount to seven long, long years, the length of time of bad luck for breaking a mirror, the minimum sentence for a felony conviction.

Preferring the "exercise" of not sitting upon the shocking pink barstool, a sit-down company man, a Desk Jockey, Les Church stood there at the end of the back bar next to the shocking pink jukebox smiling, seeming to glow alive, while the shocking pink lit up his teeth, his mouth zig-zagging up and down into the letter "w" that gave him a worried, watchful but friendly Smoky the Bear countenance, his disheveled permanent-press navy blue suit sprawling wearily like smog-beaten dead fur across his slump-shouldered, worked-stiff bod. Instead of a natty handkerchief in his breast pocket to match his loosened noose of a necktie, pencils, ballpoints and Rapidiograph pens, office miscreants and accomplices, rioted for elbow room.

When I finally began to talk to him one day as I wiped beer slop away from the cuffs of his white shirt, he told me he was an engineer at the aerospace place near LAX, same place where Stew ran things, Les on the floor below, where the draftsmen drones buzzed wearily, configuring the lofty, confounding titanium space crafts that would sock it to the Russians, ultimately make America the winner in the Race in Space. The Famous Astronaut Falcon D. Gohart, Himself, Les Church told me, once shook his hand, thanked him for his contributions to Making America Strong. Les proudly showed me an autograph signed by "The Falc" (as the elite good ol' boy aerospace Grin and Win Crowd were allowed to call him), and he carried it in his wallet next to the photographs of his three kids ex-wife Lois had taken away. Next July, I'd have a Falc autograph, too when I meet him and the astronauts when I work at the Lei'd Inn.

When the day came when Les Church finally waved me over to replace his empty bottle with a cold one, waved away the tip-hustling, avaricious sex pots Linda Alura, Suzi Q and Cher, self-admitted gold diggers who, with their shapely Las Vegas showgirl leggy-ness and I-want-you-dude-minty-breathed smiles, could woo filthy lucre from the Scroogiest of go-go girlie bar funsters and crotchwatching pervs, Les Church, his brown eyes twinkling, said to me, said it two years before Jim Morrison of The Doors said it:

"Hello. I love you. Won't you tell me your name?" just as down in front of him I placed my tip tray upon which I'd ink-markered in my inimitable script (for I was a self-styled calligrapher): "Janie Gentry."

That moment could've been not just the beginning of a beautiful friendship, which it was for a while, but a wonderful love affair too except for that dark cloud in my future six months away: Othello and his formidable, unstoppable force that would change the course of Les's life as profoundly as it would mine. And something else would ruin the possibility of Our Love, something I'm still ashamed to admit. Les had a tragic flaw, something disgusting that unshakably turned me off, and caused me to question my integrity, my good heart, my Good Woman-ness. Though he was awfully cute in his ultra-square way (what I liked best about him, in fact), sporting that sincere-ursine "w" mouth and an Orson Welles pug nose, and though one tuft of clean-shiny black hair hang-gated across his forehead just like Superman's which made him seem super-responsible, affirmed a lean-on-me indispensability, and even though I, who could not subtract numbers with zeros in them and was thrilled and mystified by his mastery of mathematics, I could not bear to look for very long at his face and that tragic flaw: his chronic zits. Always, one or two of them sprouted on his face, on the tip of his nose, middle of his forehead or Adam's apple, the shocking pink, oozy-white infected sight of them giving me the shivers, sometimes making me queasy. And one day when Les had one in the cleft of his chin and stood under the fluorescent lights near the jukebox to play his favorite song, "I Got You Babe" (to which he'd always sing along and point at me when Sonny Bono sang "I got YOU babe — ") and the zit glowed Mars-size radioactive red, I had to run to the Ladies Room to gag.

Zits, I knew, should not be someone's tragic flaw, the thing that renders anyone unlovable. Even if they were caused from nerves, as were good old Les Church's. And overwork from working days at the aerospace place and then moonlighting weeknights and weekend days at Dirkson's Drive-in Dairy out in the outer space of Lankershim Boulevard in the San Fernando Valley. Sorry, but I just couldn't help from wondering those late afternoons when Les bent my ear so often I stopped wearing earrings because it hurt my earlobes yanking them off to hear better over the blaring jukebox when I bent over to listen to his stories about the cruel but beautiful and voluptuous Lois who wouldn't cook for him or have sex with him or appreciated the olive-green tiled bathroom Les built with his own indispensable sturdy Superman hands, just couldn't help from wondering as Les listed the cruel evil ways of Lois the Wicked Witch of Suburbia, USA who took the house, the car, his kids, his hi-fi, his Frank Sinatra, Mel Torme, Ivory Joe Hunter, Elvis and Herb Alpert LPs and life insurance policies too, sorry but I could not help wondering in the mire of Les's suffering as I gazed at a zit based on the Florida Keys of his nose and a cold sore too in the corner of Les's poor "w"-wrenched lip, if those zits weren't in fact Lois's real-and justifiable-grounds for divorce based on "mental cruelty."

Mentally Cruel myself for thinking that way, I knew, but I was having it rough at the time and getting more and more hard-boiled each passing hard day's night by my hard

91

go-go girl's eight-days-a-week life and worrying about Othello after he started spying on me in March; then in April threatening to murder me, leaving nasty notes on my faded blue VW Bug's windshield, calling me all hours of the night—his mother Marie telling him where I was yet again, though I'd begged her not to. She just wouldn't believe me how frightened I was of him, thought my moving around meant I was playing hard to get. Les didn't believe me either how afraid I was as I warned Les to leave me alone, trouble was heading my way, advised him to seek the True Love company of Suzi Q, Brandi Blue, Robin, Cher, or Red-headed Penny. Otherwise Othello might mistake Les for the lover Othello constantly accused me of having.

"The bigger they are, the harder they fall," Les said after I told him how big Othello was, a champion football star, and dangerous, possibly psychotic. The process server Othello'd assaulted and battered last October trying to serve him with my divorce papers had filed a criminal complaint.

Undeterred by my warnings, my refusal to even date him, even dinner or a movie, kneeling upon one knee before me by the shocking pink light of the silvery-moon jukebox behind his favorite barstool, to the tune of "I've Got You Babe," Good Old Les Church, the first day of May, 1966, asked me to marry him. In lieu of an engagement ring, he removed from his pocket that held his embattled engineer accouterments, a sweet little royal blue velvet box that contained a sweet little half-carat diamond and white gold starburst pendant swinging on a delicate platinum chain to wear around my neck. With pleasure, he clasped it around my throat, surreptitiously in a dark corner of the bar next to the beer glasses, so no one would see. Our secret love. Until I could plot my escape permanently from Othello. Though I said No to Les's proposal of marriage, he began to court me in earnest, sent a dozen roses every Friday afternoon, those expensive lavender ones (though I preferred yellow, but yellow roses meant "friendship," said Les and he wanted more than that from me). Every Saturday evening after his day shift as manager at Dirkson's Drive-in Dairy he brought for me and my "fatherless children" as he called Sean, Leah and my baby Maureen, gallons of milk and ice cream, pounds of butter and cheese, dozens of eggs, loaves of bread, boxes of cookies, so much stuff I could give some away to the other go-go girls and some to my nanny Peggy and my friend Madge.

The first Sunday of each month Les brought me tickets to take my children to Disneyland on my Monday day off where Les would be waiting at the entrance, smiling his "w," tipping the tuft of his black hair like a hat shading his eyebrows, my silent, secret Superman who would then follow us through the park, blasé, like my bodyguard, my consort a few paces behind, watching, lovingly. And every day after he finished his three-max imported beers, he left me a ten-dollar tip, a lot of money in those days. When my hi-fi broke down and I couldn't play my Sinatra LPs when I got home from work anymore, Les donned the "Kwik-Fix" shirt he'd worn when he worked as handyman one summer and fixed it while making eyes at me and cooing fatherly advice to my fatherless children ogling his electric wire handiwork. And once a week he drove my faded blue VW Bug to the corner gas station to fill it up, check the oil, wash and wax it. Les was becoming irrefutably indispensable and possibly my Prince who'd arrived, at last, at last, to take me away from All This.

And during the weeks that this went on, I might've fallen deeply in love with Les Church as he deserved a woman to do if not for Othello who was becoming more and more bête noire brutish as he found me again that July, spied on me, darkened my door whenever he felt like it, the last time on that hot August 16, 1966 night, at two a.m., waking me up, pounding on my door till the neighbors yelled. He wanted me to cook him breakfast. While he sipped Pepsi, made wild swings at me with his arms as he pretended to yawn and stretch at the bar that looked into the kitchen, Othello made me wearily fry him a dozen eggs and a pound of bacon, courtesy, unbeknownst to him, of Dirkson's Drive-in Dairy's manager, my Potential Prince, Les Church. That morning, our last morning ever together, I'd actually amused Othello, cheered him, when I put two maraschino cherries in the middle of two over-easy eggs. Ha-ha-ha, he laughed, exclaimed, "Joyful eyeballs!"

Then he noticed my diamond.

"There is no love sincerer than the love of food," Victor Hugo wrote which I'll quote someday when I've completed the *Jane's Never Plain* cookbook I started when I was twelve years old. Othello might've remained sincerely in love with his food had it not been for my sparkling diamond starburst pendant from Les Church catching his eye that August 16, 1966 morning, twelve days after the United States Mint cancelled the production of the two-dollar bill, and the day my car payment was due. That diamond took his mind off his joyful food and placed his mind — no, slapped it, threw his mind, squarely, crazily on me.

Indispensable Les Church was very good to me after Othello did what he did to me. All pink-pocked as if from machine gun fire a-rat-a-tat-tat, broken out with four zits across his forehead, his "w" lips pinched into two tall "vees," quickly Les packed up all my stuff, the furniture that wasn't broken, lest fugitive-at-large Othello come back to finish the job of trying to murder me with his bare hands. Before the police got there, Othello, personifying a red gigantic flame in that red Hawaiian shirt of his, ran away from the scene of the crime amidst police sirens and neighbors' shouts. The next afternoon, while I sat stunned in the living room where Othello had done what he did to me, the aftermath now an abattoir stained with the bloody mess of my last night's blood, I watched Les clean up the mess, sweep up the glass, put stuff in boxes for storage, then took my three children, some clothes and toys and busted-up me to his place, a roomy one-bedroom black and red-decorated bachelor pad in Santa Monica a few blocks from the beach and pier.

Les took a two-week leave of absence from his aerospace engineering job to take care of me, holed up, in a state of shock, in his bedroom with the red drapes pulled shut to keep out the hot August California sun while he and my children lived in his living room, Leah, Sean and Maureen camping out on Les's big black sofa bed while he slept on the floor beside them in a sleeping bag. Days, Les took them to the greenbelt down by the ocean and the merry-go-round at the pier or the beach to play in the sand and surf, made them laugh to keep their minds off me while I lay benumbed in his big bed staring, staring, staring at the ceiling.

The second day, he held me like he would a baby, in his arms, told me: "All will be okay, you'll see. I promise you —"

"No," I said, pulling away. "All will not be okay. All this is your fault."

"You're in a state of shock. You don't know what you're saying." Then he went away for a while, let me be, to stare into space. Every hour he offered soup, water, anything I wanted, which I refused for days.

Late at night as I dozed, trying to sleep deeply but could not, Les would whisper from the doorway, a hovering guardian angel: "All will be okay, you'll see." Then he'd say it again, a mantra, a poem, gently, a poet reading aloud a

95

love poem while he either combed, careful not to hurt me, my tangled hair that would take days to smooth out, or fed me cool soup or crushed ice because I could not raise my arms to do so myself.

All, though, would Not Be Okay. Of this I was certain. Les did not realize that my life was over. I had no face. "Look at me, Les," I hissed at him the fifth day. Again, he embraced me, tried to calm me. But his gentleness, in my state of mind, seemed too simplistic and so cheery it became to seem dishonest, despicable, in fact, and no better, no more comforting than pure stupidity or blatant lies.

"I am the Bride of Frankenstein," I said after a week and saw my face for the first time. "A giant jack-o-lantern plum."

"No, you are beautiful."

"I am a whore."

"No. You are a Good Woman. With a fine good heart."

What a fool he was. No wonder Lois kicked him out with nothing but a fine-toothed comb. Les telephoned my parents to tell them the same thing too: All would be okay. They were very upset. But thanks to Les, they didn't worry as much as they might've. "Your father said—" and Les imitated his Texas baritone perfectly: "'—sounds to me, son, like she's in very good hands.'" So now my parents knew The Truth about me. Ashamed, I rolled over to look at the blank wall next to Les's bed where on the night stand was a Polaroid Les had taken of me in my silly shocking pink-fringed go-go girl outfit. How stupid I looked standing there holding his bottle of imported beer, smiling stupidly as if nothing bad was ever going to happen, fluorescent lights shining down on me like a halo, making my mousy brown flip hairdo look radioactive.

Les told my parents the Whole Ugly Story of Me:

what I'd been doing and going through the past year. Othello leaving. Where I'd been working. The broken furniture. The bloody walls of my apartment where Othello did what he did. The police looking for fugitive-at-large Othello. Broke my parents' hearts, my father's so much he had a heart attack later that night, the first of two that would kill him.

Les, his "w" lips stretched flat across his face jaw to jaw, somberly calmed them, told them again and again It Would All be Okay. They had his promise, he promised as he guzzled a beer. His fifth that night. I'd kept count. In four days, when he figured I'd be strong enough, he was driving us all up to them in Sacramento. Very carefully, he promised them. He'd drive very carefully, "Yes, sir!" he said to my father like a brave soldier would. "Your daughter, sir, and her children are safe in my hands. Promise, promise, you have my promise," he began to slur stupidly redundant. "Yes, ma'am," he promised my mother, who talked on the extension telephone. "You have my word, sir," to my father he said yet again before he hung up and went to the kitchen for another beer. Six! He was an alcoholic, just like Lois said. I didn't blame her at all for leaving him. I hated him too. The thought of him made my skin crawl.

"How you doing, Beautiful?" Les whispered, so's not to wake my children snoozing on his sofa bed. Les lay down beside me gently as if his bed were covered with eggs he did not want to break and I was the biggest and most breakable of all. The moon was full, just like it always seems to be every night the whole month of August. Its bright white light flashed through the row of eucalyptus trees outside the window making anomaly summer snow upon the red wall-to-wall shag carpet. Les patted, soothingly, doctorly, my right shoulder, the only place on me that was not bruised, except for one small cut from a glass shard jabbed in there after Othello defenestrated through my living room bay windows, crashing through the glass after I ran out the front door after he threw me across the room after noticing The Diamond. When he chased me out the door, I ran back in, slammed it, locked it, ran to call the police. CRASH! I will hear glass crash, see it too, in nightmares for the rest of my life. Othello's fists crashing into my face will be the last thing I'll see before I fall asleep, every night, from that day on.

Les gave me my yellow sleeping pill with a glass of water, eight nights in a row he'd done this now, to help me fall asleep before he tiptoed back to the living room to take his nightly vigil on the floor beside my children, guard them from the Boogeyman.

"Can I get you anything else, my love?" He called me "my love" because of that Herb Alpert tune he loved so much, "What Now My Love?"

Yes, I pondered forlornly: What Now?

Les hummed it to himself all the time, annoying me, before asking: "What now my love? Glass of milk? Tea? Anything. I'll give you anything." That song had become Les's Theme song, his musical accompaniment and intro to his boundless servitude to me.

No man other than my father had done so much for me and even my father had never combed my hair. So I asked Les, just as the sleeping pill's somnolistic magic took hold of me, self-pitying and feeling terribly alone, surprising myself when I did, drugs make you so unpredictable: "Do you want to sleep with me tonight?"

Immediately he answered Yes to my question, and quickly, but gently, lay down on the bed close to me. Moonlight spotlighted him, making his polka-dotted face of zits appear measled and sickly. He was shirtless because he was sunburned from the beach that day and I saw he even had red zit blotches on his shoulders and back. Looking at them and him made me so queasy I gagged. Plus Les had that yeasty smell of beer on his breath, that girlie go-go beer bar stench I hated, had grown so sick of the past year. I held my hand to my mouth so I wouldn't vomit. I shuddered.

"Are you cold, my love? I can shut the window." No, no, it was a warm August night. I'm okay, I said. Just a nervous reaction to the sleeping pill. Les kissed my cheek and I held my breath so's not to smell the reek of beer on him and shut my eyes so's not to see him, that pitiful ridiculous "w" scarring his lips, and those blotchy flaws upon his face and torso. I suppose he mistook the look of disgust on my face for rapture because Les touched my breast. For the first time, ever. The newness of this intimacy made him gasp and made me want to die.

"You've got to marry me now," Les whispered, jolly, glad to be so close like that. In bed together, about to have sex for the first time. "Think of the scandal if you don't. You spending the night like this in my bachelor pad for over a week. Without the sanction of matrimony." Les giggled. This pleased him, this old-fashioned notion in the midst of all the sexual liberation going on around us, galaxies of unauthorized orgies and accomplished revolutionary desire spinning and spinning this August night of full-moonlit free sex and love, 1966. "I must make an honest woman of you."

An honest woman. If that didn't beat all. After everything I'd done for a year trying to be an honest woman, a reliable resource to do what a mother's got to do to fulfill her biological imperative, feed and clothe The Fatherless Children, but being a dishonest one instead as I worked half-naked without my parents' approval or knowledge. A sneaky whore. All that had led me to here without a face or a home of my own in the August moonlight lying with a man I did not love but had to have sex with because he'd done so much for me and deserved it. Now I really was a whore. I pushed Les's hand off my breast, groaned so he'd think it pained me.

"Sorry," he said, not knowing what to do with his useless hand, then placed it on his forehead on top of a pink swarm of zits.

I sighed, said, "Make love to me." Before I change my mind, I wanted to add, but didn't. Because there was no place on my face that was not purple or scabbed jack-o-lantern plum, he kissed the back of my hand, leaving the moisture of his "w" lips. He kissed my one, unbruised shoulder while I thought: How could he want to make love to me the way I looked if he weren't a sex maniac? Just like Lois said. Yes, he was a pervert all right. I felt ill. I shivered.

"Why are you shivering? It's a warm August night. You said so yourself. What's wrong?"

"Just hurry, please."

"If you don't want to do this, just say so. I'm no sex maniac, you know. Even if Lois called me one." When I sighed, from abject boredom, it came out a snort. "Well? Do you want me? The way I want you, my love?"

Shivers fell over me like an avalanche of snow. Was there any place on this spinning earth in the sun where it snowed in August? I began to convulse. My whole tired body spasm'd with shivers. I pulled Les's red and white-striped candy-canes-in-August sheet up to my neck to warm myself. He sat up in bed.

"Do you? Do you want me or not?"

"No."

Then I said it again, the meanest thing I'd ever said:

"It's all your fault."

"What? What's all my fault?"

"This. My face. My life. What's happened. What my ex-husband did. All of it, it's all your fault. You've ruined my life."

"My fault? Your face? After all I've done? You say I've ruined your life? Me?"

"Yes."

Les pounded his fist upon his bed. He was drunk. He stunk. "You can't possibly mean that!"

"Yes. If you hadn't given me this diamond pendant he wouldn't've got mad." I touched it, the diamond pendant on the chain. Beneath it there would always be a dent in the middle of my chest, then a lump that will someday turn into a cyst, then a scar. "He'd've just gone away like always. If it weren't for you. If not for you, I'd still have my face."

"You don't know what you're saying. You're still in shock. And besides, you still have a face. A beautiful face." Les took my hand and gentlemanly kissed it again.

"You're such a fool. And stupid." I yanked my hand away, my fingernail accidentally scratching his cheek. A zit! It began to bleed, glowing neon magenta from the August moonlight.

"Shit!" Les said, the first profanity I'd ever heard come out of his mouth. He rolled over to the farthest edge of his bed, his back stiff, then trembling, as if he wept. "Shit!" he said, kicking the candy-cane sheet with his bare feet. We lay silently, vis-à-bas, for what seemed like hours watching the moon sail by, becoming trapped on its way in the mess of the eucalyptus branches outside the bedroom window for a while then finally working free and sailing off to safety and serenity over the Pacific Ocean, off for the pineapples and sugar cane of Hawaii. Then he began to hum again, "What Now My Love?" Unmelodious, adenoidal kazoo, irksome mantra, the eternal question always, the perplexing question every human being questing for shelter and fire and love and food has asked every minute of the day since the beginning of time from the dreary cave till now in this red and black bachelor pad three blocks from the Santa Monica Pier, California, USA: What Now?

Finally, he spoke: "That's a Rabbit Moon. They say —

101

the Chinese say, and Japanese too, I think—that it's the time of year when the mythical rabbit who lives on the moon—not a man on the moon like we westerners mythologize—sweeps and makes it bright and clean. Renewed." I did not speak. Nor move. I wanted him to think I'd fallen asleep. About five minutes later, when he heard me sigh, he asked: "Don't you care about the Rabbit Moon?"

"No."

"Why not, my love?"

"I care about nothing."

Frowning forlornly, I supposed, his lips a wavering "w," I supposed, I didn't look—I was staring at the ceiling at the shadow of a eucalyptus tree—Les got up from his bed and went back to the living room to sleep on the floor beside my fatherless sleeping children. And I was very, very glad to be left alone, to remember:

This hot August day was the third anniversary of the death of Othello's father, Reave Gentry, Senior, the man who taught his son how to be a Man and taught him, too, everything he knew about how to treat a woman.

Four nights later, on our way to my parents' house up in Sacramento, five hundred miles north of Los Angeles, around ten o'clock p.m. after Dirkson's Drive-in Dairy on Lankershim way out in the boondocks of San Fernando Valley was closed, Les, who had his own keys to the place, stopped by to fatherly fetch my children cheese and crackers, cookies and chocolate milk to snack on in the back seat of the car before they fell asleep for the long, boring eight-hour drive up Highway Five which they did and I did too while Les made his red Volkswagen Bug fly past the oilfields outside Bakersfield, the vineyards of Fresno, Modesto, cornfields and stock yards of Stockton, Lodi, getting us to Sacramento in a record-breaking seven hours.

I'll never forget, though I've tried, the looks on my parents' faces when they saw my face. None of us said a word, though, about how it looked like blueberry pie. My father, bent over from his ten days' ago heart attack, wearing paisley pajamas and his Romeos, the oxblood leather house slippers his mother Viola bought him at Sears for Christmas last, shook Les's hand more vigorously and gratefully than I've ever seen any human do. No rescuer has ever been so welcomed as was Les Church. My mother offered to fix him breakfast but all he'd accept was black coffee, four, five, six cups of it, chug-a-lug and then he said, Must be off. Work tomorrow. Back to the salt mine that was aerospace engineering. Standing his full six-feet tall, with his hands on his hips the way men do when they're fed up and tired, leaning on himself while bolstering himself, Les Church said Goodbye. First to my children, patting each on the head, gently admonishing them—an enormous irony in light of all they'd lately seen and been through—to "be good." They'd been good beyond belief, true little guardian angels hovering about, gently speaking to me as I lay silent in Les's bed all those days and nights.

To me, he said simply, monotonally, "Goodbye." Then placed his hand on my one unbruised shoulder as if anointing me with his eternal blessing while also blocking any superfluous vibes or any former emotional ties between us. Then he pulled from the back pocket of his perma-press navy-blue polyester engineer's trousers an envelope that said "Manager Les Church, Dirkson's Drive-in Dairy" on it, Les's hands shaking the way they always did when he used to talk about how mean Lois had been to him, but it might have been from jangling nerves from all the black coffee, the helter-skelter 500-mile drive up to Sacramento from Los Angeles in a record-breaking seven hours.

"For you—" he said of the envelope. "From me. With

luck. And love." With "w" lips like Smoky the Bear again looking like he did the first day I met him: friendly, worried, watchful, Les smiled at my father, gave him a little bow like a good soldier would to his commanding officer, turned around, got back into his red VW and drove the grueling 500-mile drive back to L.A.

Monday the telephone rang and rang. The Los Angeles County Police Department calling. Detectives, police officers, even the Chief of Police himself, returning my father's incessant eight days' worth of phone calls to them hounding, badgering as only a Man's Man with a Texas baritone voice could and get away with it: "When the hell dammit are you going to find that maniac son of a bitch who tried to murder my daughter? WHEN? I want to know!"

Tuesday, one of the police calls was for me. A San Fernando Valley Sheriff Department investigating officer who asked questions about the night in question that wasn't the night Othello did what he did to me but the night Les Church had packed up me and my children to head up to Sacramento. Where was I during the hours of ten o'clock p.m. and midnight? And I told him that Les Church and I'd stopped by Dirkson's Drive-in Dairy on Lankershim for such and such. Yes, Mr. Church had keys to the establishment, he was the Manager. Yes, Mr. Church showed the keys to me. Yes, he had permission to be on the premises after closing time. He was the Manager, wasn't he? At least I thought he had permission. Dirkson's Drive-in Dairy, it turned out, had been robbed of $500, the investigator informed me sternly, during the aforementioned time period. Was I involved in any way? Have any information regarding this matter?

"What the hell is this all about?" yelled my father into the extension in his bedroom, eavesdropping. "How dare you harass my daughter like this after what she's been through, sir! How dare you imply Mr. Les Church would commit any wrongdoing when the maniac son of a bitch who just tried to murder my daughter August 16 goes free and roams the Los Angeles city streets as we speak. Why aren't you out looking for that maniac son of a bitch instead of pestering the likes of Mr. Les Church a fine young man who wouldn't harm a fly and who's as honest as the century is long and I would bet the farm on it!"

After many weeks, after my father died of a coronary occlusion in the front seat of his company car on a rainy morning, November 22, 1966, as he turned on the ignition to head off for work as a traveling sales rep for Boynt Oil, Automotive Paint Division, Les Church telephoned me at my newly widowed mother's house in Sacramento where I still lived hiding out with my children while waiting for my face to heal.

"How are you?" he wanted to know, matter-of-factly. I told him all the aforementioned, concluding, sarcastically: Just great. Then I waited for the sympathetic reaction I expected from him regarding my father's sudden death, my mother's and my and my children's grief, my pitiful and slow recuperation. Also, Othello's capture (the police found him hiding in his mother Marie's bedroom closet); Othello's proclamation of innocence as he said how I had made him do it; his defense: I'd provoked him. And there was a chance he might be found innocent. He'd requested a judge not a jury at his trial at which I was to testify. But Les didn't respond to any of that. He wasn't even listening I could tell because I'd heard him humming some off-key melody as I spoke, some song I'd never heard before. Finally, when I got quiet, he told me his own news of woe: Car accident a month ago. Totaled his red VW and one of his kidneys.

"Got all cut up. Mostly my face. Went through the windshield. Pretty bad. Scarface Church." Ha-ha-ha, he chuckled, rather maniacally. How awful, I said. Why didn't you tell me sooner? "I called you right afterwards. Asked you to come down and see me. I needed you like you once needed me. But you didn't come." No, Les, you never called. This is the first I've heard of your accident. I would've come had I known. He laughed again. "Ha. Must've slipped your mind." No, Les, you didn't call. I'd never forget something like that. "Ostensibly," he snarled, "you did. My love. My good heart," he said, snidely. "The shock of your accident must've caused you some permanent amnesia. Love." Luhhhv, he pronounced it.

"The shock of your accident, Les, must've caused *you* some permanent amnesia," I said, trying to sound kindly, concerned diagnostician.

"It did not! I'm just fine!" he yelled into the receiver. I'd never heard him angry before. I imagined his "w" lips twisted barbed wire. I changed the subject. Dirkson's Drive-in Dairy. The night of such and such. Why did that police officer call me and ask so many questions about that night? After moments of long-distance silence, he finally said, blasé:

"Oh. Nothing. Just a misunderstanding. Just like everything that has occurred in my shitty life. And all that which did not occur between you and me." When we said goodbye, simultaneously, ending our mutual accusatory misery, I was very glad.

But I was even more glad to say Hello to Les Church five years later, in 1972, four years after I'd erroneously married a no-good hippie I didn't know was a no-good hippie, to be my bodyguard, protect me against Othello, the muscular T.J. DuRong with twinkling blue eyes who won my heart (not my love; I'd hang on to a lingering crush on Big Don Maraschino for years). T.J. DuRong made me laugh till I cried as he sang his imitation of Popeye the Sailor Man: "I goes to

106

the finish when I eats me spinach."

In 1972, T.J. DuRong was serving a year in an honor farm convicted for possession with intent to sell marijuana and amphetamines while I, still an "Eke Girl" after years of being the "Eek Girl" Othello made of me, worked part-time at the Strand Hotel in downtown L.A. as a cocktail waitress in their swanky Matador Lounge and going to junior college part time taking shorthand and typing, literally trying to clean up my act and amount to something after all, when Les Church walked into the Matador Room during an August heat wave with a gang of fellow engineers with whom he was attending an engineers' conference in one of the hotel's fancy crystal-ball-chandeliered ballrooms.

Hello! Hello! Gladtaseeya! we cried, then embraced.

Les Church looked even cuter than he used to, wearing his extra five years well the way most men do in their late thirties. He still had those infernal zits all over his face, though, but now they gave him an eternal youthful ever-boy insouciance rather than looking like a bumpy hangover mask of a geeky adolescent. The facial scars he'd lamented about on the long-distance telephone five years ago, I thought, only made him look more manly, as if he'd been roughed up by thugs. And won. We quickly made plans to meet that night to talk over "old times."

When "old times" are only five years old, though, they're often not very romantic, nor remembered fondly. The not-so-old times haven't had time yet to grow enough yesterday-all-my-troubles-were-so-far-away moss-gauze to mask memory of the rough edges and allow forgetfulness to allow forgiveness. Everything I remembered about our old times, Les'd forgotten. And vice versa. All of our quaint personal trivia fell ker-plunk into the nepenthe cracks of short-term memory loss or still-held-tight grudge. He remembered my not liking the lavender roses he sent me every Friday when I worked at La Pink Pantera because I preferred pink. Not true, it was yellow I liked best so I know I never said that, that I hadn't liked those lavender ones.

"Ah, Les, a rose is a rose is a rose—" I said, what-the-heck. Les even argued that the song he played all the time at Pink Pantera was "What Now My Love?" instead of what it really was: "I Got You Babe." Sammy Glassman the owner wouldn't't've put any love songs like "What Now My Love?" on the jukebox. Slow sad love songs got the drinking men to thinking and stop drinking beer. And the shocking pink fringe I wore at La Pink Pantera, according to Les, had been purple. Then why hadn't Sammy named the place La Purple Pantera? I joked. No chuckles. Les Church was serious as a heart attack—and church.

One thing was certain and which we both agreed on: Neither of our parallel lives of misery and misfortune had been better off without the other. In fact our lives had gotten worse rather than better: Les had married badly, too: a go-go girl of all things. A topless dancer named Cathy he met at La Pink Pant after Sammy changed the name and turned the place topless for real. Ha-ha, we laughed. Hadn't Les known better, learned his lesson after hanging around with the likes of me? Ha-ha. Should'a known better, he said and laughed as I poked him in the rib and said, Yeah, Les, us-love-em-and-leave-em go-go girls! Us avaricious sexpots! Heartbreakers, all. Wooing filthy lucre from the Scroogiest of Scrooges! Us Sweat Hearts of Stigma Sties. A dirty job but somebody had to do it! Right? Right! In 1972 I was only 32 years old, yet we were talking about me like I was an ancient memory and a ridiculous-and obsolete-wretch of one at that.

Gazing into the ice cube as if into a crystal ball floating in the middle of his cocktail, a pepperminty Stinger that made him reek of toothpaste, Les sighed forlornly, tired of our prattle, then looked at the poster on the wall behind me of Marilyn Monroe and Joe DiMaggio. We sat at Their Table, where they always sat in 1953 the one year they were together and where Joe DiMaggio still sat when he stayed in the hotel. I'd met him as he sat in the same chair Les sat in, got his autograph that I gave to my son. Joe DiMaggio touched the thigh of my black fishnets when he ordered another cappuccino and when I got home, I "x"-marked the spot with a dab of pink fingernail polish, still there today.

"Yeah. Yeah, them old go-go girls," Les said, sighed. He wore the sorrowful face of a man who'd made a million mistakes and couldn't figure out Why. "They probably even hocked the diamond starburst pendants some of us schmucks gave them in lieu of engagement rings."

Simultaneously, we looked at my bare chest where there was a dent now but no diamond starburst pendant dangling from a platinum chain had I worn one with my yellow tank top and blue jeans bellbottoms that night. I couldn't for the life of me remember what happened to that diamond starburst pendant. I missed it. It had meant a lot to me, even though it had been The Thing that almost got me killed. I'd loved jiggling it to catch the light to reflect off things. Its sparkle made me feel like I owned two hearts, one made of immortal, unbreakable diamond and the other of blood, sweat and tears. I suspected T.J. had something to do with its disappearance. For the next 19 years I'm married to him I'll blame 99 and 44/100ths-percent of the bad things that will happen to me on TJ. DuRong—and I'll be right.

"Oh, well, it's all water under the bridge now," Les said and sipped, sadly, every bit of his Stinger. Cathy, the topless dancer, his wife, the second one, really screwed him over, too. Money-wise. Cathy even pretended he was the father of her kid she hadn't bothered telling him she was pregnant with until after he, drunk out of his gourd, married

109

her in Las Vegas. How he got there, he couldn't remember. Cathy must've driven. It was just like being kidnapped.

"Then she tried to pass the little superfluous bastard off as mine. Well, I'd had a vasectomy when I was married to Lois. Ha-ha," Les laughed, went on: "Hell, haven't got a kidney, haven't got any sperm!" But, the judge made him pay Cathy child support anyway. Some new law. "Life is unfair," Les said, ordering us more drinks. Yes, I agreed, definitely. Life was immensely unfair.

"To Life!" Les said as he chugged half of his fifth Stinger—missing kidney be damned. "Look out teeth, look out gums, look out you poor lonesome kidney, here it comes!" He finished his drink as if it were merely water, waved his hand for the waitress to bring us two more. While Les gulped his sixth Stinger, he stared at the red velvet wallpaper behind me, intently, as if it bore the secret to love, life and happiness. I touched his hands, his heroic, sturdy, indispensable, smart-at-math engineer's hands, hands that had done so much for me, heroic hands that saved me when I needed saving. I owed so much to those good, heroic hands for packing up my stuff, my broken life and me and my confused little fatherless children and rescuing me in my darkest time and place, then or ever.

Little cedillas of black hair covered Les's knuckles. I'd never noticed that before. Gave him a manly, tough-guy look. Nor had I ever noticed the dimple in his left cheek nor how wide his shoulders were. After two more glasses of white wine for me and one more Stinger for him, when the piano bar player began to play Simon and Garfunkle's "Sounds of Silence," I leaned, sang to Les, "Hello darkness, my old friend," then, over the empty glasses of our libation, asked him, surprising myself once again when I did so: "Do you want to sleep with me tonight?"

"Hmmm. That sounds familiar. Now where or when have I been asked that question before?" A bit cross-eyed from too much drink, he winked at me. "Yeah, baby," he said, lecherously. "Let's get the hell outa Dodge," he said, tough cowboy, then tossed money on the table for the waitress, took my hand and led me, both of us staggering, leaning on each other, practicing alcoholics getting damned good at it, out the door of the Matador Room and went to the cheapest and nearest motel Les Church could find, a cute little place with cute yellow-rosy chintz curtains hanging in front of thick, old 1940s wooden Venetian blinds. A 1930s Craftsman sofa was covered with the same yellow-rosy chintz as was the bedspread on a big, soft, squeaky bed. In five years the owners of that cute 12-unit motor court will get rich and move to Honolulu when they sell the place to the Holiday Inn for them to build a 30-story skyscraper and decorate the rooms in orange and beige. Naked, in between the crisp, yellow and white-striped sheets, Les and I embraced vis-à-vis for the very first time. As I reached to turn out the light, Les suddenly pulled away and turned his back to me.

"What's wrong, my love?" I asked, pressing my cheek against Les's naked back, listened to his good, heroic heart go thump, a wild rabbit running away over his teeth and gums and out his mouth onto the wooden floor to hop over my brown shoes with the cork high heels.

"It's all your fault," he said.

"What's all my fault?"

"My car accident. My face. My kidney. Cathy. All your fault."

"Mine? How?"

"If you'd married me, none of it would've happened. You ruined my life."

I lay on my back to look at the ceiling and the matching yellow-rosy chintz wallpaper up there. Suddenly it was 1932 in that place. The Great Depression all over again.

111

No joy in Mudville or on Wall Street or the Dust Bowl. Crops and banks all dried up. Men needing six-bit shaves and haircuts stood in soup lines. Dirty little boys with holes in the knees of their knickers sold newspapers on street corners. Then it was 1944. Les about to ship off to war. Then 1952 and we were in this motel room to hide out from the Commies and the H-bomb. November 21, 1962 and we were Jackie and Jack Kennedy here for a quickie the night before Dallas. No hope. No possibilities. No place to turn to change the tide of events. No one to talk to about this. No messages to explain life and love wrapped into those golden rose petals up there on the yellow-rosy chintzy ceiling, circa 1972. Les rolled over too, to take a look. He sighed. Coughed. Out the corner of my eye I looked at his Orson Welles pug nose. No zit. The lamp next to him, glowing amber from the burnt-umber shade from 40 years' worth of 40-watt light bulbs made his skin glow amber too. And the one, two, three tears that streamed down his cheek resembled little amber drops, little jewels I might dry into beads to string and wear for Love Beads if I could.

"Les, look — There's a Rabbit Moon —" I pointed at the milky stream of hot August full moon dripping through the crannies of the ancient Venetian blinds and making stripes across our naked feet and legs.

"That's not a Rabbit Moon," he scowled. "The Rabbit Moon comes in September this year."

"A beautiful moon nonetheless. Don't you care about the beautiful full moon?"

"No."

I pressed my cheek against his shoulder, kissed the silky black hair there. "Les, there's nothing wrong with your face. It doesn't look scarred to me." I pushed aside from his forehead the tuft of black hair that looked just like Superman's. "You have a beautiful face, Les. A beautiful, handsome heroic face." Glowering, his "w" lips became a straight line across his face, an "m" in Gregg shorthand I was learning in junior college secretarial science. "M" the easiest letter in Gregg shorthand and the classic letter of many human emotions: moan for misery, mmmm for pleasure. Or Marilyn Monroe. Or:

"Moronic," Les sneered. "Can't you see the scars?" He ran his hands all over his face as if thousands of horrible things sucked and sliced his skin. "Are you blind? No, I think not. I think you are a moron." He got up, grabbed his khaki pants draped over one of the four posters of the bed. I tried to pull him back to me but he slipped away. Summertime sweat or a tear sliding down his arm making his skin slick and ungraspable.

Four years later, during the proud-full 1976 American Bicentennial, after I'd boringly, laboriously learned to type 75 words per minute and take shorthand 100 words per minute, my secretarial skills suddenly made obsolete by the prevalence of the office Dictaphone and the emergence of a new-fangled machine, the personal computer, and I'd gotten accepted to grad school to study for a Master's Degree in — of all stupid things — French literature after I'd gone a year to law school looking for respect by peppering my palaver with per ses, prima facies, and res ipso loquiturs, I had a dream Les Church died. So I called his parents' old telephone number in my book. Still good, his mother Naomi answered, repeated my inquiry: "How's Les? That bum. Haven't heard from him for two years. Nor have his kids. Fine kids. All smart. Les Jr. attending Stanford. Lois Jr. got married. Little Ben, though, he's smart but a bum. Wants to be a rock musician of all things — an Elton John! Can you imagine?"

Naomi Church asked about me. She always remembered me because I once gave her a one-ounce bottle of Joy parfum I was allergic to given to me by Crazy Ted,

Man #113 I met my first year as a go-go girl at La Pink Pantera. Les had told his mother, though, I was a secretary, not a La Pink Pantera go-go girl and that my Aunt had given me the pricey perfume. Naomi loved it. Who wouldn't? Joy parfum was the costliest perfume in the world. Then Naomi softened her tone and said: "Oh, well. Got to hand it to Lester. He had it pretty rough after he took that leave of absence from his aerospace job to help that La Pink Pantera floozie go-go girl who got beat up by her crazy jealous husband. And she probably deserved to get beat up. [ME! She's talking about ME!] Les lost his good job because of her, that floozie. Then he got into that car accident. Lost one of his kidneys. You really do need two kidneys, you know. Then he lost yet another good job. Absenteeism again, that time because of kidney stones caused from his drinking too much alcohol and then his plastic surgery that didn't help all that much. His face didn't look any different to me. I never noticed any scars. But then I'm his mother. He'll always look pretty to me. I'd love him no matter what. Les had a hard time finding another good job, aerospace dying out and all. And he'd got into a lot of debt spending money on that floozie go-go girl. [Me, again.] He probably never told you about her. I never met her, thank goodness. You're such a good girl. So he probably never told you how he sent her expensive lavender roses every week. The florist bills came here to us. And he was living with us rent free, never a dime did he pay. Just so he could live like a playboy to impress her, then got himself a bachelor pad he couldn't afford in Santa Monica. Got behind in his child support to Lois too. Then got in trouble at the Dirkson's Dairy he managed. Accused of pilfering milk and ice cream, cheese and eggs. Larceny they called it. Almost went to jail but we paid Mr. Dirkson restitution, the $500 he said Lester stole in cash right out of his safe Lester had the keys to. A lot of money $500 was 10 years ago. Les promised to pay us back but never did because then he married that awful Cathy. A topless go-go dancer! Such nasty business all that go-go! You probably never met any of those floozies who worked in those whorehouses—if you'll pardon my French. But thanks to my good, decent neighbor ladies and me, us H.A.D.I.T.S., we helped close La Pink Pant down, got petitions signed and raised a stink at city hall. Nasty business."

"Well, good for you," said I, not one dab of butter melting in my duplicitous mouth while I deep-down wanted to tell her The Truth about me, that I was a F.A.D.I.T.T.—a Floozie Against Disrespect In This Time. But I didn't.

Les Church's mother sighed, sniffed her nose at all that nasty business. "But, oh dear, my poor Lester. He never did have any sense in the ways of love. Always let his heart get in the way of his head. You wouldn't think someone so smart, so good at math could be that way. Oh well. Thanks again, dear, for that perfume. Best darned present anyone ever gave me. And I really mean it."

It's really strange how things happen to us and we don't notice them happening at the time, like how it never really sunk in that day (or any of the days that followed for years) when Les Church gave me, his hands shaking, that envelope that said Dirkson's Drive-in Dairy. on it in the living room of my parents' Sacramento house as he was saying goodbye to us. What I noticed then, that day, that moment, was not the envelope, but Les Church ruffling my little son Sean's blonde curly hair while Les told him to "be good." And how Sean, who only came up to Les's belt buckle, smiled up at him, admiringly, lovingly.

Out of the eyes of babes, we should notice more often, because little children have a way of seeing goodness, you know. If you believe in auras, some say children can see them. Black auras for bad or crazy-mad people like Othello.

115

Blue ones for sad people like I was that day. And I was wondering that day, that moment when Les handed me that envelope: What color did Sean think Les's aura was? And I forgot to ask Sean later, like I forgot all about the envelope until a week later when I finally remembered I'd crammed it, unthinking, into the back pocket of my stretchy beige jeans and opened it and found inside the Dirkson's Drive-in Dairy envelope: five one-hundred dollar bills, each one of them as crisp and clean as cool, wet lettuce.

Chapter 6 | Nervous Breakdown Number Nineteen

"You must do what you think you cannot do."
— Eleanor Roosevelt

Hell's bells. I am having a nervous breakdown, and Linda Alura's having her second fifth of Dom Perignon, chugging it straight from the bottle. Stinking drunk, she reeks of a thousand bistros and ashtrays at only three o'clock in the afternoon. What a bitter disappointment. Or, more modernly, as hipster in-crowds along the Strip and hippies at Love-ins timespeak in February, 1967: BUMMER! Fuck, I think, still too timid and Good-Girl to utter such a dirty word out loud, though I've sure been around the block a lot, am a Ph.D. candidate at Hard Knocks U, and only 27 years old. Miserable, jittery from throes of Nembutal withdrawal, I sit, back in Hollywood at Sammy Glassman's penthouse off Los Feliz, my 98-pound bod sucked into the plush of his penthouse royal blue velvet sofa the size of most human beings' entire living rooms. I bury my face into my hands, freezing cold from the icy wind blowing in through the open sliding glass windows where out on the huge balcony, behind a potted palm, I can see between my fingers the last letters of the Hollywood sign: "O.D." To the east of it I can see between my pinky and ring finger the edge of Griffith Park Observatory where James Dean in *A Rebel Without a Cause* had his switchblade fight with bad boy Buzz. If they were up there right now, I could wave and they could see me, say Hello and I could hear them and maybe I could ask Jim and Buzz to go with me to do something I don't want to

117

do, but must: go to court with me tomorrow when I have to testify against Othello, and they'd say Yes, they'd be my bodyguards, along with Linda Alura and Big Don Maraschino.

"Drink, be merry, my friend, my dear sob sister, Janie brainy," Linda says, pouring some bubbly for me, sloshing much on her purple silk caftan, filling a goblet the size of a goldfish bowl and then chugging it.

"No, thanks," I say, bitterly disappointed. "You know I don't drink."

"Well, drink the fuck up anyway, Miss Sourpuss Party Pooper. We got stuff to celebrate, baby. I will soon become a famous movie star. I'm gonna be the next Jean Harlow. Come on, drink up." She holds the goblet up to my lips as if coaxing me to take my medicine, spilling some of it on my beige stretchy jeans, slopping me up.

"Why are you always trying to corrupt me?" I ask.

"Why are you so fucking boring? Who made you Fun Monitor, anyway?"

"You're drunk, Linda," I accuse.

"Oh, you're so square—" She begins to sing, throaty baritonal, imitating Elvis; she's a very good mimic as well as actress. "—But baby I don't care."

This isn't what I'd expected of my "soul sister" as she'd begun to call herself in her countless cheer-up letters and get well-quick cards she sent me my months of catatonia during my exile in Sacramento as I tried to heal up after what Othello did, after my father died, waited for my face to mend, tried to gather my emotions that had scattered like overturned popcorn in the movie show inside my busted-up brain. Linda'd even sent me Edgar Cayce books on spiritualism, reincarnation, to help me try to figure out, however far-out and soft-headed, maybe even nutty, Cayce's notions were, What It Was All About, Why Othello'd Done

It. Karma, Linda'd decided. None of it My Fault, helping me hope, cope, carry on with my big load.

"You just wait and see," Linda declared. "That rotten brute's really gonna pay in his next life for what he did to you in this life." He was probably — maybe — going to pay for it in this life. Tomorrow, maybe, I hoped, after I testified against him in Los Angeles Superior Court, Criminal Division for his attempted murder of me, Linda Alura and Big Don Maraschino going along to be my bodyguards. But from the looks of Linda now, she's going to be too hung over tomorrow. Fuck. And I don't want to DO this!

So, instead of us and our 'jammies, spots of tea, china plates filled with crumpets, parcels of heart-strung sympathy, lingering soul and sob sister chats about the Meaning of Life next to a roaring fire I'd expected, instead I get this Big Bummer: Linda chugging Dom Perignon out of the bottle like a skid row bum, empty pizza and Chinese take-out boxes, piles of dumped ashtrays inside a stinking, black-cold fireplace the size of one that might be found in a castle in Xanadu — and on the coffee table in front of me, next to Linda's purple fuzzy slippers, a candy dish the size of a hubcap filled with rainbow drugs du jour: oblong yellow-Doll Nembutals, cherry-red Seconals, white amphetamines, powder blue Midols, beige tablets I think are Carter's Little Liver Pills and staphylococcus-shaped Good 'n' Plenty pink and black licorice rods — Linda Alura's favorite snack candy. From inside a cigarette box, Linda takes out a cigarette and a joint of marijuana and lights up both from a book of La Pink Pantera matches that has her doing a Betty Grable pose on its cover. "Oops!" she says as a marijuana seed pops out of the Zig-Zag paper and sears a black hole on top of the right breast of her purple caftan. I glower at Linda for the betrayal I expect tomorrow morning.

"You, Janie Gentry, are looking at the next Jean

Harlow." (She doesn't notice that I glower.) She smiles the beautiful white teeth that got her picked a couple years ago as a Miss California runner-up. (How can she not notice that I glower?) "Any minute my agent is going to call to announce that I got the role of Jean Harlow in this big movie. Me. The Real Jean Harlow. I'm going to be a famous movie star. My acting career is about to skyrocket." She puffs on the marijuana and then the cigarette, blows smoke in my face. "And look at this loot —" She removes a wad of money from the cleavage of her purple caftan. "Money, honey. Look —"

"Did you rob a bank?"

"Fuck, no. Got this from Dr. Bill. Fuck man, fuck man, isn't it groovy?" She rolls the bills on to the royal velvet sofa, the wad ker-plunking between the cushions like a big softball. "Fuck Sammy, fuck La Pink Pantera, his fucking hellhole, I'm never gonna have to marry him now, I'm gonna get rich on my own. Outa sight! I'm diversifying —"

While I am still very uptight about these changing times, maybe because I'm four years older than Linda and from another generation, I'm a War Baby, she's a Baby Boomer, Linda Alura assumes with the greatest of ease the nouveau identity of the tres chic and hip 1960s contemporary young American woman, rides high, hanging ten, on the tsunami zenith of the Sexual Liberation wave and the first rogue wave of Women's Liberation when it's just becoming not just Okay, but utterly right-on, for women to talk dirty. Though she repeats her profane mantra, gleefully, I wince every time she says it: "Fuck, man."

Dr. Bill Somebody is Linda's Sugar Daddy, that rich and famous playboy scientist who lives off his enormous royalties for some chemical invention so vile he won't even tell Linda what it is; she suspects it's either DDT or napalm. Once a week he pays her $300 to dine with him, be his arm candy at a steak house on La Cienega, after she dons first one of the many designer gowns he keeps in a walk-in closet in his manse in Bel Aire. An Oleg Cassini one time, the same one Grace Kelly wore in *Rear Window*. Then, while Dr. Bill sits in an easy chair in front of the fireplace, Linda strips for him while he sips cognac, watching, taking an occasional Polaroid. That's all she does, for all that money which, in 1967, buys Rudi Gernreich minis, Joy parfum, and cases of Dom Perignon Champagne. I'm disgusted that she'd do something I wouldn't do.

"I do not approve," I tell her again. "All that money is ill-gotten."

"Oh, baby, you're so square!"

"And you're a call girl."

"No. I'm self-employed. An entrepreneur. And this is a good business. Better than working in Sammy's fucking hellhole eight days a week slopping beer," Linda Alura sneers, scratching with one of her long pink-enameled fingernails the embroidered, billboard size "S.G." initials on the back of the sofa, same script, a florid curlicue, that Sammy Glassman had painted on the doors of his shocking pink Coupe de Ville Cadillac. I'll work at La Pink Pantera day after tomorrow to earn my airfare back to Sacramento—IF, that is, Othello's found guilty—and there's a chance he won't be because he's got a male judge.

"At least I stay clean, don't stink of beer. And I'm about to expand my business. Dr. Bill's setting me up for a weekly dinner date with one of his colleagues, Dr. Hector."

"Isn't that called pimping? Dr. Bill fixing you up with a colleague like that?"

"Fuck, no. It's called diversification."

Chugging the last drops of the Champagne, Linda Alura drops the bottle, thud, upon the coffin-size coffee table on top of today's newspaper. She wiggles her slender body from the billows of the huge sofa's suck, struts across the huge living room's royal blue shag carpet to the kitchen to pop open another bottle. When she walks onto the royal blue Spanish tile floor, her high heels clatter echoes off the far-flung walls of this huge penthouse, so roomy you could set up nets and play a game of badminton in it if you wanted to.

This is the Decade of Big. Everything is BIG: cars, parking lots, freeways, hairdos, breasts, movies, basketball players, Sammy's TV set; an entertainment center that includes a stereo radio, record player, cabinets for thousands of LPs covers half of one mirrored wall like a Big Kahuna surfboard. The royal blue lamp base in the corner is the size of a pier piling. USA, in 1967, seems to be a huge platter just waiting for Big Things to be placed upon it, spread out, ad infinitum, make room for all the chunks of space from outer space brought back by the famous astronauts to plunk it all down right here: to make Excessive Ecstasy for All.

Linda drops the new bottle of Champagne on top the front page photo of the Black Panther activist who's just been sentenced to life imprisonment for some heinous crime against White People; she wiggles the wet Champagne bottle bottom carefully to create a halo over his Malcolm X-bespectacled face that resembles that of a Nobel Prize winner instead of a psycho cop-killer. You don't have to be an Edgar Cayce, Victor Hugo or Martin Luther King Jr. to know this man has been framed. She sighs, kisses the tip of her finger, then presses it, a gentle lipstick-kiss fingerprint on the handsome Black Panther's distraught lips.

Then Linda burps Champagne, snarls, imitating Sammy's Brooklyn-Jewish accent: "Sammy just gave me an ultimatum to marry him, now or never. He'll give me anything, he told me, if I will, even a mansion in Beverly Hills. A fucking Taj Mahal. He showed it to me." She snuffs out her cigarette, lights another, waves it around in circles, and begins to imitate Bette Davis: "What do I want a mansion for? I'm no interior decorator. He wants to own me too! Turn me into a fucking housewife! That old fart!"

Sammy is only eight years older than Linda, four older than me, but an old codger nonetheless, Linda thinks, with an emerging pot belly she pokes every time she sees him eating too much liverwurst on rye and chocolate cheesecake he buys from Steli's Deli on Fairfax. I think Sammy's kind of cute, looks a little like Marlon Brando when Marlon played Marc Antony. But Linda's in love with another man. Who, she won't tell me, so I don't think she'd go for Sammy even if he looked like Rock Hudson in a powder blue suit. Plus he's going prematurely bald and swoops strenuously what hair he still has on the sides of his head over the top that makes his shiny pate look covered with skinny bicycle tire skid-marks. Linda Alura and I have hair nearly the size of Monet haystacks piled on top of our heads. All this hair, we are both certain in 1967, proof positive that we will stay forever young.

"An easier $300 no one has ever earned in the history of western civilization, and I'm not about to give up this gig to be someone's fucking housewife," Linda proclaims. "Money, honey," Linda sings, falsetto, imitating Paul McCartney, then kisses the money.

"Does Sammy know about the Jean Harlow thing?"

"Nope. But when it happens, I'm blowing this scene."

"Does Sammy know about Dr. Bill? The source of your ill-gotten goods?"

"Nope. He'd probably kill me if he knew. So let's not be telling Sammy our little secret."

"Hells bells, you think Sammy might really kill you?"

"Never know. It's rumored he's with the Mafia."

"Is he really?"

"I dunno for sure but it's rumored that Sammy's hellhole is just a front for a Vegas money laundering ring."

"Really?"

"Yep."

It was hard to tell when Linda was telling the truth, when to take her seriously or to laugh, she drifted so easily from reality into fantasy all the time, propelled and fueled by her many drugs and drink and acting ability. When I first met her, the first day I walked into La Pink Pantera looking for a job, she was drunk as a skunk at noon sitting in Sammy's office, chugging vodka from a paper-bagged pint she kept in her orange tote bag.

"Sammy's got a gun—" Linda says, pulls a key from her bra inside her purple silk caftan and unlocks the middle drawer of the coffee table. "See?" Inside is a gun, all right, a big ugly thing like you see Nazi spies carry in old World War Two movies.

"How do you launder money, anyway?" I ask.

"I dunno," she says and slams shut the drawer. "Who cares? I got money of my own. Fuck Sammy. Fuck Vegas."

I shake my head, disapproving of her tarty language and her tarty money. "I wouldn't do what you're doing even if those guys paid me a thousand dollars an hour."

If Linda wanted to be cruel or at least painfully honest, she could easily say, Well no one would ever pay you that kind of money because you're a square and you're not alluring and beautiful like me. She truly is beautiful with all that naturally blonde hair, big hazel-blue eyes and graceful ballerina body. She personifies literally her Spanish adjective name Linda that translates: "Beautiful."

She swings her legs around, like Elvis, imitates him again: "Baby, you just keep on a-go-go-in', that's all right with me, mama. Go-go your little heart out till you're an old and gray went-went girl. Besides, I'm gonna be the next Jean Harlow. When I get that movie role, I'm leaving Sammy for good. Keeping the diamond, of course—"

She blows on a huge diamond sparkling brightly on her left ring finger. "Ohh, looky this—a bribe from Sammy, to try to get me to marry him, said I could keep it—This rock won't lose its shape," she sings, imitating Marilyn Monroe, then she lowers her head, glowers at me and says, imitating Orson Welles as Macbeth: "Fear not till they come to Dunsinane!" Linda's very drunk.

She pops the cork of the Champagne bottle, offers me some of the foam. I shake my head no and she glubs a fourth of the contents, making me say: "Haven't you had enough? Linda, you're going to drink yourself to death."

"Hey, baby, I'm Mexican-Irish, you know," Linda Maria O'Hara Alvarado says, stage name Linda Alura, movie star-to-be-named Linda O'Hara. "I can hold my booze, baby. It's in my blood.

"And looky this: For us—" She pulls something out of her bra, holds it in her hand, these three gray gobs of goo that look like toe jam or wads of used chewing gum. "Tonight, baby. Sammy's gonna be our guide. We're gonna trip, baby, you and me. And Brandi Blue, too. Find our yellow brick road to paradise and pick the lock on the gate."

"What's that crud?"

"Mescaline. Organic. The best money can buy. From Bearded Bob."

I groan, thinking of my Bitter Disappointment of tomorrow as I see morning come and Linda too hung over, too messed up to go to court with me like she promised. "Oh, no, Linda. Not tonight. Linda, Linda, *Linda*. You know what I got to do tomorrow."

"Why are you always trying to rain on my parades? Fuck, man, you could fuck up a wet dream."

"Why are you always trying to corrupt me? Trying to convince me that this counterculture stupid stuff is the Right Thing?"

"Because it is the Right Thing. It's not corrupt at all. I'm merely trying to help enlighten you. Have some fun, won't you? It'll make you more interesting."

"You know how I feel about drugs. Even prescription stuff. I just two days ago swore off sleeping pills. After taking ten, twelve. I forget how many and crashed at Big Don's for 13 hours straight. That was scary to fall sound asleep like that and not wake up for so long. And I haven't slept since. If I were to drop mescaline in this state of mind in the middle of a nineteenth nervous breakdown I'd probably freak out and jump out the window." Sammy's penthouse looking out at the Hollywood Hills is on the ninth floor. I imagine myself splattered flat as a pancake on the sidewalk griddle of Los Feliz Boulevard. I scowl at the mescaline lying there in her palm and sneer: "This must be what the cyanide pellets look like that they drop in the buckets of acid in the gas chambers on Death Rows."

"Janie Baby, this is mescaline. Organic. From magic groovy good stuff. God made it with his own hands. It'll expand our minds. Make us clean and new. You need this, Janie Gentry, after all you've been through." She holds the gobs gently like they are tiny teeny breakable little babies, holds them up to show me: "It'll make us strong to face together that brute in court tomorrow. Don't hang with the brutes—"she says, mimicking Blanche Dubois from *A Streetcar Named Desire*, a recent role at the Pasadena Playhouse she didn't get because she was too young to play Blanche. Linda pats, lovingly, a there-there my bony knee bulging inside my beige stretch jeans. "This mescaline will help us understand what makes the universe tick. "

"I understand, all right, Linda. I can see it all ticking right now: You won't be going to court with me tomorrow morning."

"Yes, I will. This stuff'll be worn off by morning." She

126

pops one of the gobs in her mouth, chews a little, winces from its bad taste and swallows. All was lost. The mescaline, though I couldn't see it, could only sense it, was falling down, down, down, down into the black hole of Alice's gullet in Wonderland to make her larger, make her smaller, make you see her, now you don't: no Alice beside me tomorrow morning in Los Angeles County Superior Court, Criminal Division. Alice will be in her Thunderland Wonderland.

"No," I say, glowering some more. "That stuff will not be worn off by morning. And you can't go to court all hung-over and messed up on mescaline. The judge will cite you for contempt of court."

"No, he won't." And she's probably right. She's so beautiful she can get away with anything, I'm sure. I've seen her shoplift a bottle of Dom Perignon while giving the liquor store clerk a wink and blowing him a kiss and he blew a kiss back and let her walk right on out wielding the Dom Perignon like a baton twirler leading a 76-tromboned parade. Scofflaw Linda loves to break the law and defy every social convention she can. She drives her 1966 avocado green Mustang convertible at least 30 miles over the speed limit even in a school zone, passes cars from the right lane and she never gets a traffic ticket because the cops always let her off with a warning because she's so beautiful. She smokes cigarettes and sometimes marijuana in movie theaters even after she's asked by the management to cease. She mails all her letters without stamps. And she had a baby out of wedlock she named Belinda two years ago and gave up for adoption. But that's a long story, she always says, and never tells me more. And I want to know.

"Come on, baby," Linda teases, wiggles her palm holding the two remaining weird entities. "Times . . . they are ... " Linda sings, imitating Bob Dylan: " ... a-changin'."

127

She smiles at me. Her teeth are big and white and perfect and sparkle poetically like stars in the night. "You gotta get with it, Janie, strainy. Don't be uptight. Be out of sight!" She speaks brightly, believe-you-me, a chucklehead face in a TV commercial: "Baby! Get happy!"

I don't get happy, though. But Linda does. And so does her other best go-go girlfriend Brandi Blue (née Lucille Louise). Three hours into their getting happy business, just as their mescaline really kicks in full blast, Sammy arrives at eight o'clock with containers of supper shrimp chow mein and sweet and sour chicken. But they want no part of this meal because Sammy's blank white walls have become unbearably amazing and beginning to turn kaleidoscope. Outside, the lit Hollywood sign you can see only the "OD" of out the sliding glass doors that sprawl across the whole north living room wall, they imagine, if spelled backward: DOOWYLLOH is a message from God who must be Celtic, they're sure of it. As sure as I am the biggest square on earth, they accuse me in unison when I groan, Oh, dear god. When Linda gives me the finger and they both glower at me glowering at them, I get fed up. I've seen the same scenes dozens of time on the six o'clock news on TV reporting the latest Haight-Ashbury Love-ins and Be-ins. Linda and Brandi Blue aren't being the least bit original in their alleged heightened awareness. What is so mind-expanding anyway when everyone sees the same cliché psychedelia neon-nonsense?

Bored with their lack of imagination, however subconscious, I go to Sammy's spare bedroom, for I am his houseguest.

Exhausted from not sleeping in two whole days and nights, I crawl between crisp, clean sheets, but cannot fall asleep. The bells of Othello Hell and Nembutal withdrawal keep clanging inside my mind. Also, it doesn't help that next to the bed on a little table there's a hamster—Linda's—in a cage on a night stand next to the bed. The little creature is running round and round on a spinning treadmill, going crazy, it seems, from being caged. As Othello surely will go crazy too in prison if he's convicted tomorrow after I testify against him. Though there's a big chance he will go free. He's got a male judge; Othello's claiming I "made" him "do it." I "provoked" him. And he thinks a male judge will understand how true it is how women make men do things they don't want to do, *must* do because women are witches. How true, how true, how true, I hear the judge confirm, all night long as the hamster's treadmill goes: squeak-squeak; squeak-squeak; squeak-squeak while I feel, know the silent hamster's desperation to Get Outa This Place, take the Last Train to Clarksville Before It's Too Late Baby.

Around midnight I listen, too, to the squeaking of Linda's and Brandi Blue's mescaline dreams from beyond the guest room door, faraway in the caverns of Sammy's badminton court of a living room. Then I hear their squeaks turn to shrieks, the loudest, Linda's. Then I hear a big bang, as if someone's slammed the door and left forever. Or maybe it was a gunshot? Sammy's gun? Sammy shouts LINDA! Did he take mescaline, too? Sammy has never taken any drugs before that I knew of. I suppose Linda has finally corrupted him, as if he hadn't committed enough dirty deeds being a go-go girlie bar owner. When I hear a thud, I can't tell where it comes from, out there or did the hamster do it?

"Stop it!" I yell at the hamster. I rattle its cage. "Shut up! SHUT UP!" I yell louder, terrifying it, making it run faster and squeak the thing it runs on faster, louder, the hamster's flight as it runs for its life becoming one long incessant screech. After I hear a pitiful faraway squeal I can't tell is the hamster or Linda's voice in the living room, I

129

whisper an apology to the poor hamster for my cruelty. But its noisy panic does not cease. Giving up trying to communicate with the animal netherworld, I cover my head with the sheet and count not sheep but hamsters and I count not my blessings but my miseries. I do not sleep one wink.

Come the next morning the penthouse is so quiet it is as solemn and holy as an abandoned cathedral. Empty Dom Perignon Champagne bottles lined up around the Notre Dame entertainment-center of TV-stereo-et al, stand like noble monks lonely at Stations of the Cross. The lobster pot filled now with gone-cold water some sort of kitchen catechism font. Overturned clumps of empty Chinese take-out cartons and stained, deranged chopsticks upon the coffee table resemble a lesser intelligent race's skewed notion of a Stonehenge. The air is filled with the stale smoke of a million tobacco and marijuana puffs at a pow-wow café and the dying-breath narcosis of sleeping things: the exhausted, unrequited hamster curled fetal in its sad cage, Brandi Blue sprawled on the big-big royal blue velvet sofa looking misplaced and broken as if she'd fallen out of the sky from an airliner and landed there. Sammy and Linda lay leaden lumps in his big-big, round bed in his big-big rectangular bedroom painted the royal blue color of a gigantic bruise.

I am certain I will never forgive Linda if I live three hundred years, like Big Don Maraschino says the long life-line in my palm says I will, when she does not say one word to me when she throws a set of car keys at me. No Good luck, Good-bye, out of her mouth; not even "Have a Nice Day, Baby." Especially no regretful: I'm sorry Baby I'm hanging you up like an old hat, won't be your moral support, your bodyguard. Even though there was a big, big chance I might not be coming back alive. If Othello is found Not Guilty by that male judge, I won't, because Othello's

130

vowed to Finish the Job: Me. I catch, when they bounce off my chest, the car keys, Sammy's, to his shocking pink Caddie that Linda throws at me. Well, at least I have my other bodyguard, Big Don Maraschino.

Nope, I don't. Big Don isn't home when I go by to pick him up. My big, bad, brave bodyguard left for Texas — yet again — in the middle of the night, Sonny Buoy, his surfer buddy roommate informs me, showing me half of his scrawny nude bod as he peeks from behind the half-opened door. Sonny Buoy can tell by the look on my face I don't believe him because my mouth is so twisted agape I hack and croak from a dry throat. Because I can smell Big Don in there. His lemony cologne he slaps on his handsome face every hour he's awake. Big Don is in there, I just know it, smell it, and some girl crashed in his arms like I was three nights ago, the last night I slept. "Big Don's in there," I say, "don't lie to me, Sonny Buoy."

"Really, babe," says Sonny Buoy, not too convincingly, his voice pitched high, a little guilty, smirking curl on his sea salt-chapped surfer dude lips. "He really had to split, babe. Some dudes were after him. He told me to tell you when you showed up he was really, really sorry. He'll make it up to you when he comes back. Next week, maybe. Maybe not."

"I may be dead after next week. I may be dead after this afternoon."

"Hey, bummer, man. What you want me to do about it, man?" asks Sonny Buoy, raising his arms in futile, phony despair, then brushes a shawl of bushy-bushy blonde hairdo'd sun-and-sea-streaked bangs out of his beady brown eyes not unlike a hamster's, while his semi-hard penis hiding halfway behind the door, dangles no-no at me. Oh, dear, just what I didn't need: a Phallus in my Plunderland.

131

Dear God, I gasp, two hours later, not dead.

Othello's trial over, I drive back to Sammy's penthouse from Los Angeles County Superior Court, Criminal Division. Maneuvering Sammy's huge shocking pink Caddie through a driving rainstorm, I shake all over nervously as if I transport ill-got goods and feel like an even worse criminal sort after the parking lot attendant said, "Nice car, baby," and gave me a knowing wink as I paid him the parking fee, thinking me a prostitute, probably. How else would a girl like me afford a brand new Coupe de Ville like that anyway?

In the middle of a cloudburst just as I drive past city hall, a Rolling Stones medley begins on the radio with "Let's Spend the Night Together" which was officially banned in Los Angeles County last week for its obscenity and the anti-establishmentarian deejay playing it will get arrested tomorrow. Mick Jagger, my nagging nemesis for nearly two years, turns schizo and instead of telling me how I can't get me no satisfaction no matter how hard I try and try now woos me, groans that he needs me more than ever as I sigh, remember fondly three nights ago when I spent the night with Big Don and slept peacefully and platonically in his arms because he was too messed up for a romantic encounter and so was I. "Stupid Girl" plays as I turn north on to Los Angeles Street, Mick Jagger reminding me what an idiot I was in that time and place of 1967: age 27, an accidental go-go girl, mother of three fatherless children, twice divorced, one of my exes on his way to maximum security Soledad Prison for three-to-ten years for attempted murder, thanks to my testimony 24 minutes ago.

"And are you the victim?" the male judge sternly asked me, shutting up my irrelevant and immaterial babbling about the Night in Question. I was trying, via this babbling, you see, to dispute beyond a shadow of a doubt: Motive, Provocation, how I'd been so nice to Othello that night in question, that he'd really done what he did after I cooked Othello eggs over easy and put two maraschino cherries in the yolks for eyes of Joy and the little starburst diamond was innocent, too—

The judge repeated, louder: "Are you the victim?"

"Yes," I whispered, into a microphone that roared across the courtroom.

"Would you please point to your assailant, the alleged accused?"

Nervously, the 98 pounds of me pondered for a moment. Suddenly I'd had a loss of memory when I looked at Othello sitting there, all alone, in the defendant's chair behind the big rectangular table. Othello, with his 250-pounds of six-foot-two, former champion football player-might, chomping on chewing gum while he looked at the ceiling, nonplussed, awaiting acquittal, a done deal.

As soon as I pointed, silently, the judge hammered his gavel, Bang, and proclaimed: "Guilty as charged."

And it was over. Done deal. Easy as that. Othello's decision backfired not to have a jury, go man-to-man with a man judge, a man who'd know how witch women make men do things they don't want to do but *must*, and when this sunk in that this judge didn't see it man-to-man the way he did, Othello, after shaking his big wolf-black Bête Noire head, disbelieving his ears, beast unchained by truth, Othello went berserk, threw back his chair, shouted at the judge while the bailiff offered me his hand to step down from the witness stand: "WHAT?!" Othello's basso profundo bellowed and rattled the courtroom windows.

When the judge banged Order! Order! Othello bellowed at the judge:

"You MOTHERFUCKER! Can't you see she's a lying

WHORE?!"

Tossing over the courtroom table to get at me, Othello lunged so close as he reached for my throat, his fingernail scraped and gashed against my neck, and made it bleed. As two policemen rushed forward to restrain Othello, I clasped my bloody neck and ran, track-star ran, out the courtroom, looking back only once over my shoulder for Othello who surely would've chased me this one last time were he not handcuffed and being shoved and scuffled away grimacing the most monstrous look, ever, on his astounded face.

And I ran. Down the courtroom hall, down the down escalator, and out of the courthouse and into the rain and across the rain puddles in the gutter and street and into the parking lot and hopped into Sammy's Caddie. Slammed the door and locked it. As I paid the parking lot attendant for one hour and ten minutes, had he listened closely to the Rolling Stones' rock and roll drumbeat of my heart, he could've danced a little boogaloo right there in his wet raincoat and kiosk. Wet, all wet I was, wearing my two-piece avocado-green suit, a Coco Chanel imitation I'd worn to my father's funeral, blood stains now down the front of it. Othello'd worn his wedding clothes he wore when he made me marry him three years ago; 70 pounds overweight now, he'd stuffed himself, huge meaty sausage, into his dingy white shirt, maroon blazer and navy blue flannel trousers. I almost wore, inadvertently, my wedding suit too, but the beige three-piece was now too big for me. And, crazily, our court day was the third anniversary of the day we got married in Las Vegas.

Now, 30 minutes later after Othello's conviction, I am wet and woozy, yet wired, my brain wiped dry from exhaustion on my third day of Nembutol withdrawal sobriety and sleeplessness. As I drive down Sunset Boulevard to turn right on Vermont, the Rolling Stones' "Mother's Little Helpers" jeer and indict me: "What a drag it is get-teeng oh-old." And I do feel old and ancient, stiff and prematurely arthritic from the icy, pouring-down rain, yet another worst storm of the 20th Century hitting the whole state of California.

Then "Nineteenth Nervous Breakdown" begins to play, coup de grace of my personal serenade from Mick Jagger. I can barely see out the rain-splattered and fogged-up windshield. Stupid Girl, me, I can't find the defroster for the life of me in this new-fangled Cadillac. Nor can I roll down the windows because they're those electric button ones, no handles anyplace. But I do know a bit of French. Know who Victor Hugo is. But I don't know how to type nor how to roll down the windows in a 1967 brand-new car. So instead of turning left off Vermont onto Los Feliz to go to Sammy's penthouse, I drive straight ahead by mistake and am on my way up to Griffith Park.

Right past the Greek Theatre, I pull off the road beneath some eucalyptus trees that are going wild, twisting verdigris helixes in the go-go dancing tornado wind. I take a deep breath of the freezing, rainy air. Snowflakes are melting in the February sky up there at the tips of old pines. Shivering in this avocado-green skirt I made into a mini, my kneecaps turned snowballs, I try to find the heater button but it is the air conditioner and more icy-cold air sprays in across my scrawny bod devoid of the armor of fat I will have in a few years that will keep me warm in my old age. I rub my icy hands, stiff from clutching the shocking pink steering wheel as I wait a few moments for the cloudburst to subside. When it abates, I make a U-turn just as a eucalyptus branch snaps off an overhanging tree and falls hard, crashing loud behind me where the pink Caddie windshield was just a moment before.

"FUCK!" I shout. "Even Mother Nature wants to fucking murder me!" I shout to the eucalyptus trees. But they have troubles of their own.

When I finally make it back to Sammy's penthouse, unscathed, but all wet, my hair one big sticky bun, I find Linda Alura all alone. She sits on the big-big royal blue velvet sofa, a lit cigarette dangling from her mouth as she reaches into her box of stash for a marijuana one. Her long, loose, shiny naturally blonde hair and long bangs that need trimming bounce off her nose and cover her face. She peers out from this golden cavern but she is not looking at me, the frenzied friend she abandoned this morning. She is looking at the red glow of her meaningless cigarette ash. She scrutinizes it as if it talks to her, is telling her what makes the universe tick and she is memorizing every single word. I suppose she's still fucked up from last night.

"Confucius say," I say, looking at all the Chinese food cartons sitting around beginning to stink: "Never is one so low after one has been so high." Confucius, of course, never said that. I did. With more actressy sarcasm I knew I could emote. I glower at her again, and again she does not notice.

"Right on, Confucius, right on," she says, drearily, huskily. Looks up, hair shadows covering her face: "Well, well, if it isn't Janie Gentry. How'd it go, Janie Gentry, this Day of the Brute?" She lights her marijuana wand with shaking hands, puffs hard, does the ritualistic sucking, squeaking, choking, coughing, wheezing of the marijuana user. What is the point of marijuana when it's so much trouble and getting all fucked up on it hurts so bad?

"How the fuck do you think it went?" I scream, my voice echoing down the hall where the bedrooms sprawl. I kick over an empty Dom Perignon Champagne bottle, but it falls comfy, soundlessly into the royal blue shag carpet. Linda does not flinch or care one bit that I have said the word "fuck" in the presence of another human being for the first time in my life. Nor does God reach down and grab me by the throat even though I am now thus corrupted. I stand in front of the electric fireplace to dry off my profane self.

"Fuck!" I say it again, this time my voice echoing out from the kitchen and bathroom. I kind of like the way it sounds. Goody for me, good girl no more. Again, Linda does not notice. Absorbed in the dry cloth of her Self, she stares at the ashes on the top of the smoking thing and ignores me. When I throw Sammy's car keys on the floor, on the marble entryway so they'll make a loud crash, she ignores that too.

"Well, baby, guess what? We're finally going to do it." She sighs. "Me and Sammy are getting married. Might as well. My agent called. I didn't get the Jean Harlow role. Fuck!" She puffs her marijuana. "I hate Las Vegas. The desert. The gambling. The casinos. Sammy talked me into it. As if I got much of a choice." She adjusts the neck of the purple silk caftan she wears to caress her own neck and when I lean forward I can see bruises there the same width and size of Sammy's hands and fingertips, exactly what my neck looked like after Othello did what he did to me. Then I see a big black bruise across her forehead, blotches of it, like oil slick, ecological disaster, spreading down toward her eyes turning her eyelids black. Dented over her eyebrow, a red, eyelash-size cut looks just like the tiny cut Othello made minutes ago on my neck with his fingernail. I touch mine, then reach down to touch hers, hoping to make it better.

"Sammy found out about Dr. Bill, didn't he? And tried to murder you. With his gun! His Mafia gun!" Murder, murder, everywhere. Some Wonderland this is.

"No, no. Sammy wouldn't hurt a fly. Nothing to get hung about. I brought this on myself. Really. I did. Tried to kill myself last night, that's what. That mescaline was some bad shit. I must have a word with my purveyor. Bearded Bob sold me some bad shit." She takes a long hit off her marijuana. "You were wise to decline. Freaked me fucking out. Got me thinking about Belinda, my baby girl I gave away. Remember me telling you about her?" She snuffs out her smoked-down cigarette, lights another, juggling her lit marijuana on the ashtray. Having bad habits like Linda's really keeps your hands busy. Perhaps in another time and place she would've busied them with quilt making and spinning wheels and churning butter.

"Without Belinda I have nothing to live for. Nothing. Not even being Jean Harlow. Oh, well, maybe that would've helped a little. So I decided to jump off the balcony. Good ole Sammy. Grabbed me just in the nick of time and threw me back inside and I fell against the TV console. Cut my head." She touches her forehead near the red, toothpick switchblade slit there. "Sammy saved my life. So now I owe him. When he saw how sad I was, he promised to find Belinda for me. Hire a detective to look for her. It'll cost a lot of money. But he said he'd do it. Buy her back for me if he can, if anyone's adopted her. At least try to get me some visitation rights. So the least I can do for Sammy if he's going to do all that for me is marry him. Right? I even told him I love another man, that I can never love him." She puffs the marijuana, then the cigarette, blowing smoke and more back-and-forth smoke into the living room all around her until she is a human chimneystack.

I notice the newspaper's still there, the halo on the Black Panther now a round grey wrinkle, but the pal pink kiss still there. The way the Black Panther's mug shot of his handsome face looks straight at me, makes me feel psychic enough to ask: "Is that Belinda's father? The other man you really love?" She doesn't answer, says instead:

"Didn't you hear all the ruckus last night? Me and Sammy yelling our heads off? I cried out for you and I heard you yell back 'Shut up. Stop it.' I needed you, Janie Gentry.

138

And you didn't come. You know how I came in a hurry when you needed me when your father died. Went with you to his funeral at the Veterans Cemetery. When the soldiers shot off the rifles and played 'Taps.' I put my arm around you." Little tears glisten the dark circles around her eyes, making them look like onyx pools. She wipes them with her purple caftan. The caftan is a mess: Champagne, Chinese food, you name it, streaked all over it. "I sent you books and get-well cards after that Brute did what he did to you and you were holed up hiding out in Sacramento. And I needed you last night and called out for you so why didn't you come help me?"

"I was yelling at the hamster in that cage next to the bed. It kept squeaking that thing. All night long. I didn't sleep a wink all night."

"Poor little thing. Hamsters can't help it. They're nocturnal, you know. All he's doing is looking for love. And a home." She wipes another tear on her caftan. Out of pity for the hamster, not me. She shivers. The sliding glass doors to the balcony are still open, just the way they were, I guess, when Sammy threw Linda through them back to safety and the living in the living room. "Fuck! I don't want to get married! Sammy's so old! When I'm 40 he'll be pushing 50!" She stomps her bare feet, feigning tantrum. "Old!"

My stomach begins to growl. Not only have I not slept for 75 hours, neither have I eaten. "Should I offer you my condolences? What? I really don't know what to say to someone who makes walking down the aisle sound like a trek to Death Row."

Linda laughs.

"I guess marrying Sammy means you'll have to give up your diversifications. Your Drs. Bill and Hector."

"Ohh," she groans. "I forgot all about them — and all that." She laughs again. "Oh, baby, you always have a way of making me laugh and cheering me up. You've got to come to Vegas with us. Witness my execution. Tonight."

But I can't. I've got to go home to Sacramento tomorrow. Back to my children and my worried mother. First though, tonight, I have to work at La Pink Pantera to earn the plane fare. I sit down on the big-big royal blue velvet sofa, suddenly very tired, and rub my stomach to quiet down its loud growls. Linda sighs. Linda puffs. Exhales. Sighs. Puffs. Exhales. Smoke and more smoke wafts and wiggles and circles around her beautiful blonde head and heads for the open sliding-glass doors like nervous, miserable, leaving-town halos. But the rainy wind blows them back in, dissipating them.

"So, Janie Gentry. How did it go this lovely morn between you and the Brute?"

"Great. Just great. This has been one of the greatest days of my life."

"Great. As it was mine," she says, huskily, my sarcastic sob sister. "And did our Brute go to jail or go free?"

"Guilty. Three-to-ten at Soledad."

'Wow. What Karma, man, He must've done some bad shit in his last life to get such payback, being so crazy and all, in this life." Then she falls back, her head upon the fat royal blue velvet throw pillows, big royal blue shoulders to lean on that cradle gently her bruised shoulders. She sighs, says: "I know you want to know more about Belinda. My baby girl I gave away. But it's a long story. I'll tell you when we're little old ancient ladies."

"Are we going to be friends for that long?"

"If we live long enough to be old and ancient."

Being old and ancient seems so far away, I feel queasy from the time-travel motion sickness of just thinking about it. I get up, and, leaving Linda lying there, smoking and sighing, her banged-up raccoon eyes staring at the ceiling searching for more secrets to the universe, I tiptoe into the tulips of Sammy's kitchen, look in the refrigerator for something to eat. But all there is inside are bottles of chilled Dom Perignon, a log of kosher liverwurst, an empty box that once held a chocolate cheesecake from Steli's Deli. And, a coincidence, a pleasant surprise, one of my favorite foods from childhood: a jar of maraschino cherries. I always vowed when I was a little girl I'd always have them in my refrigerator when I was grown up. And I always have. Beautiful red shiny maraschino cherries to top off every dessert. My children love them too.

After I place two maraschino cherries on top of a slab of liverwurst and eat it like a pizza, I go back into Sammy's guest room with a view of the cloud-covered Griffith Park Observatory where I could see those rebels without causes, James Dean and Bad Boy Buzz, step on each other's blue suede shoes as if they were up there right now. From the window I watch wintry wonderland snow flurries flit around the "HO" part of the Hollywood sign while I step out of my rain-sopped avocado-green two-piece suit, put on my salmon-pink pajamas.

I take a good look at the bloodstained jacket, wonder if it will ever come clean, and it won't. I will never wear it again, not because of the blood but because of the memories. I'll think I've thrown it away and in 2004 will be astonished when I see wearing the faux Chanel avocado-green jacket while she sets the table for Christmas dinner sweet-sixteen Clara, Othello's and my—*our*—granddaughter whom he never saw, who will find my old clothes in an old box, think the turned-dark brown bloodstain is chocolate and I won't say otherwise. I will hug her and say how cute she looks wearing this Blast From the Past, ha-ha-ha.

This happy amazing 2004 Christmas encounter with this beautiful descendant I never, never could've imagined,

141

not in a million years that February, 1967, when I did not expect to live to be an ancient woman, as I sat, stunned senseless as stone, feeling old as yesterday's popcorn, in Sammy Glassman's guest bedroom.

Hugging myself to try to get warm in 1967, I then crawled, done, done to, and done in, in-between cold, cold sheets, and into the cold, cold bed next to the cage that held the hamster, now a brown, snoring fur ball, to rest up, both of us, rest up for yet another hard day's day and night, a respite from yet another nineteenth nervous breakdown of Being Young and doing it, doing it, running, running, go-go going, looking

and looking

for Love.

"Love is a smoke made with the fume of sighs."
— William Shakespeare

Wallflower

The Playgal Club owners had photos
of all us go-go girls
wallpapering the wall of their office:
8"x10" glossies of all of us,
past and present, bending over
or turning around showing off
breasts or bottoms or our faces
marabou or leopard skin draped
across our boobs pooching over our top

all of us photographed
by a guy older than our fathers
who called himself the Silver Fox
and still wore a 1954 bowtie and crew cut
and fancied himself a hot lover man
a Hugh Hefner harem-keeper
instead of a dirty old man
rutting around shirtless
while he snapped our pictures
in his apartment taking hours
touching us here and there
wiping his balding head and bushy eyebrows
sweating from the hot lights and his libido

and it was rumored that you
only got photos of yourself for yourself
if you went to bed with the Silver Fox although
all the girls denied it said What?
Me go to bed with that old fart?
Yet, Bunni, Wendi, Suzi Q and Delilah
got portfolios, Barbie 50 8x10s
she sold for $50 each to her

boyfriends and sugar daddies
while all I ever got after coffee
at Denny's with the Silver Fox
was one for me and one copy for the boss's office
which they tacked near the trashcan
and every day during the 2 years
I worked at the Playgal Club I watched my face,
cleavage, smile and hairdo
become fly-specked, cigarette ash-dusty
beer-, coffee- and rain-stained
as the strange wallpaper of myself
became a ruin in my own lifetime—
a squalid impertinence
of my inestimable unimportance.

Chapter 7 | The Night After I Helped To Kill A Man

The Summer of Love, August 16, 1967, the hot night after I helped to kill a man, my cup runneth over with guilt as I worked the night shift at the Playgal Club, a go-go bar, a pagan blight, in the midst of Raptures Gardens, California, a suburbia do-right bedroom city filled with assorted Christian churches a beer keg's throw from Disneyland, when suddenly that inimitable Mr. Hot Stuff, Big Don Maraschino, the man I once thought I loved, reappeared into my strange and hectic life. Wearing a white linen suit, powder blue silk open-collar shirt, white linen espadrilles, no socks, duds more suitable for a Hawaiian wedding or an inspection of his own personal pineapple plantation than a night out at a sticky-stinky girlie go-go bar, his Italian pompadour blow-dried into a Mount Everest of fastidious handsomeness, six-foot-five Big Don strutted in just as "I Can't Get No Satisfaction" began to roar on the jukebox. First, though, Big Don, former bouncer at La Pink Pantera, the first go-go bar I ever worked, on the Sunset Strip 40 miles away, paid his respects and mutual admiration of muscularity by giving five, slapping the ham-slab-sized palms of the Playgal Club's ferocious and buffed bouncer Ernesto who sat, always rocking, always rocked-out on uppers, on a broken-down, three-legged barstool at the front door. Ernesto was the man who actually killed the man last night. I, rat-fink, only helped.

Always pissed off, too, Ever-ready Ernesto, as he called himself, a Puerto Rico-born, former Marine and Vietnam vet, raised on the mean streets of Brooklyn, was always itching for a fight, to "get things off his chest and let

145

it all hang out," he said of his hard-boiled pent up hostilities. So it was with the greatest of ease like a man on a flying trapeze that Ernesto quickly, if not eagerly, responded to my complaints about the man cramming his hand down my cleavage, swatting my rump, calling me a whore. Jumping Jack flash, Ernesto grabbed the man in a choke-hold though the man was a head taller, dragged him out of the place and tossed him, ker-plop, light-weight as a Raggedy Andy doll, dumped outside on to the sidewalk. Died instantly. Never knew what hit him: not Ernesto, but that concrete, still blistering enough heat at seven p.m. you could've sizzled an egg next to where he lay that August 15, 110-degree dog-day. Dead. Really Dead.

"Baby! Long time no see!" Big Don roared over the jukebox noise, Mick Jagger, who, a multi-millionaire with thousands of groupies by 1967, had everything he wanted, yet still complained of not gettin' no satisfaction. I was still all shook up over the man dying the night before, so I wasn't in the greatest of moods to be suddenly reunited with the man I once thought I loved and hadn't seen in six months. I shouldn't've told Ernesto. Mea culpa, I supposed, pondering this guilty horror as I poured eight pitchers of tap beer for two floor girls waving at me to hurry. The Playgal Club was packed. A new band, the Beethoven Boogaloo, a groovy group comprised of pseudo-scruffy intellectuals, was starting that night after much publicity in newspapers and television. And how did Big Don find me, anyway? I'd been hiding out here in Orange County after I paid down on a house in suburbia with the money my father left me after he died, with great hope Othello, my ex, would never find me here if/when he was released from Soledad State Penitentiary where he went last February for the attempted murder of me a year ago this very night, August 16th.

Voluntary Point Girl, because after last night I'll never

serve the floor again, I plopped the slopping pitchers down, four on two trays, took the money, still warm, from Dee Dee and Blonde-haired Patti's cleavage—their "money boxes" where they stored their paper money tips—and then they wiggled away, balancing all that beer with magical powers only practiced by human contortionists, to serve the howling, fun-seeking Playgal Club habitues: Nam-bound Marines from nearby El Toro, aerospace execs, real estate brokers, construction crews, couples on dates, assorted pervs and alkies sitting at red-topped tables scattered all through the brothel-red velvet wallpapered walls. Except for our white costumes, everything was red in the place: red lights, red pool table tops, red stage, red-red-red reminding us girls of menstruation, though the Playgal Club owners had in mind cherry lollipops and lipstick-sticky lips.

"Baby—" Big Don crooned as he reached up to me standing behind the bar and grabbed me by the neck and pulled me down where he stood behind the bar to his lips to kiss me. Wow. He smelled the same, of pricey lemony aftershave you can only buy at Saks Fifth Avenue—and in Paris, France. "Lookin' good," Big Don said to me, eyeing up himself reflected all dressed in white in the mirror behind me while he pretended to eye me up in my white fringed bikini, white high heel sandals, flesh-colored dancing tights, Playgal Club Government Issue garb, sold to us at 300% markup by the owners, the rich playboy Durton Diehl and former pool hustling champion, Fast Eddie Barginer. They made us buy new fringe weekly so we could buy that from them too.

"But you still smell a lot like smoke," he said, frowning. Big Don was neat and clean. Took three showers a day, he proudly told me long ago. Odors and immaculateness meant a lot to him and he often complained about how overpoweringly we go-go girls smelled of ashtrays and stale beer, barroom stench clinging to our hairspray. I hid my fingernails stained with cigarette ashes from his view. I sighed, tried to pretend I was glad to see him, leaned toward him to hear his good news babble about his new job making big bucks as a personal bodyguard for a celebrity; I'd know his name instantly if he told me Who but he was sworn to secrecy. He slapped a hundred dollar bill on to the bar for me to bring him a glass of 45-cent tap beer. When he left me a nickel tip, the tightwad, that's when I remembered he owed me $40 for unrendered bodyguard services from the summer of 1966 when Othello started threatening to kill me and Big Don promised to protect me and did for only two nights.

"Do You Like Good Music?" began to play on the jukebox, the song last night the man I helped to kill kept playing over and over as he danced to it a gawky, stupid Boogaloo. The man shouldn't've died from simply falling like that, the investigating police detective said, the coroner agreeing, both suspecting foul play by Ernesto or me, suspected hit man and gun moll, questioned for an hour in the Playgal Club's office. But an autopsy—which we just learned of today—showed that the man had such an enormously high alcohol blood level that he would've died in an hour anyway of brain saturation, even if he hadn't hit his noggin. Turned out the man'd been making martini runs to the cocktail bar across the street; also he'd hidden a pint of rum in the breast pocket of his Richard Nixon navy blue three-piece pin-striped suit. Turned out, too, the man was the Mayor of the City of Raptures Gardens. And, until yesterday, a teetotaler.

Yesterday, the Playgal Club owners, Durton Diehl and Fast Eddie Barginer, p.r.'ing, had invited all the city's go-go bar protesters trying to take their beer license away, the Chamber of Commerce board members, Raptures Gardens City Council members, and the local H.A.D.I.T.S. (Housewives Against Decadence In This Society), for a freebie afternoon shrimp, prime rib and assorted salads buffet and beer to provide them with a chance to look and see for themselves, so's to prove to them that there was no nasty business going on upon the Playgal Club premises, show how nice we go-go girls were, working girls in our own way not unlike ordinary secretaries, some of us working our way through college, not the wrongdoing call girls and secret prostitutes those decent people, most of them do-right Christians, imagined us. We dressed in conservative white-fringed bikinis, child-like derring-do compared to the topless bars emerging on the go-go horizon, including my former place of employ, La Pink Pantera, now called the Pink Pant. Owner Sammy Glassman had built a huge middle bar to showcase the topless hypermammiferous Linda Alura after she got silicone breast enlargement injections to size 40D. We playgals at the Playgal Club were not obscene at all, merely girls-next-door types not unlike the clientele's very own wives, sisters, nieces and daughters, dancing goofy dances like the Mashed Potato, James Brown, The Monkey, Funky Chicken, the Jerk, Boogaloo, Temptation Walk, Shing-a-Ling. You know, all that harmless, silly stuff they could now see hippies do on the six o'clock news at Love-ins and on *Laugh In*.

By the time us night shift go-go girls came on last night, most of the city dignitaries had gone home to their wives, 2.3 children, and casserole suppers, except for that one hanger-on drunken guy, Raptures Gardens' esteemed Mayor, who lugged around an on-the-house sloppy pitcher of beer into which he'd poured some of that rum, chugging it like water, singing yo-ho-ho and a bottle of rum. Har har, me matey, he pirate-talked as he leered at Blonde Patti first, who pushed him away and then, pinching my bosom, calling me a serving wench, he stuck his entire hand down my cleavage, then, into my ear, his tongue. Then he got mean. "WHORES!" he yelled as the jukebox played up loud. "All of you bitches are WHORES!" When he punched me on my rear end, missing my tailbone by an inch, causing me to fall against a table, spill two pitchers and twist my ankle, that's when I told Ernesto on him. I'll always wish I hadn't.

Ernesto didn't mean to kill the guy. Only eighty-six him, kick him out, show him the Playgal Club didn't put up with such rough stuff disrespect to us go-go girls. Ernesto felt bad about it too, though he'd seen plenty of guys die in Vietnam. However, when the Raptures Gardens city cops checked his criminal and military record, turned out Ernesto'd not only been a Vietnam war hero, but also a juvenile delinquent with a record of assault with a deadly weapon — his hands. He'd been a Golden Gloves champ. As I sat shaking in owner Durton and Fast Eddie's claustrophobic broom closet-size office, the cops ran a make on me, too, insinuated conspiracy between Ernesto and me that implied, the more they talked about it, a possible love triangle that included the Mayor, that turned into a story (alleged "Shocking!") on page one of that day's city newspaper.

After the man died, Spike, the manager, my mean Edward G. Robinson-faced boss, wouldn't let me go home, so all night long last night, as I shook serving beer, nearly fell off the stage from vertigo when I go-go danced, I felt the mayor guy's ghost hovering over me. A terrible feeling. To know that you are the last person on earth someone touched before he died. Making it even more horrible, the ghost kept calling me whore, as if I'd been the one who shoved him out the door. I suppose the ghost thought I'd helped, and I suppose I did. Mea culpa. I'm sorry, I'm sorry, I said to the

150

ghost all night. Ernesto didn't care, thanks to being hardened by Vietnam's horrors and to smoking marijuana on his breaks with Spike as they took drives in Spike's white Caddie up and down Harbor Boulevard, back and forth in front of Disneyland, getting higher and higher.

"BABY!" Big Don shouted, "Aren't you listening? I said I got something for you —" He pushed two twenties at me. Oh, so he was finally paying me back for his bodyguard services unrendered. He only protected me two nights at $10 a night. "But first, answer me: Do you still love ol' Big Don?" I smiled, wanly. I nodded, lying. "Good, because here's what I need —"

I thought he was going to say he needed me, decided during this long six months of not seeing me that I was the one he really loved. I was still young enough to think silly thoughts like that, even though I'd been around the block a few times. Something about your ex-husband trying to murder you makes you grow old very fast. This was the night, August 16th, of the first-year anniversary of What Othello Did To Me. I had a lot of crazy thoughts running around in my head all day: the dead man, Othello. I figured all these months that if I just didn't THINK about what Othello had done to me, I'd forget what he did. But when I remembered that morning when I woke up what day it was, I remembered Every Thing: every blow from his fist, every drop of blood I shed and I was awfully disappointed in myself. August 16ths for the rest of my life, disappointing me all those days, too, would always be my days of If Only — If Only I'd run the other way. So it was hard to pay attention to what Big Don was yammering about, especially with my memories and the jukebox up so loud. Then finally it sunk in: Big Don wanted me to do something, naked.

"What?!" I said. "You want me to do WHAT?"

"Please, baby, it's such short notice and I can't find anyone else. Please, I need you to do this for Sonny Buoy," he said, pleadingly, just as that scrawny little surfer dude, Big Dan's Best Bud, Sonny Buoy, Himself, strolled in, saw Big Don and saddled up beside him on a barstool.

"Fuck, man, sure is hard to find a parking spot out there, man," Sonny Buoy snarled. "This place packed or what? Did they assassinate a President in here or what?"

What a jerk, that rotten little Sonny Buoy, to make joke of President Kennedy's 1963 assassination.

Bursting into laughter, Big Don spat a big mouthful of beer across the bar, most of it landing on my white fringe bikini bottom, near my thigh. The beer streamed down my flesh-colored pantyhose (skater's tights, actually), into my high-heeled sandals, sopping more my beer-soaked Dr. Scholl's foot pads. I stood in a puddle of slopped beer that in five minutes would be mopped by the Playgal go-fer, Wild Willie, a Vietnam vet whose hands shook all the time, results of Agent Orange exposure. "Swabbing the deck" he, ex-Navy man, called this janitorial duty, payment for which he got all the beer he wanted and to sleep for free nights he needed to on one of the pool tables.

A month ago, Kelli Kate, one of the cutest go-go girls ever, slipped on the spot where I stood in a flood of beer, a Sea of Absurdity, all this go-go stuff, and broke both of her cute kneecaps. She was suing Fast Eddie and Durton; I didn't know if she'd ever get any money out of them even though she wasn't expected to ever be able to walk again.

"Man, you are the funniest!" Big Don said to his Good Bud, patting Sonny Buoy's back. I cringed. I almost hated Sonny Buoy (because he ostensibly hated me so much), could not understand what Big Don saw in him as a friend. Strung out, as usual, probably on Nembutals and amphetamines and maybe LSD, too, since it'd gotten so

152

popular the last few months thanks to Timothy Leary and the hordes of hippies turning on and tuning out, Sonny Buoy twitched, twisted his hair and looked stupid. The Beethoven Boogaloo was warming up, so it quieted down for a moment so Sonny Buoy could say loud enough for all the drinking men at the bar to hear, holding his nose at me bending toward him:

"Is it true you go-go girls wash your hair in clam juice?" Big Don laughed some more, along with a couple burly machinists sitting next to them. In 1967, after two years of all this go-go stuff, I was really getting tired of being the brunt of put-down go-go girl jokes.

"You're not funny, Sonny Buoy," I said. Misogynist, I could've said he was, but I was only 27 in 1967, that Summer of Love, and hadn't yet heard that word. (The Feminists were coming and would teach us a thing or two about such male chauvinsts like him.) Big Don pushed money at me to fetch Sonny Buoy his usual cola. As I poured, Big Don, behind my back, fickle as always, began to flirt with Red-headed Carol, whispered to her, probably gave her his telephone number. I gave Sonny Buoy his drink, deliberately spilling some so the bar around his elbows would get sticky, stain his weirdo tie-dyed Nehru shirt, and left the bar to dance. My turn, every eighth song, my turn, this time: "Mustang Sally." After go-go dancing for two years, I had a rote routine now, just "did my thing," jerked, bent my knees, shook my imagined tail feathers (that white fringe), waved my arms around, snapped my fingers, tried to remember to smile my "Ain't we got fun?" smile, thought about my life, what went wrong, why Othello did what he did. If only I'd run for my life, it wouldn't've happened the way it did a year ago. Dance, dance, dance, one-trick pony, in the frying pan, into the fire, hard day's night, eight days a week.

All my life I'll remember those dances. A rock song

from that day might pop out of a Muzak intercom speaker in a grocery store in 1984 or 2001 or 2014, "My Girl," say, or "Land of a Thousand Dances," "What's New Pussycat?" or "I Got You, Babe," "Lady Madonna," and, remembering my routine, I'll almost break out into my old moves next to a pile of tomatoes in the vegetable department, take a chance of slipping on a wet lettuce leaf strewn on the floor to do the Pony, a Temptation Walk, Boogaloo, the electrical unforgettable past jerking me around, shocking me alive when I'm an old ancient woman. Done dancing in 1967, I ran back to the bar, robot serving-wench, to wash glasses, pour beer, empty ashtrays, and smile. "I'll give you fifty to do it," Big Don said when I returned. "Please—"

"I wouldn't do it for a thousand."

"Hey, I don't got that kind of money. Aw, baby, come on, it's no big thing."

"NO!" I shouted.

"Shhh—" He waved for me to bend over to whisper in my ear. "Don't say anything. It's supposed to be a surprise for Sonny Buoy."

"Surprise him with someone else."

"Hey, I just thought you could use the money, baby, that's all. Hey, baby, you don't have to get hostile—" He held up his hands, backed off, as if I held a gun to him trying to rob him.

What he wanted me to do was jump out of a cardboard cake at Sonny Buoy's going away stag party in his honor. Tomorrow night. NAKED. Sonny Buoy got drafted and was ordered to go off to boot camp by September 1st. Good, I was about to say, and add that I hoped he got his salty little sunburned butt shot off, the meanest thing I'd've ever said up till then, when my Simon Legree, Edward G. Robinson-gangster-faced boss, Spike, shined his flashlight, crisscross, in my face, the sign it was my turn to take a pee break. Then Spike waved another crisscross over my head as I pushed, rushing through the crowd to the ladies room, to remind me I better make it snappy. We go-go girls only got three-minute pee breaks three times a night on our nine-hour shift. Spike had a stopwatch to make sure that's all we took. *Le roi s'amuser*.

The Playgal Club's Ladies Room was also us go-go girls' dressing room, the only place I ever worked that didn't provide us with privacy, not even a storage room filled with wharf rats like The Fort had. This go-go thing had lightened up so much the past year, become such a no-big-thing, pervs moving on to gaze at topless dancers, couples out on dates now came to see us go-go girls dance, so harmless we'd become with our mere show of bellybuttons. So the ladies room was filled with ordinary women, some becoming groupies, wannabes, asking questions about our makeup, where we bought our false eyelashes, eyelash glue; where'd we get our hair done so cute, how did we learn to dance so good. These younger, ordinary women were the baby sisters of the harpy-heroines, the H.A.D.I.T.S., wannabe Aphrodites, femme rebels with applause for emerging decadence in this society Sometimes they even asked for our autographs, which was what I thought at first the woman waiting for me that night in the Ladies Room wanted from me when she asked:

"You Janie Gentry?" The woman didn't smile, seemed shy. Sometimes the housewives were in such awe of us, we seemed so exotic wearing all that fringe, they could barely speak. I looked for a pen she might be holding so I could autograph a paper towel for her like I sometimes did.

"Yes," I said, quickly unpinning my fringe so's to pull down my bikini bottoms to pee. Relieving myself quickly, quickly wiping, flushing, vacating the stall, gathering my pins from the table next to the full-length mirror to re-pin quickly my fringe to my bottoms within my allotted three

155

minutes, I finally had a second to notice she held up her left hand, showing me something, but not a pen for me to sign my autograph. She showed me her wedding ring.

"Guess you know who I am," she said, solemnly, waving her hand wearing the ring.

I looked at her ring. "No. Who?"

"I'm his wife."

HIS wife. The only masculine pronoun on my mind right then was related to the proper noun of Othello, Reave Gentry Jr., my ex-husband, the man who tried to murder me a year ago this very night. Othello's wife? Petite, trembling, wearing dark-cherry lipstick, she looked like a 1950s girl of the chickie run, what Natalie Wood would look like when she's forty, if she wears a blonde wig then. That ring, a silver wedding band, looked somewhat like the cheap dime store one Othello bought for me the summer of 1956 when we were sweet 16 and he was trying to get me to marry him. "LUV," he'd had engraved for 25 cents inside it. What was she doing with it? How had Othello's wife found me? Was Othello out of Soledad State Penitentiary so soon?

"What do you want?" I asked Othello's wife.

'Wanted to see what you looked like. Tell you what I thought of you for what you did to my husband."

"What I did to HIM? He tried to murder me. A year ago this very night."

"Oh, so it's true. You do know him. Have known him for some time."

"Yes. Since I was fourteen years old."

"Dear me! For that long he's known you?"

How long had she known Othello? She looked a lot like his high school Latin teacher who bawled me out for doing Othello's homework. How could Othello've hooked up with his old high school Latin teacher after all these years? Persona non grata, I remembered from my help-

156

Othello Latin homework days, when she began to weep, said, "It's all your fault—you, you—" And I was just about to ask her about Othello, where was he, why had she married him, when suddenly:

"OKAY, TIME IS UP! YOU LITTLE TRAMP!" yelled Spike, yelled it every night, as he shoved open the door of the Ladies Room, then: "GET YOUR LAZY BUTT DOWN THE RAMP!" Then he laughed. Spike loved it how it rhymed. Spike liked thinking of himself as a poet, a Bob Dylan or a John Lennon.

The little, but older, woman began to sob. How exceptionally ordinary she looked. Respectable far beyond the primness of a Latin teacher, so much so she seemed illuminated, the mirror behind her making a halo surrounding her blonde wig. She looked more like the dutiful, casserole-making good wife of an accountant, a doctor's wife, not the babycake of an incarcerated convicted attempted murderer. Finally, I noticed that the wedding band was actually made of platinum and had a small sparkling diamond in the center. Finally, I realized who she was, recognized her from a photo in today's newspaper. Wearing that conservative brass-buttoned royal blue suit and those sensible shoes: she was a politician's wife. This was the good wife of the dead Mayor of Raptures Gardens, California, glowering at me.

"I'd like to scratch your eyes out!" the good wife of the dead mayor snarled, holding up her pale, perfectly manicured fingernails. Her tiny royal blue shoulders shook with furious grief.

"Grief can make you very angry," I said to the sad, good woman, remembering how my mother felt last November after my father died suddenly of a second heart attack, how she tossed with a great fury all his inflammable things into the fireplace, his books, his letters, his business cards. My grief over my father's death took the form of

157

catatonia as I sought solace and comprehension, but not finding it, in Victor Hugo, Darby and Joan, The Book of Job, Edgar Cayce, Freud, Jung, finally that diamond sutra: my father's World War Two journal he kept when he was a medic in Algeria I'd rescued, only partially scorched, from my mother's roaring fire. I'm so sorry for your loss, I was going to say to this grieving Good Woman, when:

"Grief makes you angry? You, you— What do YOU, nothing but a party girl, know about such sensibilities as grief? Half naked! Working in a terrible place like this! Why, you're nothing but a SLUT!" Being called that—a slut—even though I wasn't a slut—by this Good Woman was the dirtiest, ugliest I've ever felt in my life. Men say ugly things like that all the time; ugly words can spill out of men like trash, proliferation, out of overstuffed bins and brains, mere gender-glitch testosterone overflow. But a woman, especially a Good Woman, should know better, be able to crystallize her latent knowledge. But I was beginning to realize how stupid we human beings are, even us women. Especially me.

"I've never talked like that to anyone before! Never been in a terrible place like this before—This Sodom and Gomorrah—" A fair lily in this Playgal Club's pagan blight, she looked in horror around the filthy Ladies Room at the empty beer glasses on the table left by ladies, "Dee Dee is a Dyke!" lip-stick-written on the mirror, toilet paper strewn about. I knew how she felt. I'd been terrified, too, raw like her once, too, the first time I stepped into a go-go bar, La Pink Pantera, all by myself, ages ago. She took a hanky from her clutch bag, blew her lovely nose, and wiped her pretty brown eyes. Tears sparkled upon a tiny golden cross she wore on a chain around her neck and when she caressed it feebly and said, nobly: "I'm a Good Christian Woman—" I believed her. Her role models had probably been Eleanor Roosevelt, Mamie Eisenhower, and Doris Day.

158

I'd simply been a Good Girl, a War Baby who'd been told not to ever try. "Girls are to be seen and not heard," they told me. My role models Betty Crocker, Olive Oyl, Lucy Ricardo, Lois Lane. Always, a baked-goods loving Mr. Hot Stuff or big galoot Superman would come running to my rescue. But, so far, nothing.

"My husband was a fine man. I just can't believe he cavorted with the likes of you." She began to blubber, thinking of cavorting with the likes of me. "He was deacon of our church. A pillar of society. A good father. Husband. Never drank a day in his life — And YOU killed him!"

When Spike kicked the door one more time, then stuck his head, shoulders and big foot inside the door, flicked the lights on and off, and yelled at me: "NOW, BITCH!" the woman shrieked. There's always something very scary, loathsome and violating about a man in the Ladies Room, like finding a cockroach in your teacup or a cobra in your tote bag.

"OHHHH—" the grieving, Good Christian Woman screamed, scared, loathing, violated.

"WHO the fuck's THAT!" Spike yelled. "SHUT UP LADY! I got a business to run here! There're ladies out here waiting to use the ladies room!" Waiting ladies out there peeked inside the door.

The woman screamed: "Help, Help! Dear God, help me! They've killed my husband!"

Spike waved for Ernesto, who came running. "Hey, lady," Spike said, lowering his voice to a growl, as gentle of a voice as his mean self could muster: "Lady, shhh, shhh, lady, we've never thrown a woman outa here before, but we will if you don't shut the fuck up!"

Hysterical with grief, the dead mayor's wife shrieked again, louder. "OHHHHHHH! HELP! GOD HELP ME!"

"SHADDAP!" Spike roared. Pool hustlers began to

look inside the Ladies Room door.

"Don't, Spike. She's that man's wife," I said. "That man last night, you know, the man who died. I think she's having a nervous breakdown—" El Toro Marines looked inside the Ladies Room.

"Oh, noooo—" Spike groaned. "Fuck, man, we don't need any more trouble than we already got. She says she's gonna sue our asses! For a million dollars! We're screwed! Get her outa here, Ernesto!" The Beethoven Boogaloo looked inside the Ladies Room.

I nudged Spike's torso and snarling face out of the doorjamb, waved Ernesto toward me. "Leave her be, Spike. She had to get something off her chest and let it all hang out." Ernesto nodded; he understood.

Okay with Spike to leave her be, because he had another goldbricking go-go girl to crisscross his flashlight at: Red-headed Donna who was talking, smiling at Big Don. "And hey! You: Doris Day—" Spike warned me, "—no more jaw-jagging, no more pillow talking, with your Rock Hudson over there. If he doesn't stop pestering the girls, I'm gonna have Ernesto throw out his big ass." Grandly, with his flashlight, Spike crisscrossed Big Don's big, but shapely, ass.

"Okay, boss," I said, and went back to the sobbing woman, took her gently by her elbow, led her to Ernesto standing alert, ever-ready to kick some ass. "Escort this nice lady to her car."

"I've never thrown out a woman before."

"No, Ernesto, I said escort. Walk her all the way to her car. See that she locks her doors and drives safely away. She's a grieving widow and a good Christian woman."

And, tenderly, Ernesto did and I went back to work.

I never again saw the widow of the dead man I helped to kill. Her lawsuit against the Playgal Club, Does: Ernesto, Spike, Patti and me, for Wrongful Death, was dismissed for lack of evidence to prove negligence, malice aforethought or culpability of any kind on the part of any of us. Spike and Ernesto were just doing His Job. No charges were brought against me, arguably the Victim, an Exhibit A. Blonde Patti Exhibit B. The shocking story of the dead man's alleged love triangle in the newspaper was never retracted, so that poor distraught widow's worries of her husband's shenanigans were never laid to rest. I wish I could've explained to her and his ghost that hovered over me at night and sometimes, to this day, still does, told them the truth: I wasn't a slut, or a whore. Her unfortunate husband, pillar of society, maligned on the last day of his life on earth as a lech and lush, had not cavorted with the likes of me. Respectable uptight teetotaler Jekyll turned street-thug rummy Hyde, Mr. Good Christian Mayor Man was simply a bad drunk. Proof that you've got to watch your step through life up to the very last inch, and *never* fall off the stage, no matter how bad the music is and you can't dance to it. Life is often unfair, but Death is always a dirty, rotten, cacophonous Trickster.

Spike fired me that night for jaw-jagging and taking too long of a pee break. But he rehired me the next day. No, I didn't jump out of a cardboard cake, naked. Red-headed Carol did, but never got paid for it. Sonny Buoy didn't go to Vietnam anyway. His rich oil magnate father, Sondringham Boynton, Senior, owner of all of California's Boynt Oil gas stations, finally forgiving his sonny boy (aka "buoy") for being just a Go-fer, bought off the draft board. (Big Don luckily 4-F due to his flat feet.) The new band, the Beethoven Boogaloo, didn't turn out to be as much of a crowd pleaser as expected. In fact, too gifted as musicians to be popular, they were often booed when they lapsed into long flute riffs playing "Light My Fire" so Durton Diehl fired them and replaced them with Dick Dale and his Surfing Guitar who turned out to be a smash, packed them in, twistin' and shouting nights away, for years until he bought the place and Durton and Fast Eddie published a magazine called *The Playgal*, and made millions using nude men as centerfolds, Big Don Maraschino and Ever-ready Ernesto a couple of them. The Beethoven Boogaloo, though, made me an offer Summer of Love 1967 they didn't think I could refuse: to go with them on their gig up to Alaska to go-go dance for $500 a week—topless, in a go-go bar where men up there hadn't seen a woman in three years. Wow, I said. And then: No. But, baby, it's daylight 24 hours a day up there right now, said rumored-to-be-gay Little Davy, the cute flutist, thinking that piece of heliology would change my mind. Up there in Alaska, all that sunshine assuring it, I'd've surely had many hard days' days.

Working at the Playgal Club for another two years before I went to another place to conclude the course of my seven years as a go-go girl, the length of bad luck for breaking a mirror, the average prison sentence for the commission of a felony, I watched up close and personal the go-go thing die, that *"ye-ye phenomene"* —as the world-weary, but right-on, Jean-Paul Sartre had called the yeah-yeah pop culture emergence in 1964. And as it all went-went away, choked like an old horse at a drying-up gulch, as it all devolved, all that Beatlesiana seemingly soulfully Beethoven now, in retrospect, when compared to today's dismissive, impatient, yeah-yeah-yeah mantra of the me-me-me anti-culture, I continued my comings of ages, my low-life Odyssey of Wonderment about What now? Why? And: If only—If only I'd run the other way—none of the above would've ever happened. Nor this little piece of my latent knowledge that crystallized big and bright:

What work it was, being young.

@ The Playgal Club, 1969
photo by "Big Dave"

Painting the Topless Dancer Till We Glowed

Maida the topless dancer lay naked on her motel bed
smoking marijuana and giggling, ticklish
while my hippie boyfriend and I painted yellow
fluorescent daisies and green vines and leaves
up and down and all around her breasts, arms,
back and thighs and then we painted orange
fluorescent butterflies on her shoulders, nipples
bellybutton and knees, and then, my idea, we
painted all over her bod purple, blue and white
fluorescent dots I told Maida to tell the guys
at the topless go-go bar was "rainbow rain,"
drunk guys sometimes liking a little poetry
and Maida did and she was so popular that night
because she was so beautiful that night with all
that beautiful fluorescent paint all over her while
she danced and glowed at her topless dancing job
she made $200 in tips plus another $100 when
a good-looking guy paid her to let him come home
with her to her motel room to watch her wash off
the fluorescent paint and he wound up loving her
so much he bought her a house where they still live
today and later that night because my hippie boyfriend
and I'd had so much fun laughing and painting till we
glowed like Maida, he asked me to marry him and
even though I knew he'd never amount to anything
with all that fluorescence on his mind, two weeks later I did.
It's really amazing how
a coat of paint can change how
everything really is.

Chapter 8 | Went-Went Girl

California dreamin' on a pre-winter's day in northeast Kansas, day after Thanksgiving, 1969, after seeing goofy go-go girls on tv just standing around, goofing off it seemed, doing nothing but look cute and happy, waving arms, go-go dancing the Swim, the Jerk, the wa-wa-Watusi, then seeing even cuter and happier Goldie Hawn giggling and wiggling on "Laugh In," Mary Kay Randall figured being a go-go girl was the brand new Gold Rush for Girls, an easy way to get rich quick, maybe get famous too like giddy Goldie, meet and maybe marry one of The Righteous Brothers. Mary Kay Randall had a crush on the tall one. Plus it'd be fun. Gosh, a hundred times more fun than being a root beer girl in her hometown's A&W. So, leaving her little two-year-old boy, Josh, too young to even know she was gone, with her mother to care for till she got rich in California, Mary Kay Randall packed up everything she owned in her rattletrap yellow VW Bug and left her home state of Kansas where they grew corn the color of her hair and wheat to make white bread the color of her skin and came to L.A., first stop for gold in them thar California hills, so she thought: the Hollywood Strip.

Trouble was, tired from driving 32 hours straight through from Kansas to Colorado and Utah and Nevada to California, Mary Kay Randall took the wrong freeway fork in the road at the juncture in Colton, California, veered south on the Riverside Freeway towards Orange County instead of going west to L.A. and the Hollywood Strip. By then, so exhausted she was falling asleep at the wheel at midnight, taking an off-ramp for gas, she wound up in the small town of Gustin in the packed parking lot of Daisy Mae's á Go-Go where a supermarket once lived before get-rich-quickers turned it into a beer bar dirty dive.

In the middle of a strip mall five miles from El Toro Marine Corps base, Daisy Mae's á Go-Go shimmied, twisted and shouted in the middle of all the world's orange groves that in five years would be leveled for upscale tract housing, the orange grove owners becoming overnight millionaires.

Inside Daisy Mae's á Go-Go that night, Ike and Tina Turner, working it on out, playing their hearts out, got down, performed their last Saturday night after a month-long booking that had not attracted many fans in that very white and sometimes white supremacist-conservative Orange County, the birthplace of the high and mighty John Birch Society and stern reborn Christianity where in 1969 dwelled descendants of the indigenous San Gabrieleños and Mexicans, 1890s no-nonsense German homesteaders (who'd planted the orange groves) and 1950s working-stiff G.I. no-down-payment suburbanites — most of them, if not all, future Ronald Reagan fanatics. That night Daisy's was packed with Vietnam-bound Marines, free-love loving tatterdemalion hippies and scofflaw dope dealers. In a lull on Ike and Tina Turner's meteoric rise to fame that would happen in a year when "Proud Mary" became number one on the pop charts, Ike and Tina's show-stopping sweat and stomp Revue had been wasted on and merely bored that see-and-be-seen motley young in-and-sin-crowd.

I couldn't keep my eyes off the show, though, the most fun dancing I'd ever have as a go-go girl except for a couple nights at The Fort in 1965 when I was a go-go girl in the raw and got to hear and dance to some of the best of the blues, live, and lush. I loved Tina Turner's athletic wonder-woman dancing, fresh wild alive every time she danced no matter how tired she got and I loved Ike's rhythmic soul music abounding in 1969, hoped it would win in the pop music race instead of Jimi Hendrix's, The Doors', et al ad

166

infinitum psychedelic rock 'n' roll the younger generation, those ubiquitous Baby Boomers breathing down my War Baby neck were liking best, ear- and mind-busting music for them to tune in, turn on and drop out to. When Ike and Tina took their breaks, Ike and his band leaving the place to ride around the block for some "fresh air," meaning, doing drugs du jour, whatever it was they were "into," wherever they were "at," I'd always catch Tina Turner's eye, hand her the cola in the glass I iced to frosty in the beer cooler especially for her. She never knew I did so, cared so much for her. She never spoke to me except to say Thanks and I never dared speak to her because she seemed so sad as she sipped the cola solemnly while she leaned in the corner against the jukebox, hugging herself as if cold though the huge room was hot with drugged, alcoholic breath and young energy. Tina Turner stared into space as if wondering, as I often did, too, in 1969 at Daisy Mae's á Go-Go: "Where am I?"

Often, trying to conjure courage to speak to her, I imagined telling Tina Turner how my mother was half Cajun on her father's side that meant maybe I had one-sixteenth black blood in me, maybe one-32/nds. Black was Beautiful in those days of 1969 during the supposed Dawning of the Age of Aquarius. After Otis Redding died in 1967 and then Martin Luther King Jr. in 1968, I felt so utterly pale and nondescript. But it was only a rumor that my grandfather Old Robert was half Cajun, and even if I could prove that he was, what would Tina Turner say about this? Not, "Gimme five, Sister!" as I imagined, then an invitation to go on the road with her as her back-up soul sister, but, most likely a cursory glance at my mousy-brown hair only sometimes curly, a blank stare and: "So?"

Once I tried to get her to notice me by volunteering to dance on the ten-foot-high circular stage in the middle of the dance floor Spike, my mean boss, had built just for her. But she

167

refused to dance up there, on that "dangerous thing" and run the risk of falling off and breaking her neck. I played "Proud Mary" on the jukebox and tried to imitate Tina's Funky Chicken steps, looked pretty good, too, I might say, but Tina Turner just stared on into space thinking her own thoughts and didn't notice how I'd risked falling from that awful contraption and breaking my neck. My sense of balance hadn't been too good after Othello did what he did to me in 1966; often I experienced serious vertigo on stages higher than six feet and needed help getting down the narrow stairs.

During Ike and Tina Turner's last break, wearing a zipped-up corduroy jacket and baggy, farmer type work jeans, Kansas square, not California Girl modish, slim-thighed cool hip-hugger bellbottoms, road-weary Mary Kay Randall pushed her way to the bar through the crowd wanting drinks from me, waving money and empty glasses. Mary Kay Randall looked up at me, her round white face glowing lemon meringue pie beneath the black lights and asked if I could give her a job. I guess I looked like the Boss since I was doing so much work, washing glasses, emptying ashtrays, giving all the floor girls their drink orders for the two hundred-and-some drinkers that night, then ringing up their money on the cash register, giving back change. But bosses of go-go bars didn't do much work. I pointed to the Real Boss, Spike, near Tina Turner leaning on the other side of the jukebox.

One black stripe of an eyebrow across his smirking face, fat pink lips sucking a cigar, Spike was the spitting and dangerous image of Edward G. Robinson. He smirked, showing no teeth like Edward G. smirked, teeth hidden behind his snarly big teeth contemptuously because he'd just smoked some marijuana in his incense-stinky-smoky office he called his "Orifice." Some good stuff, some Thai Stick that came already rolled, looking like mere cigarettes in Lucky

Strike packs that came from Vietnam, smuggled into California somehow and at great risk by brave entrepreneur American soldiers. Spike'd just bought a bunch from Bearded Bob, a handsome devil, a blonde one with a curly beard like some of those ancient Greek god heads without noses in museums. He stood bodyguard close to Spike, Spike's arm snake-slung around his shoulder, Bearded Bob a bro', a favored henchman, the main Orange County purveyor of ill-gotten goods. I know because my no-good scofflaw third husband, T.J. DuRong, was one of his flunkies.

After Spike hired Mary Kay Randall on the spot because the joint was jumpin' and he needed an extra girl, Mary Kay didn't mind at all the show-nearly-all scanty costume. She beamed as happy as a little girl in Mommy's best satin dress as she smiled nice white teeth, just one little barely noticeable crooked eyetooth. So happy was she with the red and white polka-dot off-the-shoulder peasant top cut so short and low down, letting-it-all-hang-out, it bared us girls' midriff and most of our cleavage, she giggled, sounding a lot like Goldie Hawn on tv. With the red and white polka-dot Daisy Mae peasant top, we wore black French cut bikini bottoms that showed off her round and chubby thighs, pleasingly plump, though, that seemed to have white pockets filled with cotton poofs sewn to them. Her ribcage, amply covered with white-fleshed pooch, turned into a little roll of angel food cake and bobbled sweet baby fat over her bikini bottom. Mary Kay Randall, according to her Kansas state drivers license, was twenty-one years and two days old.

"Right on! Outa sight! I DIG this! Guh-ROOVY!" she said, sounding so very-very square with her mid-western twang, turning around for me where I stood behind the bar. I was what was called The Point Girl. Bartender, I'd be called in a cocktail lounge except that I never saw a bartender anywhere who ever worked this hard. And I worked this hard behind the bar because I preferred the protection it provided against the lushes and lechers on the other side of it reaching to pinch or cop a feel. And every night I paid the price for this safety from salacity by pouring every drop of beer, cola, lemon-lime soda, and wine cooler, plus popped open bottled beer, tomato juice, warmed up poor boy sandwiches in an electric toaster oven, snatched bags of Beer Nuts and potato chips, corn chips, beef jerky from racks and plopped it all, eight days a week, onto the trays of five floor girls, now six of them, counting Mary Kay.

Newly named "Merry," she'd written floridly this "stage name" on six tip-trays Spike'd just sold her for a dollar each, plus $10 for the Daisy Mae go-go girl garb. Hardly any of the young drinking generation knew who or what a Daisy Mae was, the once-famous horny gal friend of reluctant runaway lover man L'il' Abner from cartoonist Al Capp's daily syndicated newspaper cartoon satire of rube buffoonery, snide white supremacist jabs, actually, at hardscrabble Deep South hick hunks and dumb love-starved farmers' daughters as obsolete and cornball in 1969 as a Papa Hemingway marlin tail-finned 1949 Studebaker.

"Lookin' good," I, being a go-go girl, said, 1969 slangily. Then, the Real Me, a square, said: "You look utterly adorable." And she did, the hick girl, the innocent that she was, go-go girl in the raw, oblivious, not knowing or caring about le scandal extraordinaire of her Daisy Mae costume, her anachronistic persona. And what spunk; she reminded me of me my first day on the job back in July 1965, enduring the noise, the bawd and wages of skin and sin, enjoying and amazed by the instant wealth provided by this mother lode go-go thing. During the last set Ike and Tina Turner Revue would ever play in Orange County, Mary Kay, I mean

Merry, made as much in tips in one hour serving beer, wine coolers, colas and Beer Nuts, et al, as she made in a WEEK at the Kansas root beer stand as a root beer girl.

"Thanks to Bobby," she said to me after Daisy Mae's closed at 2 a.m. for the night, helping me behind the bar wash the millions of dirty beer glasses, pitchers and ashtrays in a sink full of yeasty, ashy scummy water I, a cynical, wearing out factotum by then, imagined clogged if not with cholera, at least with euglena I learned about in my prerequisite microbiology class I attended twice a week for nursing school admission next fall. Soon, I hoped, with adequate education and a respectable job, I'd literally clean up my act, Get Away from All This.

Bobby? I asked. Bobby Who? Fluttering her thick, pale blonde eyelashes, she nodded at Bearded Bob. None of Bearded Bob's go-go girlfriends I'd known had ever called him Bobby. I cringed at her naif familiarity with this wicked wolf in tie-dyed t-shirt's and patched jeans' sheep's clothing.

"Bobby gave me this little white pill that gave me the strength to work tonight. I was really tired after being on the road for so long. For free he gave it to me. Really nice of him. You don't find guys like him in Kansas. He's so cute. He looks like a movie star. Don't know what it was but boy did it do the trick. Woke me right up!"

Handsome devil Bearded Bob, no Kansas boy, that was for sure, smiled at her from where he always stood by the jukebox while Spike counted the night's profits in his Orifice, Bearded Bob waiting like he always did for the go-go girl of the night who didn't have a date, take her with him to spend the night at Spike's nightly pot party filled with partygoer go-go girls, gofers and house bands from other go-go bars. Amongst this assortment of derelicts and users, Bearded Bob would make record-breaking sales that would cop him a CEO post if he worked for a corporation

171

instead of being self-employed at Spike's big rented house in the middle of the orange groves over the hill east of Daisy Mae's á Go-Go strip mall locale.

At one of those boring, scofflaw parties a year ago I met my no-good third husband, T.J. DuRong, sharing a joint with him one of the few times I tried to like marijuana. Un-stoned, marijuana giving me asthma rather than a groovy high, I perceived, clear-headed, I thought, T.J. DuRong as an intellectual, interested in me as a person, not a sex object because he looked at me straight in the un-stoned eyes, not at my chest, with his twinkling blue eyes. He actually talked to me, stoned though pretending not to be. He listened intently to every word I said which I didn't know then was his modus operandi. A Love Trickster, T.J. DuRong wooed me so gently I mistook as sociological experimental his peace-sign strapped sandals, patched jeans, rabbit fur vest, wilted hibiscus in his unkempt hippie hair. Worse, I misconstrued as sincerity T.J. DuRong's bullshit promise to be my bodyguard, My Superman, my big galoot, and kick the shit out of Othello, my psychotic second husband who'd be getting out of prison any day now.

"Bobby asked me to go to an after-hours party with him!" Merry gushed, merrily, not knowing, of course, she was The Go-Go Girl of This Saturday Night. "I think Bobby likes me. Don't you?" New go-go girl in town, she smiled at Bearded Bob who smiled back, big, just like I'd seen him do to how many was it now, four different go-go girls the six months I'd worked here? Every one of them falling madly in love with him: Sally the bored housewife who left her aerospace engineer husband for some fun. Some fun, working in this dirty dump, getting strung out on Bearded Bob's drugs. Her husband dragged her out of here one night while she screamed Help but neither Spike nor Bearded Bob wanted any part of her anymore. Those dumb housewives, Spike said, make the worst go-go girls. Then came who? Little Carole G., a little Barbie doll of a girl with long blonde hair and tiny waist, who broke up with her career Marine boyfriend, an Annapolis grad lieutenant jet pilot who was shipping off to Nam. Left that fine boy. For Bob. She got strung out too, got pregnant, had an abortion; she thought having Bob's baby would change him, make him get a "real job." Cher (not the real one) wasn't so dumb. She'd been around. She blacked Bob's eye when she caught him with Linda Lee. And so on. Bearded Bob was a looker. Big hairy blonde chest, good in bed, too, I heard. Not many dope dealers were.

"Be careful, Mary," I said, always meaning Mary when I spoke her name, never "Merry." "Bob probably gave you amphetamines. They're very habit forming. Be careful. My advice to you, Mary, is to get a good night's sleep. Then you'll have the energy, real energy to work here and you won't need drugs. Like I don't." Though I did get awfully tired, sometimes fell asleep driving home to my three children in suburbia until freeway ghosts hiding behind off-ramp cement boulders jumped out at me, to scare me the hell awake with: BOO!

"No, not drugs," merry Mary informed me. "Prescription medicine. Same stuff doctors give you, Bobby said. It can't be bad for you, can it? If doctors give it to you? Doctors never hurt us, do they?"

"No, I guess not," I said. "Who am I, a go-go girl, to disrespect and denounce the medical profession?" Then didn't say: But Bearded Bob can hurt you. Maybe I should've. But it seems that all of us, though I didn't think this then, need to learn life's lessons for ourselves. Warnings never seem like Truth. Only Maybes. And I had enough troubles of my own living my own life lessons with T.J.

DuRong, trying to learn the Truth about him. I didn't have time or the strength to go sticking my nose into anyone else's business, though Mary Kay was awfully sweet and young, a go-go girl in the raw; raw material of this hard reality. Bearded Bob, a handsome devil, was irresistible; nothing I could do, I knew, to cool the heat, dim the bright, the hot moonlight of New Love, stop her moving in with him and she did, that night.

Right away, after Ike and Tina Turner and their Revue moved on and a new band booked, a psychedelic band whose LSD-corroded lead singer croaked when he imitated Jim Morrison, The Mamas and the Papas' "California Dreamin'" became Mary Kay's theme song, the song she always had Spike play on the jukebox during the band's breaks when we go-go girls had to take turns and dance. "All the leaves are brown—" Mary Kay sang along in her girlie Midwestern twang as she did her funny little go-go girl imitation of Goldie Hawn, not knowing Goldie did it as a goofy go-go girl satire, a joke. She flipped and flopped her arms like Goldie; made awkward slow-motion jerks that often threw her off balance, often caused her to almost fall off that Mt. Everest four-foot-wide, ten-foot-high stage in the middle of the dance floor where hippie couples down below Boogalooed, fast-motion from cocaine or amphetamines. Stoned hippies slow-motioned ballet on reds, yellows, pot or THC or remained seated, inert, literal stones, tripping out on our Daisy Mae peasant tops' white polka-dots that glowed orbed, pupil-less eyes beneath the fluorescent lights. Many of those hippies, some I knew the names of, like Kandi Kane a wannabe stripper, Johnny Jump-Jump with a nervous tic people made fun of (I'd realize someday was Tourette's syndrome) and Gypsy Rose who read our palms sometimes for free (and verified that long life line in my palm), would o.d. before summer, 1970.

174

Mary Kay danced for Bearded Bob's eyes only that glowed too, stoned, beneath the lights, her innocent gawky motions so childishly sweet they were sexy with sincerity, so arousing to the young stoner fantasizing tripping-out hippie males, virile Marines and Bearded Bob, they all leered shamelessly when she danced, her new, raw sexuality. Her hominess so nakedly and joyously obvious she seemed to dance in the nude. Amazing. She was getting strung out on Bearded Bob's drugs faster than any of his other go-go girls I'd known. Probably because of her rawness, the tabula rasa of her niceness, fresh, blank. Ready, available for wear and stain.

By Christmas, because of all the amphetamines, constant and raucous sex with Bearded Bob, and dancing — she'd volunteered to dance for the rest of us go-go girls when it came our turn, fine with us and Spike too who liked looking at her best for now — Mary Kay had lost 20 pounds and looked great, could pass for a slender, photographable movie starlet. Her face no longer round lemon meringue pie now resembled a curved oval-shaped Proustian vanilla Madeleine. And since she'd begun to make so much money, tips from her sexy little girl dancing, Bearded Bob started charging her rent money and for her amphetamines plus the cocaine she'd started liking. To advance her "career," Bearded Bob got her a job on the side as a photographer's model, posing for soft porn.

"Got me some boob shots. My boobs look great now, don't sag anymore since I lost so much weight," she bragged to me. Boobs. Three weeks ago she'd referred to her breasts as her "chest." All of us go-go girls got hard, cool and hip, eventually, but none I'd ever known, even myself, as quickly as Mary Kay had. "Can't wait till summer to get my first California Girl tan!"

For Christmas Bearded Bob asked Mary Kay to marry

him, gave her a diamond ring. "Cheapo Zircon!" proclaimed Mitzi Malone, my Friday night co-Point Girl, Fridays our busiest night, though it wasn't busy much anymore at Daisy Mae's. The hippies, the main fans of this rotten psychedelic band, drank less and less as they worked less and less, unable to for turning on and tuning out more and more. Mitzi Malone knew diamonds when she saw them; she came from a good family. When her attorney father, in deep debt, died when she was 18 she married right out of high school a man she thought would amount to something but didn't. To pay the mortgage on the tract home they bought, Mitzi worked part-time here, growing to hate her husband more and more each day for letting her. But she got even; she had a cute secret lover, Kenny, a hunk of burning love construction worker.

New Year's Day, 1970, Mary Kay told me she and Bobby were getting married on Valentine's Day in Las Vegas. By then she'd have three thousand dollars saved and she was going to quit being a go-go girl. Best of all: Bobby was going to quit dealing dope, get a real job, pay down on a little house near the beach—she loved the Pacific Ocean! Easter they were going back to Kansas, get married a second time in her hometown Baptist church, then bring back to California her little boy, Josh. Gosh, she missed him, she said, showing me recent photos her mother'd sent of a little yellow-white-haired boy the spitting image of Mary Kay, fast, fast, fast, she talked, a rapper, a motor mouth, strung out, strung out, she was. "Bobby can't wait to be a Daddy to Josh. Also—don't tell Spike, he might fire me—I'm pregnant! Bobby will be a REAL Daddy! Next September!"

As Mary Kay walked away with a tray full of beer and beef jerky, Mitzi Malone rolled her eyes at me, twirled her index finger screwy around the side of her pretty head. "La-la-la-la-la—" she sang, a riff from the rock song "Land

176

of a Thousand Dances," our secret song covenant between us when we agreed that some of the go-go girls we worked with weren't very smart. Some go-go girls were too smart or cruel and mean, like Michelle Ma Belle, about whom Mitzi Malone sniped: "She wouldn't give you the time of day if she wore two watches."

Not that I was so smart myself, having picked a third Bad Husband. That New Year's Day found T.J. DuRong doing dead time in the Riverside County Jail busted three days before for possession of a bag of organic Arizona-made mescaline, best in the state, and 20 kilos of marijuana cops found after T.J. was hit head-on in my beige Volkswagen Bug by a pickup truck, T.J. on his merry way, making a delivery run for Bearded Bob. T.J. refused to turn state's evidence against his Good Bud, his bro' Bearded Bob, making it sound like some bro'-is-beautiful esprit de corps when I really knew T.J. was scared shitless by the Big Guys Bearded Bob fronted for, some bad-ass Mafioso-type Biker dudes, and Ku Klux Klanners, who dwelt in the outskirts of Riverside. A very cold California winter that year, all the leaves brown, the skies gray, T.J. DuRong's breath wafted ice smoke when I visited him visiting days in January, as he chattered to me on a telephone shivering looking at me as I looked through a triple-glass jail window at his pitiful, broken three front teeth, a gash on his forehead from the car crash.

"Patsy," I wanted to call him like they call fall guys like him in B movies, but didn't because I felt so damned sorry for him, the sight of him incarcerated and freezing in that cold jail, making me weep while I visited him and later, wept again home alone without his sorry ass as I read his begging, remorseful letters all Jailhouse Rock men write women. "janie angel," he wrote in his lower-case neat handwriting, emulating e.e. cummings not knowing who e.e. was, T.J. DuRong one of the few hippies who didn't read or write poetry. "please forgive me. i've had plenty of time to think with a clear head, not one 'fogged' by drugs. you were right warning me that i was ruining my life ..."

"Son of a bitch!" said Mary Kay January 30, 1970. "Know what that son of a bitch did?" she asked me while that rotten band played "Light My Fire." "He found my money! Three thousand! Took it! RIPPED ME OFF! FUCKER! FUCKING ASSHOLE!"

"Why didn't you put your money into a savings account where Bob couldn't find it?" I asked, leaning over the bar to speak to her, be heard over the rotten noisy psychedelic rock 'n' roll band. She shrugged. I knew why. She was too screwed up days these days to do anything real, legitimate. It now took all day for her to wake up, Sleepyhead, come down from the high of the night before. It always amazed me how fast Bearded Bob's go-go girls got strung out, now Mary Kay winning First Prize. He didn't come into Daisy Mae's anymore. It was "too hot." Meaning that narcotics agents hung out there now and I knew it too, knew a narc when I saw one and every night there were at least ten sitting around, pretending to be hippies in their ratty long-haired wigs. Ridiculously worse, pretended to be El Toro Marines with their gone-flabby police officer arms and guts, talking phony slang, grumbling about having to ship out for Nam, sniffing out Bearded Bob whom they knew knew who the Big Boys were even though T.J. DuRong hadn't told them a thing, didn't have to, they already knew, just was giving T.J. a break to be a rat fink, cop a plea, make it easy on himself, but T.J. was too scared. And stupid.

Bearded Bob, I heard, after he made Mary Kay get an abortion, was now hanging out at the Blue Bunny in L.A. near the Strip, 35 miles away from Daisy Mae's, hustling a go-go girl named Charlee. "ALL THE LEAVES ARE BROWN!" shouted Mary Kay now when she danced, not dancing sexy at all anymore, but waddling droopy eyed, a broken down marionette, strings snipped. When the rotten psychedelic band lowered their amps and played slow songs like "When A Man Loves A Woman" and you could hear yourself think, Mary Kay began to tell me stories about her little boy Josh, how sweet he was, had blue eyes like hers, told me about Kansas, how big and bright the stars were at night and how big the sunflowers in the summertime were. There wasn't any GODDAMNED SMOG back home in Kansas. No SONS OF BITCHES either! Sometimes she'd burst into tears, lay her head at the point area right into the slopped beer and yeasty yuck there, getting it all over her beautiful yellow hair, and sob. I'd motion for the other girls to hover around her so Spike or any of the customers wouldn't see her.

The Valentine's night that was supposed to be her wedding night she was so hysterical I had to motion for Mitzi to take over so I could take Mary Kay into the Ladies Room, splash water in her face, sit her on a toilet stool, wipe away her tears, pat her shoulders, hug her shaking head against my stomach, help her pull herself together, put back on her mascara that made her thick blonde eyelashes look like chocolate-covered coconut and, making Spike give me a couple amphetamines from his personal stash, became a dope dealer for the first and last time, gave it to Mary Kay to wash down with a full glass of cola, hoping the caffeine in it would help wire her up too, so she could go back to work, finish the shift, before Spike got sick of her.

And one night, every go-go girl's worst nightmare, Mary Kay fell off the ten-foot-high stage. She didn't break her neck, but she did break her thumb. Samaritan Spike drove her home. And fired her. "Something I been wanting to do since I hired the little square," he said, walking back into Daisy's. "She's gone. A went-went girl," he said, cracking a cliché, a joke du jour, we go-go girls gone the past tense punch line. "Those out-of-staters make the worst go-go girls anyway. Squares. They don't know what's happening. Where it's at." He slapped his fingers and palms together as if brushing scuzz off his hands, dropping it onto the barroom floor amongst the cigar and cigarette butts and ashes and slopped beer.

The next night when she came in for her pay check and a hippie played "California Dreamin'" on the jukebox, though her thumb was in a splint, she jumped back up on that skyscraper dance stage. Wearing her Daisy Mae top that now bagged across her dwindled chest, old Kansas work jeans that fit her like a sack now that she was skinny as Twiggy, gangly, geeky with her scrawny girth, she wiggled around, wobbling. Out of it, weird and wild in the eyes, her pale pink lipstick on wrong smeared all over her front teeth and glowed anemic blood beneath the black lights, she big-mouth screamed, a raving, Dionysus-intoxicated-gone-mad Maenad for all the world to hear: "ALL THE FUCKING LEAVES ARE BROWN! YOU ASSHOLES!"

No ancient serpents, however, harmlessly licked the sweat from her het-up, heated crimson cheeks as Spike, with the help of big galoot gofer, Wild Willie, speedily sprinted to the stage and yanked her down as easy as if she were a rag doll, easy now anyway since she weighed no more than 100 pounds. As they jerked her around, her old Kansas hick girl jeans were so baggy now they came half off her scrawny bod and showed the wide crack on her rear end, turning her into a writhing bottomless dancer. Mean, mad, Maenad no more.

"HELP!" she hollered, pitifully, kicking the air and then a table full of dirty pitchers, causing it all to topple over into a glassy crash. "SOMEBODY! PLEASE HELP ME! I NEED SOME BODY! JUST ANY OLD BODY! PLEASE!

180

PLEASE HELP ME!" But nobody helped her. She was a damsel in a dire distress of her own mess-making. The stoned hippies looked away, not wanting their reveries disturbed with bad vibes. The rotten psychedelic rock 'n' roll band minded their own business, kept on tuning their cacophonous guitars, adjusting wires and amps. The Nam-bound U.S. Marines, angst'd-out zombies, shooting pool, had too much future to think about to care about the present and pretended not to see. And her hardhearted fellow go-go girls, her former sorority sisters of sin here on the campus of Hard Knock U., Sweethearts/Sweathearts of Stigma Sigh, had seen it all and didn't want to see any more. And I'd done all I could.

Across the big barroom that used to be a supermarket Spike and Wild Willie, a couple white bwanas, carried her, a squirming portage, above their heads to the door they pushed open with hurricane force with their boots to throw her, rotten lunch, outside into the parking lot, and slammed the door behind her. When she banged on the door, Spike, alone, went out to tend to her. Mary Kay Randall screamed HELP! one more time and was never heard from again.

I suppose she drove, nine fingered, thumb pointing splint at God, back home to Kansas dressed like that, former go-go girl gone anachronism before her very eyes, un-suntanned in March, all the leaves brown along the way. I suppose she knew now how temporary the wages of skin, knew the limitations of a wearing-out mother lode for young mothers. I suppose she knew too that her skin, once white bread-colored when she lived in Kansas a sweet young girl now resembled the pale airy color of stinky beer foam. And knew too that her waist-length hair once the color of Kansas corn might now be likened to the color of California beer, cheap and fizzy from the tap I would pour for another year and a half at Daisy Mae's á Go-Go while I waited for T.J.

181

DuRong to get out of the honor farm where the hardnosed presiding judge sent him to serve the maximum sentence for a misdemeanor drug possession because he wouldn't fink on his friends, held fast to his popular anti-Establishment pro-bro' beliefs, Butch Cassidy and Sundance Kid male mythos.

Spike got busted that next Thanksgiving when the sky turned to gray on a pre-winter's day. Arrested in his Orifice when he sold to an undercover narc, believable as a real hippie because of his real long hair. Sold the fraud some excellent Acapulco Gold Spike got from Bearded Bob. But Spike, neither scared nor stupid, turned State's evidence. He finked, turned State's: "Quick as a fucking jumping jack flash," Spike said, against Bearded Bob. Bailed out a week before Christmas, Spike bragged to us Daisy Mae á Go-Go go-go girls before his one-year sentence at a minimum security facility began January 1, 1971. Yeah, he did it. Ratted out Bearded Bob. Saw to it the son of a bitch got the maximum at Folsom Prison.

"For Merry."

From a pack he always kept inside his shirt pocket, Spike jerked out and lit up one of his El Cheapo cigars that reeked of dirty socks and flatulence. Spike inhaled deeply, sucking the stench and smoke down into his Edward G. Robinson lungs made of steel, two black fenders off a 1936 Cadillac sedan Al Capone getaway car. Spike hated being compared to Edward G. Robinson; so much so he once fired a go-go girl for calling him "Little Caesar." A "fucking softie" Spike called Edward G. Robinson, who'd led a cushy life as a movie star whereas Spike at age 37 had done, so far, ten years' hard time in two prisons, one Leavenworth, not to mention the time he did as a kid in reform school for running numbers and stealing a Studebaker. A "pipsqueak" too, Spike called Edward G. Robinson, who would've stood only as high as Spike's upper lip now sprouting a black handlebar moustache to match his mutton-chop sideburns he was going to have to shave off before he went to county jail, get a Johnny Straight Arrow hair cut too. The seven years I am a go-go girl, the length of bad luck for breaking a mirror, the minimum sentence for a felony conviction, I will know many gangsters, but Spike will be the only one who looks like one.

"Yeah," Spike growled, blew smoke into the barroom sky of Daisy Mae's á Go-Go, and held his stinky cigar up high and nobly as if it were a brandy snifter full of fine cognac and he paid homage to a wondrous Dionysian god.

"Yeah. Got even with that son of a bitch Bearded Bob for what he did to our poor little Merry."

"Yes, our poor little Merry," I said. "You're a veritable saint, Spike," I said, scrubbing the beer-stinky scuzzy bar with a bleach-drenched towel.

"Damn' right I am, a saint, a goddamn' saint, yeah," Spike said, meaning it.

Bukowski Chugs Cheap Beer @ the Go-Go a No-No

Charles Bukowski laughed har-har when I told him I'd
been a go-go girl for 7 years, the length of bad luck time
for breaking a mirror, minimum sentence for a felony
conviction. In 1973 Bukowski's thought me one of
those feminists who wanted to kick his butt, booed,
stomped en masse out of his poetry readings. Worse,
he'd thought me another bored housewife going back to
college, my hard working schmuck hubby buying my
books, tuition and bellbottoms, cooking his own supper,
diapering the baby while I read Sexton, Plath and Jong
and flirted with cute professors. Bukowski never drank
at any of those go-go bars I worked those 7 years. Too
expensive, too uppity and all that rock 'n' roll too noisy.
No, he preferred the bossa nova and cheap beer at the
Go-Go a No-No's where barmaids wore overalls, not
fringed bikinis and could toss out any drunk, including
him, with one bare hand. Midnights Buk phoned me long
distance, drunk because his Woman had left him again,
he listened intently to my go-go girl Tales about men like
him, broke, lonely who drank too much, said wild things,
talk of men not like him: astronauts, murderers, rich men
wearing diamond pinky rings while Bukowski chugged his
cheap beer in his cheap apartment in L.A., blew smoke
from cheap cigars into the telephone at me sipping cheap
white wine 40 miles away till one night Bukowski finally
said: You gotta write about all that madness, Kid.
So I did.

Chapter 9 | Beer Can in the Garden

"I love women ... especially when they love me."
— Charles Bukowski

Henry Charles Bukowski, age 54, the wannabe, almost-gonnabe Famous Poet, sat in the most comfy spot in my living room, a cavernous antique red velvet throne chair with hand carved oak armrests and claw feet and leaned his big leonine head toward me below him where I, his liege, age 35, sat on a footstool, looking up at him. Slimmed down, the most handsome Bukowski would ever be, he brushed my waist-length post-hippie hair away from my ear and, his breath hot with alcohol, whispered into it: "Six inches."

Then, on this Friday night of April 11, 1975, 7:35 p.m., four days before the 110th anniversary of the demise of Abraham Lincoln and the 63rd anniversary of the sinking of the *Titanic*, though we were commemorating neither of those historical facts, Charles Bukowski grabbed one of the many magnums of cheap champagne I'd bought and placed to chill in a wash bucket of ice cubes on my coffee table.

Swirling around, his baggy plaid shirt flipping apart because a button was missing, Charles Bukowski popped open the machine-gun sized green bottle of cheap champagne and poured us both goblets-full of the bubbly stuff because I, the hostess of this party in Charles Bukowski's honor, couldn't. Because my right thumb was broken and harnessed up in a contraption made of beige Velcro-clasping plastic and canvas, a thick and longish erect six-inch brace that made him laugh har-har and say once again because Charles Bukowski liked to repeat himself when he said something especially controversial, entre-nous he said it, but loud enough to set off burglar alarms in the next block: "SIX INCHES!"

"Six Inches" the title, too, of one of his raunchiest short stories in his Black Sparrow collection *Exclamations, Erections, Ejaculations and Other Tales of Ordinary Madness.* About a man, much to his horror, suddenly turning into a six-inch penis so's to forever satisfy, perpetually, whenever she wanted, his demanding, oversexed woman from hell. I'd never read that story, knew I didn't want to just from the synopsis of it even though university profs in 1975 who liked him likened it to Kafka existentialism. I wasn't much crazy about Bukowski's sexcapade fiction he'd begun writing during the mid-1960s' sexual liberation which now, during the Everything Goes Swinging Seventies, was considered, by his admirers tour de force cause celebre Theatre of the Absurd. Secretly, I thought some of it was vulgar. Porn, even. I was especially offended by his recent story in *Hustler* he'd "written for the bucks"; but I wouldn't've dared told Bukowski. I was sort of in love with him, had fallen for him after reading his poetry, *The Days Run Away Like Wild Horses Over the Hills.*

But I "loved him" in an an extremely ambivalent way, so don't ever tell anyone because I was really confused and going crazy in 1975. Five years ago I'd started out to be a secretarial science major (learned shorthand up to 110wpm just as the Dictaphone proliferated); then became a pre-nursing major but I was allergic to Escherichia coli and formaldehyde and couldn't dissect a feral cat so I got a B.A three months ago and was now a Law student, trying to make Something of myself, shed my go-go girl Bimbo reputation, find a respectable career to finish rearing my three kids, and hopefully make enough money to dump my no-good third husband T.J. DuRong who was driving me crazy. Had driven me to drink, too, a lot of cheap champagne—but, unlike W.C. Fields, I was not going to lament over not bothering to thank him.

This "six inches," my protruding broken thumb, was the reason a week ago I'd cancelled my Big Bukowski Bash to honor him, my next Feature in the fourth issue of my small press magazine *Pearl* I founded two years ago while an undergrad, funded by the university Honors Program. *Pearl* #4, a Male Chauvinist Pig Issue (that would also include Anaïs Nin, with whom I'd become friends, and hopefully her friend Henry Miller she'd promised to introduce me to that summer), I planned to produce with part of my next student loan. Bukowski had last week generously obliged my publishing entrepreneurialship with a batch of unpublished poems and one of his Thurberesque ink drawings for the *Pearl* cover he titled "Men's Lib Poster" of a little "six inch" man looking up the skirt of a gargantuan, voluptuous, leggy, garter-belted woman smoking a cigarette and blowing smoke insouciantly into the air that resembled quite a bit, in looks, not giantessness, his then-girlfriend, Lydia Kane, but was actually supposed to be Me but he told me not to tell Lydia. She got jealous, he said, when he drew cartoons of Other Women.

"But I don't smoke," I reminded Bukowski.

"You should smoke," Bukowski said. "You'd look sexy if you smoked."

Erroneously, thinking Bukowski would enjoy the mix of humanity at this party, I'd invited my all-male study group of seven from law school plus a bunch of poets and English profs from the university I graduated from four months ago. Law and Literature. A more caustic, diametrically and diabolically-opposed motley crew there'd never be as the law students shot pool out in my two-car garage and mumbled about "that dissolute Bukowski" and the poets, with their notebooks huddled in corners jotting and doodling, pretended to be invisible. This party would always be, along with going to law school and marrying T.J.

DuRong, on my Top Ten List of Things I Wish I'd Never Done.

Bukowski had warned me about going to law school: "Feed your brain on me," he'd said.

Rescheduling the Party In His Honor so pissed off Bukowski who wasn't used to being rescheduled that I held it as soon as possible before I pissed him off forever and he took back his poems and "Men's Lib Poster" (he was a pretty petulant and unforgiving cuss) although my thumb hurt like hell, still throbbing, freshly busted just Thursday night before last down by the Huntington Beach Pier two doors down from The Golden Bear, a bistro Bukowski occasionally appeared at to read his raucous poetry getting more and more popular amongst the pay-to-see crowd of young intellectuals, old hipsters and aging hippies who went there to see the likes of Crosby Stills, Nash and Young, Joan Baez, post-Woodstock maestros and old-timey rock 'n' rollers like Jan and Dean, the Rivingtons and country stars like Hoyt Axton and where, in 1966, I went with Les Church to see Lenny Bruce's last performance.

My thumb got busted at the joint when my third husband T.J.DuRong jerked loose my fist clutching his fuzzy hair I'd snatched onto after I caught him walking happy as a you please down Main Street whistling "come on baby light my fire," as he arm-in-arm'd with a cute hippie chick wearing a long orange and yellow madras cloth skirt. Seeing him like that, having such a good time while I was going crazy studying Contracts, Real Estate, Torts and Community Property law, made me crazier. So I chased him down the alley in back of the Golden Bear then up Pacific Coast Highway where he tried to make a quick getaway in his beat up gray primer-coated 1936 Chevy pickup.

But I caught the sneaky scofflaw infidel before he even got behind the steering wheel because I'd outrun him—

with only one shoe, too, a four-inch high-heeled wedgie at that — even though he'd been a track star in high school. So he said. My no-good third husband T.J. DuRong lied to me about Every Thing. Even about coming home in time for this party I was giving in Bukowski's honor.

"When's T.J getting home?" asked Lydia Kane, Bukowski's beauteous sexpot of a young girlfriend after hearing the champagne blather all the way out in the garage where she'd been shooting pool with my all-male study group. That cheap California-made stuff was so carbonated, its cork pop was as loud as a whale belch. My Wandering Third Husband, had been gone for two days and nights, obviously having forgotten this Big Bukowski Bash. He'd been looking forward to it, too, because he had a big crush on Lydia Kane, as did most men who ever laid eyes on her. I shrugged. I never knew when T.J. DuRong would ever be home or if he'd ever come home again. And maybe this time he was gone for good. Or dead. "Well, when he gets home, tell him Big Mama's looking for him," Lydia said, sexily. Jane Russell one of her Role Models, she'll tell me in 2012.

"Oh, yeah?" said Bukowski.

"Yeah, Bukowski." Lydia Kane, the Famous Lusty Lydia who'd starred for the seven years they'd been together in many of Bukowski's Women poems and would play a leading role in his book titled *Women*, That Lydia walked away, sashaying her voluptuous rear beneath her tight mini skirt as she went, then said over her shoulder, "Don't do anything I wouldn't do, Bukowski." Briefly she glowered at me, pretending to be jealous, making sure Bukowski saw her doing it. Then when he bent to light up a cigar, she winked at me. She and I were actually good friends, talked weekly on the phone long distance, her in L.A., me in the Orange County suburbs for her to complain about Bukowski, detail to me their many domestic squabbles. It was because of

Lydia, a vociferous women's libber, after I'd featured her, an emerging famous L.A. poet in her "own write," in my first two all-female issues of *Pearl*, that I'd got hooked up literarily with the well-known and notorious Bukowski.

What I, an only child, liked most about the women's lib movement was how we women were supposed to be "sisters." I'd always wanted a sister and sometimes, because the affable, gregarious Lydia was one of five sisters and well-rehearsed at mingling with her own gender and so easy to talk to about love, life, poetry and rotten men, she made me feel like a sister. And, that night, already drunk on that champagne, so cheap it wasn't even worth its weight in potatoes, I glowed with being-someone's-sister pride.

"All right, baby, sure, I won't do anything YOU wouldn't do, yeah, sure," Bukowski said to Lydia, sarcastically, blowing smoke into the air toward her as she walked away. Chugging the goblet of fizzy, then pouring himself and me some more, Bukowski winced, then growled:

"What a long drink of piss this is. You know, don't you, men only pretend to like champagne to get into women's skirts." He looked at my "starving student" attire, the Levi's I wore and shrugged. He liked women to wear skirts, to show off their legs. He especially liked garter belts and hosiery, didn't like it that this younger generation of women were wearing pantyhose and jeans all the time.

"Even Cary Grant hates champagne," Bukowski sneered and drank the cheap champagne anyway. Because it was free. Bukowski always liked to drink up the hosts' stuff first at parties in his honor (and there were many such parties back then in 1975 when he was in the process of climbing out of the Skid Row gutter to put his foot permanently and pyrotechnically onto the slippery sidewalk of American literature). When the freebies were all gone, he'd drink what he preferred, his own B.Y.O.B. usually vodka he carried in a brown paper sack.

Bukowski looked at my harnessed erect broken thumb again, shook his head, and har-har-harred again. Admiringly, you see, because when Bukowski found out the truth about why I cancelled the first party in his honor — lying at first and saying I had the flu which was what pissed him off, the apparent transparent obviousness of the excuse, the phony appeal to his presumed poet humanity (of which he was in short supply and mostly saved for his poetry) to forgive my low immune frailties. When told the The Truth about my broken thumb and how I got it, he laughed, liking the hilarious tawdriness, and said:

"I ought to bill you and Lydia down at the Olympic. Either of you would tear the average prelim boy to pieces. God save the male race or at least my part of it anyhow with two women like you and Lydia who love their men so much!"

But I didn't love that ne'er-do-well T.J. DuRong, and hadn't since 1972 when he started driving me crazy and to drink. And now law school was making me crazier and drink even more. I'd gained another five pounds since starting law school in January, three months ago. It wasn't that studying law was so hard, not when you got a gift of gab and a short-term memory like mine able to cram full of useless information for final exams. Plus law school, unlike English and literature, my undergrad majors, made sense with its specific lists, though endless, of logical rules, laws, exceptions to the rules and laws, even the loopholes foreseeable glottal stops when compared to the unfathomable, illogical raison d'etre of comma splice, homonym and "'i' before 'e' except after 'c'" and much easier to remember, krill I shoved into the gullet of my fat whale still-young mind. Yet, pure law was pure drivel. Law school a chore, a rite of passage to weed out the workhorses from the slump-backed nags because that's what being a lawyer was really all about: work. Lots of hard, hard work to file appeals, stall the law, get your way from push and shove, moving and shaking tail feathers. I hated it.

And I especially hated my all-male study group out in the garage shooting pool with Lydia, mainly the unmarried ones, Kirk the Work and Facto Jacko (all of us had nicknames in the group except me, at least not one I knew about), who, when alone with me, sexually harassed me, the last time two weeks ago when we studied Products Liability and Defamation together at Facto Jacko's cheap apartment across the street from law school and they spent two hours kidding me about trying a ménage a trois, Kirk even unbuttoning the top button of my Levi's. "A little juris-IM-prudence," Kirk kidded. Finally, after not learning a thing except to be reminded in 1975 what jerks men could be— odious vermin that made the drinking men I'd known in all the gin joints and go-go bars seem sane and sober—and like gentlemen, I went home. At law school where I was one of only three women students enrolled amongst the maelstrom of men, there were no hunky protective bouncers like Big Don or Ernesto or the ferocious 7-foot-tall Samoan Brothers to 86 these bullies. I had to fend for myself against this men-and in-crowd, this win-crowd, these future Yuppie Dudes who will soon mantra Greed is Good while I'd gone to law school to work for the American Civil Liberties Union or the public defender's office, protect people's rights, especially aid and abet damsels in distress from Bête Noires.

"Don't do it, baby," Bukowski had slurred to me one night last January after Lydia left him "for good" (yet again). Drunk, he called me on the telephone after I wrote him I was going to law school to warn me: "Law. That's a bigger mirage than LOVE. A few fat manipulative cats break through the barricades to walk the greensward but it's strictly trickery and low-class. All they can concentrate on is digging in. The most vicious people that I have known, those furthest away from reality and compassion are lawyers." And then he added: "And the college professors. And these, teach. Be careful, Jane."

Oh well. I wasn't going to be in law school much longer. I just knew it. Something was going to happen to interfere with it. I didn't know what, but it was. Something unforeseeable, odd and potentially dangerous — and not this broken thumb — was going to end my pursuit of Lawyerness. LawyerDOOM: It was coming. Peeking at me with its thousand eyes from the horizon of hell.

"Mom," said my oldest daughter Leah, aged 16 and a half. "MOM!" She was upset, nearly shouting at me, unusual for her, a soft-spoken, gentle girl, a Libra, if you believe in astrology. "Come look at this!" She narrowed her green eyes the color of her father's, my first husband, Terence Larrigan, the Black Irish alcoholic and led me down the hallway to her bedroom.

"I thought your friends were all smarty pants intellectuals. College graduates. Respectable people." That's what I'd told her about people who were educated, people I wanted her to be like, be like me and go to college. No, she hated school, knowledge, learning "stuff." All she wanted in life was to get married and have children. I hoped she'd want to DO something when she grew up. I hoped I was setting an example of what that could be: Lawyerdom.

"Look—" She squeaked open her bedroom door and there was Facto Jacko having sex with one of the women poets I'd invited, the famous L.A. one, a university PhD prof and Oleander Prize recipient who'd soon marry Facto Jacko, pay his law school tuition, then after he graduates, receiving his "License to Steal" as my all-male group called our future law degree and passes the Bar exam and dumps her for his legal secretary, she'll vanish and never be heard of ever again.

But right then they were falling in love, Doing It. In front of the green Black Irish eyes of my innocent, soft-spoken,16-and-a-half-year-old gentle daughter in her own bed decorated with koala bear sheets and comforter in her own bedroom with matching koala bear wallpaper and curtains she'd bought with her own money working at an ice cream parlor.

"My God! You guys!" I cried before I shut the door, ashamed for them and me while they scurried for their clothes flung all over the room.

"Some example, Mom, these friends of yours, these so-called intellectuals. A bunch of pervs. They're no better than those dirt bag biker and hippie and ex-convict friends of T.J.'s! And that Charles Bukowski is a horrible man. You told me he was famous, is a genius."

"Yeah, Mom, what's the deal?" demanded Sean, my 14-year-old son. "What's so special about this dirty old man?" he asked, a high school innocent who'd only read one book, *The Andromeda Strain* and did not know Bukowski had written a book titled *Notes of a Dirty Old Man*. "A genius? I don't think so. Know what he's doing right now? Peeing in a champagne bottle, Mom, and then drinking it! His OWN URINE!"

Not really. I peeked down the hallway to where I could see Bukowski in the middle of the living room. He was only pretending to, trying to shock the law students giving him a bad time, gawking at him, making snide, know-it-all lawyerly remarks like prima facie, res ipsa loquitur, non compos mentis, all to the delight of one of the university lit profs and the female feminist poets who didn't much like him, enjoyed the shameful comeuppance

194

they perceived. The gawking male tyro poets there who liked him didn't even seem to notice the caustic commotion because they wanted To Be Bukowski, wanted to garner this kind of attention however provocateur someday, any old way. Imagining themselves in Bukowski's place, they just smiled beatifically.

"Even T.J.'s never done anything so stupid. Your law school pals are all laughing at Bukowski. And laughing at you too for inviting him. I can't believe you, Mom, hanging around a dirty old man like him." My kids had never talked to me like this before. Reprimanding me, their Mom, a college grad, a Junior Bar Association member on her way to a juris doctorate degree. (Maybe.) Leah and Sean stomped away to go outside to talk about my disgusting party with Lydia's handsome nephew Mike who was Leah's age, didn't approve of the carryings-on either, all of them drinking Pepsis as they leaned on the yellow Thing Lydia owned parked out front at the curb, a strange Volkswagen product du jour, a motor vehicle resembling a Jeep that would be proven a dangerous contraption and recalled and in which Bukowski'd been hauled by Lydia, chauffeured by young Mike—all the 40-some-mile way from L.A. to my house in the suburbs to this disgusting party.

The party didn't get any better even as I got drunker and drunker waiting for T.J. DuRong to come home who never did though Lydia seemed to have a good time out in the garage dancing with the law students and poets and university profs and Bukowski too seemed to be having the time of his life, at least for a while flirting with my beautiful dark-haired and young girlfriends Marilyn and Kay in the living room, matching him drink for drink, while he held court from the red velvet throne chair like a king. He liked women who could hold their liquor and he liked women with good legs who wore skirts, he said, as he eyed up the dark crotch of Marilyn's denim midi skirt.

"What the hell?!" Bukowski bellowed after getting a gander of her lacy knee-length undies. "What in the hell are those things?!"

Marilyn answered in her sweet voice: "Petti-pants. Beaver Cheaters some call them."

"Har-har! I remember those things from the sixties! Peter Cheaters I called them. My first wife wore those things! What you got underneath them? Hmmm?" His big leonine head dawdling, Bukowski was getting very drunk; he leaned forward holding a magnum champagne bottle as if it were a flashlight to brighten the darkness of her crotch, as if she would show him.

"My regular undies," she revealed, shyly.

"You're wearing TWO pairs of underwear? One a pair of Peter Cheaters? Christ, what a cockteaser! Take them off!" Marilyn, not a cockteaser at all, happily married 12 years to a firefighter and was also my *Pearl* co-editor said No way Jose and giggled. "Take them off!" Bukowski roared gleefully, chuckling ho-ho-ho, Santa Claus in April, shaking his big head, knocking loose some dark hair slicked back with pomade.

"Take what off, Bukowski?" asked Lydia, who, I had come to realize had the keen hear-all ears of a Hound of Baskerville and the ever-presence of protoplasm, sneaky and snaky as smoke. Necessary attributes to keep a-pace with Bukowski. Then, just like I'd heard from Lydia, read about in Bukowski's many books and seen for myself recently in Taylor Hackford's 1972 public television documentary "Bukowski," their purple-passionate intensity contingent upon their alcohol consumption, Lydia and Bukowski began to argue, loudly, and the party was worse than ever.

After all, it was two o'clock in the morning; the law

students had all left hours ago anyway, after they'd chowed down two two-gallon pots of homemade Jane's Never Plain Chili, even the vegetarian one with carrots and parsnips in it they'd mistaken for chorizo. All the poets gone, too, just my girlfriends Marilyn and Kay remaining, but quietly exiting, giving me little paltry waves of fearful Goodbyes as Lydia's and Bukowski's going-on-eight-years-now give-and-take, give-as-good-as-you-get accusations, exclamations of ordinary madness and their many don't-go-down-without-kicking heart-crime grievances got louder. And my broken thumb ached, throbbed like a bongo drum. But for Bukowski, the night had just begun: he'd drunk all the freebie and now was chugging the hard stuff — straight vodka — and really getting in the partying mood, taking center stage in his outrageous Theatre of the Absurd:

"I am a beer can in the garden!" Bukowski proclaimed, slurping his BYOB wrapped in a brown paper bag, vodka dripping down his beard onto his blue plaid shirt half unbuttoned, his burgeoning belly propped on top his belt buckle.

"You're a drunk asshole, Bukowski," said Lydia.

Bukowski ignored her and went on — "I'm an umlaut in Alsace-Lorraine! The first spark of the fire from the torch that burned down the Library of Alexandria!"

"You're a firebug all right, Bukowski, you scorched all my furniture with your cigars." When she fluffed her long curly hair as a got-the-last-word gesture, Bukowski's eyes, though seeming to swirl in their sockets, gazed at her for a long moment, glistening with great affection because he did truly adore her.

As one last law student snuck out my front door, Kirk, Lydia's paramour of the night, the one she'd flirted most with and her constant dance-and-pool partner that was

197

supposed to be T.J., Bukowski shouted to him: "And you, you long drink of piss—" Kirk, standing at 6'5" was nearly a head taller than the six-foot Bukowski who hunkered down his head, a raging bull about to butt Kirk in the chest.

"Don't you think for one minute I don't know what you and Lydia have been up to all night! I got eyes in the back of my head too, Lydia. You, you elongated wormy shyster—" Bukowski bellowed at Kirk, who shrugged, totally dismayed by Bukowski's outrage.

"What the hell's he talking about?" Kirk said, holding up his arms.

"—you ambulance chasing Shylock, I got a pound of flesh for you, all right—"

Bukowski grabbed his own crotch as if a sack of potatoes bulged inside his baggy navy blue corduroy pants. Kirk jumped back in fear as if Bukowski aimed an uzi at his guts. Bukowski ranted on: "You litigious lug-nut, you are the sweaty hair on the wart of an asshole's asshole!"

Kirk shot me a dirty look that had it been bullets would've got me right between the eyes and splattered my brains all over my living room wall. When Bukowski lunged at him, kicked at him, Kirk ran out the front door and out to his car, fast as a track star.

"And you—You, Jaaane, Jaaane, you are—" Bukowski turned to me. I shivered in fear at what Bukowski thought I was.

"You, Jane, you are a honeybee upon the tundra." It would be the nicest thing he'd ever say to me except when he calls next winter after Lydia leaves him after their biggest fight ever, leaves him for good, to read me a poem he will write about my nose. Bukowski liked noses too, along with women with good legs who could drink as much as he could. But then he added:

"Jaaane, you're getting faaaat," Bukowski said as he

eyed, disapprovingly, my burgeoning bosom fattened up from too much champagne. He was, after all, a Leg Man.

"And what am I, Bukowski? An ant at the picnic?"

"You, Lydia, my great beauty, you are the woman of all women. You, you, Lydia, Lydia, you have pink and orange butterflies sewn upon your thighs." Bukowski pulled another cigar from his shirt pocket but could not light it because he was so drunk, could not focus his eyes to see the match's flame.

Finally Mike, Lydia's nephew arrived, as if SOS'd via secret telegraph wire, and helped Bukowski, bent and staggering, out the door to be driven home safely back to Los Angeles in that strange yellow motor-vehicular Jeep-like contraption the VW people had named in 1975 The Thing. And the party, one of the biggest mistakes of my life, was finally over. Thank God. I could at last relax so, all alone, I chugged the very last goblet of the cheap champagne, warm as urine—my God, was it urine?—the urine of Charles Bukowski? I sniffed it. No, it wasn't—a rumor after all— t'was just plain old cheap California champagne gone flat and caustic as sandpaper as it scraped dry my esophagus on its way down.

I heard a shuffling of feet in the hallway. "T.J.?" I called. "You sneaky bastard! Is that you?"

"No. S'me," said the last law student. Yet another one. My God, the law students, those odious vermin, were like ants at a picnic. Yawning, stretching, it was Nicholas the Ridiculous (the only good-looker) from my study group, nicknamed that by Facto Jacko, not me, called that behind his back, but called Nick the Quick to his face, again, not by me but the rest of the group, though Nick did not know that was a slur too, referring to his flabbergasted filibustering when called on in class to summarize aloud our daily case studies, law school teaching all of us "to think on our feet" which Nick was not good at, at all, poor guy. Nick would flunk out with a pitiful 1.65 GPA this first semester after our June finals. I was never called on in class, the profs already pushing me to the side of the pack, not worthy of even the humiliation of being called on, presumed a bimbo, I suspected, because I'd gotten so bosomy from all my drinking.

After Jacko the Facto receives a 4.0 and I tie with Kirk the Work for second highest score in Torts that June, a 3.75 that will so surprise my Torts prof, he will hold a special inquiry as to the possibility that I cheated (based upon a rumor instigated by Kirk). I will be exonerated but with much shame and implication that "where there's smoke there's fire," substantiating the "But for" Law. No, intentional infliction of mental distress and malicious prosecution and disparagement won't be any of the reasons I won't finish law school.

Nick the Ridick yawned again, looked around, asked: "Where's that snide prick?"

"Bukowski?"

"No. Facto Jacko. He took my car keys after I fell asleep on that couch in your dining room. Man, I'm tired, all the time tired, tired. Law school's really tough, man. Where's Jacko?" I shrugged, not knowing that at that very moment Jacko and the Famous Woman Poet were, carpe diem, eloping to Las Vegas, Nevada in Nick's red 1971 Datsun. (With her Oleander Prize money, she will pay Jacko's fall tuition.)

"Bukowski? What's a Bukowski?"

"My guest of honor, Charles Bukowski, the famous poet." Nick looked confused. "Bukowski—the loud one who sat in the red velvet chair all night in my living room."

"Famous? That pervert? That repugnant reprobate? Famous for what?"

"His amazing poetry. He's widely published. Makes a

200

lot of money. He'll read at the Golden Bear next week. He's a poet." Nick still looked confused like that clueless, but sweet innocent, malapropping older lady in the liquor store in Taylor Hackford's "Bukowski" documentary who, after Bukowski told her he was a Poet, asked: "Pollock?"

"A poet? You're kidding. That debauched derelict? We all thought he was some deranged alcoholic you'd known when you were a go-go girl or some rummy bum you'd found in skid row and invited to your party. You mean to tell me people PAY to hear that drunken slob read poetry?"

"Yeah. His books are for sale in all the bookstores all over the world."

"Well, bookstore owners better post big caveat emptor signs next to his books to absolve themselves of products liability. Man, what a show he put on. Your name's mud, baby. You'll be the laughing stock of law school after Kirk and Jacko get through telling everyone about this party."

My name really will be Mudd, as in Samuel A. Mudd, the ill-fated Good Samaritan bandager of John Wilkes Booth, Abraham Lincoln's assassin, beginning that Tuesday we all return to law school, April 15, the day the *Titanic* sunk and Abraham Lincoln died of assassination wounds.

"Ms. Mudd," nicknamed that by my own study group who will blackball me. But my libelous besmirched reputation won't be the reason either I don't become a lawyer. It'll be because of an Attractive Nuisance as it's called in Torts: Another Party, another Disastrous Bash. One even worse than my Big Bukowski Bash and the one that would change the course of my life and it happened June 6, 1975, right after I took my grueling two-hour Contracts One final exam, barely squeaking through it with a 1.75 (me gabbing erroneously on and on about disparagement and got even further off track with detrimental reliance instead of the correct cut-to-the-chase summary of per se breach of contract which I misspelled "breech" — how could 1?); 1.75 GPA the bottom line for any class in that law school and I was feeling like shit anyway when I arrived home with my usual two bags of groceries plus toilet paper and dog food after my ordeal and saw the police helicopters circling my house. Then when I drove onto the street where I lived I saw at last the thousands of eyes peeking from the horizon of hell: hundreds of cars, motorcycles, dune buggies, pickups, RVs, bicycles and skateboards parked all over the street and on my front lawn and driveway.

There must've been at least 300 people (newspapers will cite 500), mostly teenagers, many bikers and hippies and thugs and firebugs and repulsive reprobates and debauched derelicts at Leah's Last-Day-of-School Party I'd told her she could have, but said she could invite no more than 20. That was the early days of copy machines in supermarkets and some funster had reproduced her invitation with a map and stapled it to telephone poles and hallway bulletin boards at three high schools. The Disastrous Party, The Fracas, The Melee, My Nemesis, whatever words to describe disaster, disillusion and mayhem I could think of over the years to call it, would be not as much a free-for-all as it was a Bad Omen, a sign from Wherever that I was NOT being admitted into the rarefied society of Lawyerdom that, in the length of time that it takes to call 300 of your friends and tell them about a cute chick's beer bust (T.J. DuRong had bought four keggers), had become my LawyerDOOM.

That summer of 1975 turned out to be a hellish one for me, a true saison d'enfer, as I labored strenuously with my law studies, floundered in confusion wondering whether I should keep on carpe dieming, or, truckin', as they called it in those days, or drop out of Hell and go back to the university and study what I really wanted to: French. Get a self-satisfying, blissful but miscreant Masters Degree in French which would surely seal my fate as a failed careerist. My misery, though not half as bad as Lydia Kane's and Charles Bukowski's who started fighting so bad and ugly they would soon break up for good in such a horrible way, Lydia would say: "Our love turned sick."

And I had nothing to do with it though Lydia thought I did and Bukowski said to me: "I believe Lydia thinks that I am in love with you so you'd better not mention a casual friendship. Lydia is ambitious, despondent, sex-oriented and a damned women's libber. There is something about her energy that is fragmented and near-hysteria."

Lydia's energy and hysteria turned toward me, unfragmented, in the form of a steamroller, four-page, single-spaced typewritten letter wherein she accused me of being in love with Bukowski, setting up my Bukowski Bash just to get Bukowski off alone, have him all to myself. "Reach for the steel, Sister!" Lydia warned, prefacing each paragraph of her irate, kick-butt letter—one of Utah-country girl Lydia's role models was undoubtedly Annie Oakley. Sisters, I remembered, often warn each other to stay away from their misters.

"What did I do to deserve this?" I asked Bukowski. Bukowski laughed his har-har-har amongst the trumpets. He liked making Lydia jealous. He liked it a lot. "A hundred years from now, Bukowski, all these women of yours are going to make you seem like the biggest stud poet of this millennium, replacing Lord Byron. You're responsible for all this, you know. I just want to be friends with Lydia, be her Poet Sister. And be friends with you, too. Why don't you two just get married, settle down in a nice little L.A. stucco home, make a baby, and write poems about Grecian urns?"

And he replied: "Basically Lydia's complexity is out for victory, that American-bred shit to win, win, win. Her basic lack of reality is that just to win don't win ya a cold hot dog. As the years grow shorter and the catch gets less close she becomes more vindictive, demanding, caustic, cantankerous . . . hell, you've got a dictionary. I'm drunk."

I begged Lydia to believe me that I wasn't in love with Bukowski. I just wanted to be his friend. And hers, be a "sister."

"Don't give me that. You've become one of his groupies just like all these women hanging around wanting a piece of him. Disgusting. Friend, sister, my foot."

"Lydia, why would I want Bukowski when he's yours? I'm not a groupie, I'm your friend. Why would I want to be a groupie for a dirty old man like Charles Bukowski?"

"Because he's a genius. Because he's the most exciting man you'll ever know."

After Lydia left him for good, December, 1975, selling her house in Los Angeles and fleeing in fury to Phoenix, Arizona, where she stayed, Bukowski, drunk as usual at midnight, called me: "Lydia, Lydia? Is that you my beauteous woman? My woman with little green and golden moths sewed against the sides of her thighs? Love, Lydia, is not having to pretend that you care. Remember, Lydia?"

"This isn't Lydia, Bukowski," I said. "It's Jane."

"Ohhh, it's you. Jaaaaane, Jane. Jaaaaane, you have a way of sounding like all women. Shit. All you women are either named Lydia, Smith or Jane." He hung up and called, I suppose, the Real Lydia.

On his 56th birthday, August 16, 1976, Bukowski called me so I could wish him a happy birthday. He was all alone and, as usual, drunk. His new girlfriend, Tammie, a young beautiful honey-red-haired babe, only 24, had abandoned him that night. I was alone, too, drinking cheap champagne and quite depressed because, coincidentally, August 16, 1976, was the 10th anniversary of the day my second husband tried to kill me with his bare hands. Feeling sorry for myself like I did every year on August 16th since Othello did what he did to me, I blubbered to Bukowski, began to tell him about that awful night, how psychotic Othello defenestrated through my living room bay windows, glass crashing all around — and how Othello grabbed my hair, pulling me down a flight of stairs, and —

"Aww, yeah, well —" Bukowski muttered, August 16, 1976, Beethoven's Fifth Symphony playing on the radio da-da-da-dahh — in the background of his cheap apartment on Carlton Way in Hollywood: Then Bukowski took a long chug of drink and said: "Yeah, sure. August 16, 1966. I remember that night well, kid. My 46th birthday. A bad day for both of us." Bukowski saving his compassion for his artful, heartful poetry. Then added, as da-da-da-dahhh — roared in the background:

"But hey, kid, you got to remember that Desdemona died. You didn't."

Seven more years Charles Bukowski amused me at his standing-room-only poetry readings I attended, a few more midnight drunken phone calls, his fabulous letters until he finally married (not Lydia) in 1985, got rich off his poetry and a screenplay, and then never spoke to me again. Lydia and I stayed friends and distant almost sisters.

Three months, five days before the tragic titanic loss of the World Trade Center, 9/11/2001, when the State of California's legal system has a seven-year backlog of impending litigation created by the largest glut of attorneys-at-law in the USA and years after T.J. DuRong is a long-ago nightmare I had when I lived on Agony Way and I am married to a poet and Charles Bukowski is famous and celebrates his August 16th birthday with Sean Penn and

205

Madonna, both born that day, too (and the day Elvis died in 1977) and Facto Jacko calls me from his 20th-story posh Family Law office in Beverly Hills to say "Hey, that s.o.b. Bukowski at that stupid party of yours really was a famous poet" and after Bukowski dies of leukemia instead of by the blood-besotted hands of a beauteous jealous woman screaming from a balcony, when Lydia calls one hot, full-moon June 6, 2001, night, she will suddenly tell me that Bukowski told her how we'd been lovers. Bukowski and ME. **NO**! I'll shout.

I hadn't seen Lydia since 1994 when she came to L.A. to be interviewed and filmed for a BBC television documentary about Charles Bukowski. But we'd written now and then during the 1990s, but she hadn't telephoned until now. And to tell me What? That Bukowski had said What? Lydia repeated What she'd said.

That sneaky bastard. That sneaky dead bastard. I will vehemently deny it: "I'd never in a million years go to bed with Charles Bukowski. Not for a thousand dollars. NO!"

"Don't lie to me," Lydia will snap. "You were crazy about Bukowski."

True. In 1975, I was crazy about Bukowski — and cheap champagne, too. But Bukowski also terrified me. I wasn't brave enough to be one of Bukowski's Women. Not one of his Real Women, scream at him from a balcony, wrestle with him, love dog from hell, get down south of no north then flop wantonly onto a water bed to kiss and make up. One kiss from him was all I could handle. That night of my Bukowski Bash, just as he was leaving, Lydia in my garage getting her purse and car keys, Bukowski and I were alone for the first and only time, standing in my front doorway. Six inches-plus-two taller than me, crouching over me, Bukowski looked down on me. So drunk his out-of-focus eyes slit snoozing cat's, so mind-blotto'd he did not know who he was, that he might be one of the greatest American poets of them all, he took me in his arms and kissed me on the mouth, so startling me, so terrifying me, I almost threw up. Maybe it was all the cheap champagne I'd drunk that night that made me so sick. But I don't think so. I think it was the meltdown of pure nervous shock. Plus my broken thumb got bent up in his embrace. When I cried out in pain, Bukowski let me go and ran out my front door to Lydia who stood on my front lawn, screaming:

"Bukowski! Get your inebriated butt out here! Else I'm leaving you to walk home to L.A.!" shouted Lydia from the curb outside my house where her funny looking vehicle The Thing was parked. Bukowski, jerking to sobriety as he must've remembered how egregious the 35-mile walk from suburbia to L.A. alongside the freeways San Diego, Santa Ana and Hollywood, staggered on out into the April dawn, the morning after the *Titanic* sunk 63 years ago, three days before Lincoln died 110 years ago, stealing a kiss from me meaning absolutely nothing to him, merely something piddling he did every day like sipping coffee, petting his cat, kicking a beer can out of his garden, because he never, ever mentioned kissing me. For me, though, drenched and dizzy from it, the secret sin of it, I felt like his accomplice in the last Great Train Robbery, Pinkerton Men all around, me all alone left holding the bag.

"I was crazy, all right, but I was never crazy enough to be Charles Bukowski's lover," I will avow to Lydia Kane, June 6, 2001.

"Oh, how the lady doth protest too much," she will snidely sneer. "Sure you were. Those were the best years of your life. You were lovers with Bukowski, all right. You might as well admit it. He was a genius. He was absolutely amazing. He was the most exciting man you'll ever know. How could you possibly have resisted Charles Bukowski?"

Lydia Kane, my don't-wannabe, never-will-be sister will always like her *Mister* Henry Charles Bukowski best.

Ah, but time marches on, and August 16, 2014, Bukowski's 84th birthday, when Lydia Kane—uh, I mean Linda King, her real name, of course, after publishing her memoir *Loving & Hating Charles Bukowski*, and reading my literary profile I wrote about him: *Charles Bukowski: Epic Glottis: His Art & His Women*, and she reads all the above and when she comes to L.A. and we meet again, she will finally believe me, that I did resist Bukowski, that he'd lied about me. And Linda will thank me for writing so favorably of her. And, unbelievably: we'll embrace—*almost* sisterly.

"well, there's beer … rivers and seas of beer/beer beer beer. and beer is all there is …" — Charles Bukowski

Chapter 10 | Love the One You're With, Darlin'

"O Fortune/like the Moon/changeable in state/
always waxing/or waning/detestable life/at one moment
hard/and at the next cares for/the witty games of the mind/
poverty/power/it dissolves like ice..."
— Boethius' *Wheel of Fortune*

The Texan, my sometimes lover, is the only person in 1979 I know who has an answering service. Though I do not love my sometimes lover nor does he love me, though he does say often "Love the one you're with, Darlin'," any time of day or night the four or five times a year these past seven years I call him when my no-good husband T.J. DuRong has disappeared again, and I talk to Shirley, Heather or Debbie Herself of Debbie's Ding-a-Ling Answering Service, and leave my message, "Call your cousin," The Texan calls me within the hour to ask: "Darlin' Cuz, is that sommabitch T.J. DuRong done flown the coop again? Can y'all come out to play?" And if I say yes, The Texan'll stop what he's doing, no matter what, even if he's with another woman, and make plans for my arrival to his abode, his "orifice," his pun for "office," his cramped but posh makeshift living quarters he illegally built and painted "orifice red" in the back of his high performance boat-building machine shop in an industrial complex near LAX.

The only time he didn't call me right back was when he went back home to Sweetblossom, Texas, a year ago to his blessed mother's funeral who'd died suddenly of a heart attack at the young age of 61, the most beautiful woman who ever lived Mae Belle was; her name, a verbatim translation of the French meaning "Beautiful May" which she was, just

209

ask The Texan, he'll show you countless portraits of her pretty face. He's the only man I've ever known, and ever will, who carries pictures of his mother in his wallet and adores his mother so much so he regretted after her death of not ever giving her the grandchildren she begged him—her only child—to provide, wished for about an hour, he said, he'd not got his vasectomy at age 19 in Juarez, Mexico to assure that no girl or woman, no matter how sweet, desirable or lovable could trap him into paternity and marriage against his will.

While The Texan sits naked, Indian chief-style this August 16, 1979, night in his red satin-covered waterbed, skillfully rolling us a large joint of Acapulco Gold, very good marijuana devotees—of which I am not one—of the stuff lovingly call a "bomber," I tell him that I have this awful feeling lately that I will wind up dying young too, like his mama. Though a California resident since 1966, The Texan's a never-die purist Texas-talking Texan who calls his mother Mama while I, born in Texas, too, was instructed to call mine Mother.

"Well, Darlin' Cuz, you better hurry up and do it, cuz you ain't gettin' any younger, y' know," he says cheerily and pats my thigh with his hand that wears a two thousand-dollar diamond pinky ring.

I am 39. The Texan won't tell me how old he is and hides his wallet when I come over, a habit he has with all his women, afraid one of them will be tempted to roll him, so I can't check his driver's license for his real age so I can only guess he's about seven years older than me because his favorite movie star is Clark Gable whom he tries hard to resemble, wears a narrow pencil moustache in 1979, very old-timey looking these days when big bushy handlebars are fashionable. The Texan smiles like Clark Gable, too, with clenched teeth, tilts his head to one side when he does, to show off his deep dimples. Also, his favorite songs are old-fogy ones from the early 1950s: Tony Bennett's "Rags to Riches" (which describes The Texan's phenomenal and lucky life of perpetuating prosperity), Hank Williams' "Cheatin' Heart" (his personal anthem which he sings in the first person: "my cheatin' heart will tell on ME—") and Doris Day's "Secret Love" which he considers "our song" since we've been secret lovers for these past seven years ever since I heard a rumor that T.J. DuRong was messing around with not just one but two hippie chicks—plus an aging glamour movie star who owned an antique shop in Newport Beach.

Though one of T.J. DuRong's anthem songs, his ode to sin, singing it often to himself, was: "If you can't be with the one you love, love the one you're with," T.J. DuRong denied his infidelities vehemently. Thus on this August 16, 1979, night, our precariously unuxorious journey on the SS Marital Wreck of a Ship continues upon tsunami high seas as T.J. DuRong's whereabouts are unknown to me, and that's why I'm here in The Texan's waterbed. Lonesome. And nervous. Because today, at 1:30 a.m. marks the 13th anniversary of What Othello Did to Me.

When I frown, remembering that horrible fact and wondering what T.J.'s up to, in whose waterbed T.J. is a-lyin' while I am lying in The Texan's waterbed, The Texan pats, there-there, my arm, then kisses the crease between my eyes. "Aw, I didn't hurt your feelings, did I? You know you are younger than springtime to me—" No, I know he didn't mean to hurt me; he's always a gentleman to me, opens doors for me, brings me a Beefeater gin on the rocks whenever the one I'm drinking goes dry, and after we make love he always rearranges my waist-length hair upon his pillow, gently spreads it like sprawls of flowers to bury his face into and takes deep breaths of my gardenia fragrant shampoo.

"You know, Darlin', I'm always asking you all these years how come it is I'm the only one of the two of us who's gettin' ole?"

True. He wears little half-moon Ben Franklin bifocals now; his red cottony hair and pencil moustache streaked gray. "Cheer up, my poor li'l' Darlin' Cuz—" he coos, kisses my cheek. He calls me cousin because we are both from Texas. The likelihood, though, that we are related is quite remote if not impossible since his place of birth in Sweetblossom near El Paso and the Rio Grande River that separates Texas in the south from Mexico and on the southwest from New Mexico, and my place of birth in northeast Paris near Dallas and the Red River that separates Texas from Oklahoma, is a landscape sprawl of humanity and dirt as far-flung and far-fetched as Dublin, Ireland is from Rangoon. His hot, dusty place in Texas once belonged to Mexico. While Paris, Texas, founded by a lonesome Parisian named Beaumont Lamar, was once a pit-stop off the Chisholm Trail, a bit of a Garden of Eden made fertile by the flood plain from the Red River where sprout and flourish thousands of pecan trees and rose-bushes. So I've heard. Haven't been there since I was thirteen years old.

"Just why is it you think you're gonna die now, Darlin' Cuz? Don't you feel good?" He squeezes my bare thigh, says: "You feels good to me—like always—" Then he looks in my face for signs of sickness, looks in my ears, kisses one with his bristly pencil-moustachioed lips making a buzzing kiss like a bee's caught in my cochlea that makes me tingle all over, makes my skin feel suddenly encrusted with sparkling diamonds. During the seven years I was a go-go girl, a course of tawdry misfortunate chicanery that lasted the length of accursed bad luck after breaking a mirror, seven years, too, the minimum sentence for a felony conviction, though I probably made the acquaintance of

212

more than seven thousand men, one thousand men per year, I have not acquainted myself with that many lovers, marrying three of them. But I am so certain I'd bet a lot of money on this: The world's best lover is the sweet-talking, gentle-touching Texan.

I have called The Texan The Texan for so long, ever since I met him in 1966, seven months, on my January birthday in fact, after I began working as a neophyte go-go girl at La Pink Pantera, I have to think to remember his name is really Abraham Moses, named that by his Bible-belting Mama Mae Belle. He calls himself "Ab" — referring to his buffed stomach muscles — rather than Abe because he doesn't want to be mistaken for being Jewish. As if, with his cottony red hair and pearly-toothed Texas grin and drawl, puddling bellbottom jeans, red alligator boots and red cowboy shirts with pearl buttons, he ever could be.

"Too many anti-semens out there in this dog-eat-dog biz-ness world," he said, when he explained to me why he doesn't want to be mistaken for being Jewish.

"Anti-Semites," I amend. "Then why don't you say you were named after Abraham Lincoln?"

"Aw, that's even worse. Lotta my customers are some of the worst red-neckers around, have John Bircher coe-nex-shuns and even some Klan ties and they still bear a grudge against that old abolitionist sommabitch Abraham Lincoln."

I shook my head, a bit appalled hearing Lincoln called a son of a bitch for the first time — in my lifetime, that is. The Texan's way of calling a spade a spade — at least how he discerned a "spade" — always troubled me.

The Texan, Drinking Man #500, I arbitrarily numbered him, blew into La Pink Pantera on a January rainy Sunday, 1966, when all the Crazy Ones, as I called them, came into the place, the unloved, unwashed, deranged and dispossessed dudes and down-and-out delirium tremens'd alcoholics bedeviled with thirst for beer, beer, beer, drying out some of them from Saturday night's revelry, in limbo Sunday, a one-day doldrum as they readied for the Cape Horn of Blue Monday to start their weekday misery high seas anew. Because of them, that motley drinking crew of misbegotten, impecunious men, men, men, I was the only go-go girl who'd work Sundays, not even the bouncers would come in that day, hung over too from Saturday night; I worked six days a week because I had to; I had three kids and needed the tips, no matter how paltry.

Only in California from Texas for two months, The Texan was a Biker then, riding with the Red Snakes, the only one of them not to have a red snake tattoo on his forearm because he would soon dump them to start up his legit business building race boats that would thrive even through the first Energy Crisis of the early 1970s, so good were his high performance engines. His latest kingly masterpiece, a pointy-nosed red-white-and-blue race boat the size of a big-rig truck, "Blood, Sweat and Gears," held court in the warehouse outside this "orifice"—his personal cubbyhole quarters he built in back of the shop—waiting for final touches from Maestro Machinist Ab, while next to it was his newest speedboat in its early stages he'd named "Moby Slick."

I met him the same day I met Crazy Ted, a six-foot-five aerospace engineer, a United State Naval retiree and card-carrying registered sexual deviate (for homosexuality) who carne in out of the rain holding open the bullet-hole-scarred front door of La Pink Pantera for the littlest woman I'd ever seen. Beneath the stretched-out armpit of his Navy pea coat, the little lady came scurrying in, looking gratefully up into his funny-looking face, then cozied up beside him on a barstool, cleaving so to him as if they'd been doing this barroom dance for years. Crazy Ted wasted no time in

214

telling me about His Gun. Patting where his heart would be on the inside of his rib bones on the inside of his pea coat, he placed my hand upon the lump there, the hard contents of his pea coat inside pocket: That Gun. He always carried it. Because the World Was Such a Crazy Place. The little woman smiled admiringly at this fact. She wore a trench coat.

And nothing underneath, I'd soon find out when she went flashing her scrawny naked bod to the Red Snakes playing pool while The Texan flirted with me, eyed amazingly that someone as slim as me had given birth to three babies, now two, five and seven years old I showed him photos of in my wallet.

While Crazy Ted, who called himself "Ready Teddy" and patted the gun over his heart like a pledge of allegiance to his every-ready craziness, chugged seven Coors in a row, the little woman left one by one, out the side exit, with a Red Snake until she'd performed fellatio on ten of them at five dollars a pop out back in the alley behind the trash bins. In the rain. I was shocked when The Texan told me what she was up to, as if she was getting a big kick out of it, all the Red Snakes laughing as if she were. I worried sick that afternoon what Crazy Ted would do when he discovered what that little woman, his woman, maybe his wife, was up to, what he'd do, incited by a jealous rage, with That Gun in his breast pocket. Turned out, though, Crazy Ted had never seen her before in his life till he found her shivering on the front steps of the entrance to La Pink Pantera and opened the door for her. Now, 13 years later, I wanted to cry when I thought of her, not much older back then than the age I was now in 1979, doing that, giving blowjobs, for a living. A Fellatrice. In the rain. Could be the name of a sad Beatles song.

"You don't got cancer, do you, Darlin'? That why you

gonna die young?"

"No. I don't got cancer. Not that I know of, at least."

"If you do ever get cancer, now, you be sure to tell me. Okay?" He pats me like my father used to pat my mother, like my father used to pat me when I was sick, medicinally, paternally lovingly, and while The Texan pats me, I don't feel like I'm going to die. I look at my palm for my life-line, to see if it's still long, and it is. Deep, too, because my palm is getting wrinkled in my approaching old age.

"Okay," I say. "I'll tell you if I ever get cancer."

I roll over onto my back, making waves in the waterbed, and look up into the mirror on the ceiling at the top of the Texan's cottony red head and notice a tiny bald spot emerging in the middle of his cranium. The Texan lights the Acapulco Gold-stuffed bomber the size of his index finger, puffs, then hands it to me. I take a puff. Cough. Choke. I hate marijuana but pretend to love it for The Texan's sake; he always prides himself on having the best pot money can buy in the whole county of Los Angeles.

God, I hate that ceiling mirror. When The Texan first installed it four years ago and I got a look at it, I turned around and walked out and didn't come back for a year. He had to beg me to come back, said he wouldn't ever turn on the lights around it ever again when I was there. Lights! Multi-colored lights all around it that when it was all lit up made it seem like some sex-crazed, all-seeing, all-knowing higher deity with a Christmas tree fetish, watching over you, while you did what you did in The Texan's waterbed. I roll over onto my stomach so's not to see even the shadowy images on the ceiling that are the naked Texan and me.

In the small indent in the small of my back I feel the

216

slow icy stream of what must be Beefeater gin from the Texan's glass. The August 16, 1979, night is hot; eggs were fried today on Sunset Boulevard sidewalks, and the cold gin feels good. I feel The Texan's warm breath as he begins to lap up the gin from the concave of my middle body. If I looked over my shoulder, if the ceiling lights were on, I could see this, and I almost want to. But I am not a kinky person, no Swinger, moi, in this year of 1979 that is the tail end of the Swinging Seventies advocating that you love the one you're with, let it all hang out, keep on truckin' and Do It In The Road. I do not want to do it in the road. Nor on a desktop nor on the kitchen floor. I'm not even particularly fond of waterbeds, those unreliable slosh buckets. I am the last person you want to invite to your Stag Movie Party. I freaked after seeing *Deep Throat*. Didn't want to have sex for months, suffered post trauma from involuntary gagging reflexes for weeks. I do not like how times are a-changin'. Never did. Never will.

The Texan puts down his dope, takes me in his arms, kisses my neck where he knows I like it best, right behind my right ear when the phone rings. Stops. Rings twice, stops, rings once and, recognizing this secret code (mine is two rings, twice) before the answering service picks up, The Texan picks up and shouts into the receiver:

"Bart! You sommabitch! S'bout time you returned my calls!" The Texan leans over to lick the last of the gin from my skin and grins at me, his companion here at this grin-and gin- in-crowd. When I roll over on to my back and look up at him on the ceiling, he waves at me up there beside him in the dark mirror, mimes, Howdy, Darlin'.

"Oh, yeah?" He goes on. "Well, Bart, you know what you can do with that check in the mail shit? You can shove it up your ass, Bart. I want my money. Now. Cash. All of it. No down payments. I ain't a used car lot. Or no bank." He clicks on the remote. He's the only person in 1979 I know who has remote controlled TV. The Fonz appears on the TV the Texan has attached to the wall near the ceiling, he laughs. Says, sotto voce to me:

"That wuz me, Darlin' when I wuz young. Ha-ha— Had a leather jacket just like that when I wuz his age—"

Yes, I know, he had it on the first time I met him that Crazy Sunday when The Texan liked me right off, me and him reunited Texans on the Hollywood Strip of all places. "Meet my Darlin' cuz—" he said to his fellow Red Snakes. If my crazy ex-husband hadn't been stalking me, in fact he was on the premises when the bikers walked in, had just twisted my arm before he snuck out quickly when they took over the way that bikers always do, The Texan might've become my lover then instead of seven years later after I'd erroneously married T.J. DuRong because I thought the "P" in T.J.'s Personal Alphabet stood for "Potential." Instead T.J.'s "P" stood for "Party Animal."

Blah-blah-blah! I hear Bart shout, then the Texan shouts: "Don't gimme no shit! I'll tell you what, Bart— There's a Clark Gable movie comin' on Channel 11 at ten I'm gonna watch. By 9:30 if you haven't brought me by my money—all of it—I'm gonna shoot you between the eyes, Bart. Yep. Simple as that. You know I will, too." Blah-blah-blah, Bart says apologetically. "Okay, Bart. You bring it to me here. I just bought this industrial complex—"

He winks at me, whispers: "My Daddy just died, rest his soul, and left me a bunch of money. So all this is mine now, Darlin'—" He spreads out his arms to indicate the width of his wealth, this vast acreage of gated, gray and greasy commercial real estate. "Nope, no one around to bother us, Bart. I quadrupled everyone's rent here in this industrial park so's they'd all move out. You come to the gate and buzz and I'll come runnin'—for my money. All of it, now. You got that straight between us?" He slams down the receiver loud as gunfire.

"Now where were we?" He clicks off The Fonz. He's breathing hard, full of testosterone. "So what's this again about you're gonna die young? You got some dread disease you ain't telling me about? My mama had breast cancer and that wasn't no laughin' matter."

"It's just a feeling. I am so stressed out, I have these awful headaches, nightmares." Since he found Maureen and me, my recurring nightmares about Othello defenestrating through my living room bay windows 13 years ago, have been coming to me once a week. "My kids are teenagers now and hate my guts, my mother is sick, grad school's driving me crazy —"

"My li'l' skoo girl still goin' to skoo? When you gonna be through with all those books and get yourself a real job? What is it you're studying that's takin' so much time?"

"French."

"French, like my mama's name? Mae Belle, which means a beautiful month of May? Which she surely was, no doubt about it. Bless her beauteous wondrous heart. But wait a minute. Lemme get this straight now. First you was gonna be a secretary, then a nurse like my mama was. Then you went to law skoo to be a lawyeress."

"I had to quit nursing school because I was allergic to formaldehyde and couldn't dissect a feral cat —" The other nursing students, all women, called me a sissy. " — and I dropped out of law school because — oh, never mind. Now I'm in grad school, in the French Department."

"Nursing skoo, law skoo, now French skoo? A bit indecisive, ain't you? What you plan to do with all your knowledge of French? Go to France? Wear some underpants? Ha-ha. I'm a poet who knows it!"

I had no idea what I was going to do after grad

school when I got my useless Master Degree in French literature. "I'm following my bliss," I defended to him and myself.

"Bliss. That was my mama's maiden name. Do you know there used to be a Blissful, Texas? My mama's uncle old Randolph Benton Bliss founded it during the oil boom of the 'teens. A pretty li'l' town it was but it got blowed away during the 1920s and '30s Dust Bowl times. I'm gonna take you there someday to Blissful, Texas, at least where it used to be, show you all the red dirt, rich ole earth around it, how it goes on and on into the horizon like a big red carpet of roses." He relights the bomber, puffs, inhales deeply, smiles clenched little elfin teeth, blissfully, tilts his head to emulate Clark Gable.

"Tell me about your headaches. Where do they hurt? You know headaches are always caused by something outside the body that makes the inside of the head ache. What's outside your body bringing you so much pain?"

I can't tell him about T.J. He likes it how T.J. DuRong's no good, does nothing but wrong. It means I get to sneak off and spend time with him when T.J.'s bad which is more often than I let The Texan know about.

"My ex-husband ..." I tell him. "Othello wants to see his daughter, Maureen—found us via the—oh, never mind—" I don't tell him the long story of how Othello found us, how all he did was go to the District Attorney's Office and pretend to be an abused ex-husband whose crazy ex-wife wouldn't let him see his little girl. The sympathetic assistant D.A. had no record of what Othello'd done to me 13 years ago. So he nicely gave him our address.

"O'Thayo? That bastard's Irish? I thought he was Mexican or Italian with all that black hair of his."

"Cherokee. He's half Cherokee."

"Ah, well, now some of them Cherokees've got a

220

mean streak. Still hold a grudge for what the white men did to them, took all their land. That's why he's so crazy. Course so's the Irish. I should know. I'm half Irish myself. The Irish side's where I got my green eyes and red hair. Y'know, ever buddy here in Ah-murr-ka's Irish or Ind-yun or Nee-grow."

"I'm German and Scottish and Welsh and—"

"Welsh? Y'see whut I mean? Hell, the Welsh—ha-ha—are the Irish who can't swim!"

"Ohhh—" I groan. "That's not funny. You're such a Texan, such a racist."

"Aw, can't you take a joke? Hey, I can tell racist jokes about Texans too. Here's one: How many Texans does it take to screw in a light bulb?"

"I don't know."

"None! Because us Texans don't SCREW in light bulbs! We screw in waterbeds!" He bounces the waterbed, making it slosh, and bursts into uncontrollable laughter. I can't help but laugh too; but I turn my head, cover my mouth so he won't see. I don't want to encourage him, but he hears me laugh, nudges me, bites my shoulder gently, makes me giggle. For years, this is the only place, lying beside The Texan, that I experience unconditional, insouciant joy. He inhales the marijuana deeply, ponders, says:

"Y'know, if I'd known what that bastard O'Thayo was doing to you back then I would've saved you—You should'a told me." Amazing how many of the men I knew back then at La Pink Pantera said that post-facto, post-bellum, after Othello'd tried to murder me. I did try, in fact, to tell The Texan, but I couldn't find him; if I had, maybe he'd've really saved me. When crazy Othello came defenestrating through my living room window after I locked him out, the Texan would've been right behind him. Maybe. I'll never know.

"If that bastard's threatening you again Darlin' Cuz, I still have some Red Snakes coe-nex-shuns, y'know. They snuff that bastard out like a candlelight." He snaps his fingers and takes a long puff off the bomber, hands it to me and I shake my head No. "Kick that O'Thayo's ass up over the top of his black head of hair."

"Never mind—" I say. "All that stuff's water under the bridge now." Though it's not; I still worry Othello will find me.

If all the men in the world who say they could kick ass really did kick ass, there'd be no men on earth who could walk upright. Crazy Ted wanted to save me too, before it happened. In fact, the month before Othello did to me what he did, when he saw pissed-off Othello snarling at me on the front bar of La Pink Pantera and then jerk my wrist, toss a beer at me and left, Crazy Ted went after him with That Gun. Trod out to the Pink Pantera parking lot to shoot Othello where he stood by my faded blue VW Bug, waiting to harass me some more when I got off work. Crazy Ted actually fired that gun but missed, shot out a streetlight instead of Othello's brains and the cops came and put ol' Ready Teddy in jail for disturbing the peace. That Gun of his. Always flailing it about, a nutty inebriated Don Quixote, it had to be that Crazy Ted would die by it a most awful death. I sip some Beefeater gin, not much left but a bit of ice.

"What you need is more of me and this—" He pours me more Beefeater gin. I chug it down. "And nude therapy—" He kisses my naked shoulder. Yes, I certainly need this: this eye of my hurry-cane, this port in the storm, this gin-and-grin in-crowd nude therapy in this waterbed bog far away from the madding crowd of loveless kids, sick mother and no-good huz number three, R and R from the worry of the foreclosure notice of my house in the mail, my defaulted student loan, my Victor Hugo translation of "Fantine" due Monday morning at Prestigious U; plus we're out of toilet paper at home and dog food and I forgot to pay the last installment on T.J. DuRong's drunk driving fine and my old car needs new tires. And this morning at 1:30 a.m. was the 13th anniversary of When & What He Did To Me. Why can't I just forget about it? Why do I keep dreaming about Defenestration? Am I having a nervous breakdown at last? At age 39? So much to remember. So much ahead. Life. What is it all about? Why can't I pull myself together like my father wanted me to do in 1966? Make myself into a ball of taffy and bounce high and get over this? It's been 13 years.

"What's in that paper bag you brought?" The Texan asks. I always bring him a "TV dinner," homemade meals I pack onto a tin pie pan he plops onto a plastic plate and microwaves. He's the only person I know in 1979 who owns a microwave and knows how to operate it. "More of your Jane's Plain Good Meat loaf I hope? And some of those bitty li'l' taters with green stuff on 'em?"

"Roasted parsley potatoes," I inform him. I've brought him this time Jane's Plain Good Old Texas Beans and a pan of cornbread. His Irish green eyes sparkle leprechaun when he sees what it is.

"My, my, my — If this don't beat all —" He gets up to warm it up on his small stove in the cubbyhole near the door to the warehouse where beyond is housed all his machinery. Back on the waterbed with a big bowl of my Texas beans and a plate of steaming cornbread, he gobbles big bites. "Mmmm, mmmm good. Better than my mama ever made. And looky all the chorizo sausage! I love chorizo sausage!" He shows me a chunk of carrot but I let him think it's chorizo. Not many people like carrots. "And did you put molasses in the cornbread?" I nod. "Mmmm mmmm!" T.J. hates my cooking. Especially Texas Food. He says my cooking tastes like earwax-covered toenails.

When he's done eating, he puts on his jeans and red

satin shirt and red alligator boots, reaches inside his closet to take out my red satin robe he bought me, red his favorite color, not mine, that has "Jane" embroidered on the pocket and my red satin high-heel slippers he bought with fuzzy stuff on the toes, and says, "Come on, wanna show you somethin' —" Then, gently as if I'm a baby girl, he dresses me, slips the slippers onto my feet, like Prince Charming would and takes my hand and leads me clip-clop through his warehouse filled with race boats and steel chains and cranes and air compressors and ceiling-high tool cabinets. Out we go into the night, out the big aluminum door down the asphalt walkway and around the dark corner to where, behind his big-assed silver Lincoln Continental with red leather upholstery, a huge mobile home stands parked.

"Looky —" he says as he flicks on the lights inside that lights up an exact replica of a 1890s' whorehouse boudoir. "Built it all with my own li'l' hands — everything except the ole-timey lamps and furniture, that is — but I picked it out." He'd fashioned old-fashioned dark wood paneling, gingerbread moldings, parlor tables, wing-backed chairs, a loveseat and an amber glass chandelier that when all lit up be-speckled golden confetti upon the copper ceiling squares. Mosaic red roses captured in reproduction Tiffany glass lamplight blush and glow off faux William Morris gold and velvet tasselated and swagged paisley drapes and in the far corner — he points to, with a big grin on his face — a big brass four-poster bed sparkling as if neon-wired with a thick red and gold velvet patchwork quilt sprawled over huge plush pillows. But in the middle of it all bubbles a steaming, gardenia-fragrant hot tub — with a mirror on the ceiling above it.

"Ain't it somethin'? My gilded bordello —" He shows me the bathroom and the claw-foot porcelain bathtub there, marble-and-mahogany wash stand and the old-fashioned

224

toilet with the oak-covered water chamber overhead with a velvet pull to flush it. A plush red towel embroidered "Jane" with golden thread flops voluptuously from a lion-headed brass ring. "Ain't it purty?" He puts his arms around my waist. "Wanna lay, lady lay? Lay across my big brass bed?" he whispers, mimicking Bob Dylan.

"Amazing. "

"Hop in, Darlin', it's been callin' your name all night—Jane, Jane, the water keeps sayin' Hear it?" He kisses my cheek, his Clark Gable pencil moustache pinking it blush, helps me out of the satin robe and holds my hand so I won't slip as I step into the sudsy warm water. A frosty air conditioner blows my hair into my face as he sinks in beside me. "Ain't this fun? Sit on this jet, Darlin'. It'll make hair grow on your butt." He snaps open a brass-handled oak door on the wall, a built-in refrigerator, containing frosted highball glasses and a bottle of Beefeater gin and a crystal bowl of caviar with a tiny mother-of-pearl spoon. "The best for the best—" he says, scooping caviar on to Melba toast for us.

Same kind Crazy Ted brought me in 1966, along with a bottle of Dom Perignon I'd pour into a coffee mug and sip sneakily Sunday mornings before the Crazy Ones came staggering in. For lack of a knife, he'd dab caviar onto crackers with the handle of my Maybelline mascara brush and laugh, like a maniac. I didn't know then Crazy Ted was crazy from drink, Cutty Sark at home first before coming in; it takes a while to understand alcoholism. By that time he called me his little sister because I looked like, so he said, the photos he showed me looked nothing like me, his concert pianist sister, skinny like her at least. And smart like her too because I was the only go-go girl Crazy Ted knew who could spell Einstein. The week before Othello did what he did, an angry pelican of a woman, Crazy Ted's landlady, came in looking for me at La Pink Pantera to tell me of Crazy

Ted's most awful death. He'd shot himself in the head. He'd left a note, leaving Every Thing to me, telling where to find me, his sister, a concert pianist who'd fallen on hard times.

"Ha. His sister. Yeah, sure—" she said snidely, eyeing me up in my shocking pink go-go girl bikini as I stood beneath the fluorescent black lights on the front bar while "Wooly Booly" blasted from the jukebox. "So you're what those go-go girls look like!" She shouted it to be heard above the eardrum-busting go-go noise.

"Sister! Ha! You're nothing but a common frump." How awful, how embarrassing it was that she thought Crazy Ted, that drunkard homosexual Knight of the Sad Countenance my Sugar Daddy; that crazy old Don Quixote who never tipped more than a dollar a day, but it did pay for my kids' daily oatmeal. Too much of a lady to tell me what she really thought of me, she shouted, she told me how she was a member of the H.A.D.I.T.S., one of those outraged Housewives Against Decadence In This Society, who picketed these sleazy girlie bars along the Strip, got signatures for petitions to close them places down. Irate with decency in 1966, she really would've boiled herself into a simmering stew had she known that times ahead in 1972 would bring the movie *Deep Throat* to that theatre on Sunset just a block away from her home sweet home.

Later, at Crazy Ted's one-room dump around the corner, to get his stuff, take possession of my dubious "inheritance," I was sternly informed by the pelican woman that I had to first clean up the mess, the blood and brains splattered all over the floor and wall behind the table where he'd sat when he did it. All my inheritance consisted of, that I could see, was a cardboard box of family photographs, a half-gone case of Cutty Sark, hundreds of empty Dom Perignon and beer bottles and some scruffy clothing. I asked for the Navy pea coat but Nope, no dice, the pelican woman snarled.

Slumlord turned neatnik, she was adamant: I had to clean up the mess. Or at least pay to have it done before she'd let me take one thing from that cardboard box so I let her keep all Crazy Ted's pitiful stuff and went back to work.

"Do you remember Crazy Ted?"

"Who?"

"That tall skinny guy at La Pink Pantera that day you and I met."

"Darlin', I can't remember that far back. I'm gettin' ole. That was more'n 13 years ago, way back, winter, 1966. Them's ancient times. Ancient." He licks wayward caviar off his knuckle then his diamond pinky ring.

"Surely you remember Crazy Ted. He was 6'5", weighed about 130 pounds, scrawny; he looked like a wobbling Abraham Lincoln on a stick. Wore a Navy pea coat. You remember him, don't you? And the little woman?"

"Don't remember no wobbly Abraham Lincoln, no other woman. I only had eyes for you—Darlin'. Darlin' you remember way too much anyways. You should drink more gin so you don't remember all the time—"

"Crazy Ted came in every day after that day, always drunk and he'd blabber then blubber and pass out on the bar. None of the girls would wait on him except me."

"Can't blame 'em much. That Pink Pantera was a hellhole of humanity. Only sorry cusses and pervs hung out in those go-go bars. A dirty job you go-go girls had to do. But someone had to do it. Shake them tattered cutie pie tail feathers. Ha-ha. I only went a couple times. Just to see you. This Crazy Ted one of your ole boyfriends? You go see him when you don' come see me Darlin' Cuz?" Othello had thought he was my boyfriend too after Crazy Ted had tried to shoot him.

"No, no, I didn't have boyfriends, then or now. Othello was stalking me. Crazy Ted was a homosexual.

227

Crazy Ted's family disowned him for it. Then he got kicked out of the Navy for it."

"See what I mean? A bunch of pervs hung out there."

"Crazy Ted killed himself."

"Over you? See? A bunch of sorry cusses—"

"No. He killed himself because he was homosexual. I meant nothing to him except to serve him beer. Occasionally listen to him talk, when sober enough, about the theory of relativity. He was an engineer. I was the only go-go girl he knew who could spell Einstein. He shot himself in the head." My slipshod shootist, my Knight of the Sad Nearsighted Countenance couldn't maim the windmill Othello with That Gun but he managed to aim on target between his own eyes.

"I saw Crazy Ted's blood and brains afterwards all over the floor and wall of his apartment. Have you ever seen splattered human brains?"

"Splattered brains? What splattered brains?"

"Crazy Ted's. When splattered brains dry up they look like black rubies." A tear streams down my cheek. I am getting very-very drunk from hot tub bubbles and a lot of old memories and cold gin. I am not a good drunk, do not hold my liquor well. I want to blubber, but instead, out my mouth comes one stifled lugubrious sob.

"Aw, kee-rice, let's not get all sorrowful now, ruin our good time talking about bloody splattered brains and death and dyin' young of headaches. Think decadence, Darlin'!" He pours us each a glassful of gin and as we sip and nibble caviar and toast, we watch ourselves in the steaming-up mirror above us. This is more decadence than I could've ever imagined: the gilt, the ruby plush, the awesome amber diamond glow of the chandelier, our naked bodies' reflections a-stewin' in the ceiling mirror above.

I sigh, think "decadence" and say: "This is absolutely amazing."

228

"Now don't go fallin' in love with it. It ain't mine much longer. I just sold it. Made a mint off it, too. Only cost me a couple thou to build it. Found this ol' mobile home in the desert, junked and all rusted up. Hauled it here and been workin' on it in my spare time. Sold it last week to this porn king. You'd know who he was if I mentioned his name but I won't. He's gonna use it for sneaky business. See, Darlin', there's a secret camera up there inside that mirror. I built a crawl space in the ceiling, see—" He points up at it. "And this porn king dude wants to have some babes over for what they'll think's an awe-dish-shun and you know—Film himself some stars, some unsuspecting cutie pie Linda Lovelaces, for his movies without payin' 'em for it—"

"That's not audition, that's invasion of privacy, peeping Tommery. That's disgusting—"

"Aw, it's jus' fun, Darlin'. The porn king jus' wants to have fun. Make some money. And all them cutie pies'll have fun, too."

This makes me remember what Joan Crawford once said in an old movie: "Men are all alike. If they ain't fresh, they're rotten." And I think she said it about Clark Gable.

"You're not filming ME, are you?"

"Aw, naw. I don't got eny more film."

In the corner near an antique mirror on the wall are five TV screens showing the grounds of this industrial complex the Texan now owns plus the locked front gate. It all looks like what a prison must resemble at 9:30 at night. "Hey, there's that sommabitch Bart!" He jumps out of the hot tub and quickly puts on his jeans and boots. From a drawer he takes a gun, shoves it in his front pocket. "Be right back, Darlin'—"

The unsuspecting black-and-white televised Bart, with a snarl on his face and a crooked nose hanging over a scruffy handlebar moustache, resembles a hired assassin and

229

looks nervous on the TV screen, looks around, anxiously, talks to someone behind him. I can't see who stands in the darkness leaning on the fender of the biggest black Cadillac General Motors ever made. Looks maybe like he's up to something. But I've got to go to the bathroom and crawl out of the slippery hot tub. I can't wait to flush that fancy old-fashioned toilet. A small brass-knobbed closet next to the claw-foot tub looks like it safe-holds something wonderful, possibly bags of gold from an olde Jesse James train robbery, and I can't resist looking inside where, I'll be a snooper's blooper, I find several satin robes of different colors and towels to match.

I unfold the top towel, a green one, and it says "Heather." As does the green satin robe. The royal blue towel and robe say "Marlene." A lavender towel and robe: "Lorri." All familiar names. Heather working for Debbie's Ding-a-Ling Answering Service; Marlene the cocktail waitress at Wayne's Wharf where The Texan hangs out weekends; Lorri the graveyard-shift waitress at the all-night coffee shop down the street. I guess I am The Texan's ancient go-go girl. I don't bother reading the rest of the towels and robes. Well, what could I expect? How dare I be shocked. The Texan is, after all, the best lover in the world and these are his patronesses of his prodigious prowess when I'm not around which is 360 days of the year. At least he assigned his favorite color, red, to me.

When I hear a gunshot, I grab the red towel that says "Jane" to cover myself—the sound of gunfire suddenly making me feel very-very naked—and I run to look at the TV screens, all blank; I mean empty of guns or people shooting guns, only the gate is there, no one around it. Other points are devoid of people, motion, guns, too, just gray stucco-walled industrial buildings and shadows of telephone poles, wires and trash bins. I hear footsteps on the mobile home porch and the door swings open. The Texan stands there, a grin on his face, a smoking gun at his side.

"My God! What happened?"

"Shot the sommabitch."

"You SHOT him?"

"Yep. Right between the eyes."

"You KILLED him?"

"What'd you want me to do with him? Ask him in for beans and cornbread? A dip in the hot tub?" Blood is splattered all over his hands and jeans.

"You didn't have to MURDER him!"

"Murder? You call extermination of a dirty ole wharf rat murder? You a spy from the SPCA or somethin'?" He laughs at me, then steps back outside and hauls up from out a trash bin next to the front door a dog-sized rat that must weigh 20 pounds, less two or three pounds because half of its head and all its brains drying up into little black rubies are gone, shot off.

"A rat! My God! I thought you shot that man!"

"What man?"

"Bart."

"Naw, Bart gave me my money and split. Then I saw this sommabitch rat a'runnin and shot the damned thing. Held him up for you to see on TV. Weren't you watchin'?" From a front pocket of his jeans he takes the gun and puts it in a drawer, then he removes, grunting, because it's so big, a wad of money from his back pocket and throws it on to the honey-colored shag carpet where hundred dollar bills flop about like 20 or 30 green baby rabbits. He smiles at me "Did you really think I'd shoot and murder a man?"

"I have no idea what you are capable of doing."

"Good. That's what I'm here for. To surprise you." He throws the rat away for good.

"You wouldn't really murder a man, would you?"

"Well, Darlin', that's for me to know and you never to find out, now ain't it?" An elegant grandfather clock, stately, staidly, in the corner, dongs mellifluously the hour often. "Ah, goody, ole Clark's on!" With his remote control he flicks on the TV above the hot tub. "That's my boy!" he says, then claps once and the amber chandelier dims, claps twice and it dims again.

I've never seen this happen before. "How did you do that? Turn down the lights?"

"I jus' clap my hands. I'm magic! See?" The third clap dims to a burnt umber glow bathing us sepia-toned. Then The Texan turns to me, tilts his red and gray cottony head of hair and smiles big ear-to-big ear just like Clark Gable and says to me, the same words he no doubt says to Marlene, Heather, Lorri, et al—all his other Joan Crawfords and Claudette Colberts and Myrna Loys and Jean Harlows. But I don't care, it's wonderful when he says it just to me, once again sounding just as sweet as it did the first time I heard him over 13 years ago on that rainy January day I first met him, say it the way Gable might've 40 years ago said to Carol Lombard: "Has anyone ever told you, Darlin', that you are the prettiest woman alive?"

"No," I whimper, his cue to take me in his arms and when he does, I let my arms fall loose at my sides, gracefully, a Swan Lake ballerina, in surrender.

"Ah, but first, Darlin', I got a present for you. Almost forgot," he says, as he opens the drawer of an ornate Victorian chest, pulls out an elaborately ribboned box and hands it to me with a big smile on his face, sunburned from a long hot summer's work in the 1979 August sun.

"A little somethin' I bet you've been wanting—"

When I open my gift, I am so disappointed, I could cry. Because it was something I did not want.

After that night, though he was magic, I didn't want to see The Texan again and only saw him one more time, two years later, for gin martinis at Wayne's Wharf where huge portraits of John Wayne hung on the walls—the one of The Duke as the Ringo Kid in *Stagecoach* behind The Texan pointed a Winchester rifle at me while I told The Texan I wasn't going to see him again. That's okay, Darlin', said The Texan; he was about to tell me the same thing because this bossy, rich woman who owned two discos he'd been seeing was forcing him into marrying her, just wouldn't leave him the hell alone she loved his butt so much, stalkin' him the way that crazy Irish Cherokee sommabitch O'Thayo had done to me.

"She even slashed all four of my tires with a big ole butcher knife, held it up to my throat and said she'd slash that, too, that's how much she wants me. And I'm gettin' ole, need somebuddy to take care of me should I become poor and infirm." That time seemed a long ways away as The Texan looked spiffy that night in a grey, silk Armani suit and a Pierre Cardin pearl-buttoned red satin shirt that matched his red snakeskin Texas boots. And he'd tinted his fuzzy graying hair the color of enchilada sauce mixed with some jambalaya roux that gave off an aura of go-go locomotion a'fire beneath the overhead sepia-tinted chandeliers. He looked pretty upwardly mobile: a yuppie, in fact. A go-gettin' mover and shaker moneymaker.

Then when the country rock band The Wild Groats 'n' Grits came on, played their theme song "Deep In The Heart of Texas," The Texan danced with me for the first time, led me around the chandelier-shiny wooden floor, danced a boot-clonking but bullfighter-graceful Texas two-step just like the one my Texas Daddy taught me when I was three years old. Later, I waved as The Texan drove away in his brand new silver Rolls and I got into my 1972 broccoli green

233

Dodge I'd just bought for cheap. But The Texan did call me one more time, in 1985, the day I brought my very ill mother home from the hospital. She was in the throes of a turn for the worse and having a horrible time of it. I was having a hard time, too, trying to administer morphine and bedpans.

"Can y'all come out to play?" he asked, explaining that he was able to call because he'd just broke up with that bossy woman who almost nailed him to the cross of matrimony. I told him about my mother, what we were going through. "Aw, my poor li'l' Darlin' Cuz. Y'know we only get one of them beauteous wondrous women in this cold, cruel ole world. So you take good care of your sweet mama."

And I did. And she died. And years later when I tried to call him after he'd sold off his industrial park in the big L.A. commercial building boom of the early 1990s and gotten very-very rich, become Ab-Mo Industries, I called his main branch to talk to him, tell him I'd divorced that no-good T.J. DuRong and married a poet who'd taken me to England where I saw a real beefeater, a yeoman of the guard at the Tower of London, tell him I'd had a Happy Ending too, my cook book *Jane's Never Plain Good for You Cookery* was a $100 finalist in this year's Best American Food Cook Book competition — though the "money" turned out to be coupons for canned tomato sauce. I wanted to say Goodbye Forever to him. Tell The Texan a joke I'd made up: "How many dead go-go girls does it take to screw in a light bulb?"

Of course, his answer, the wrong answer, would be: "None, because they don't screw in light bulbs, they screw in waterbeds." And I'd have to emphasize the trick of the joke-question, so he'd get it: "*Dead* go-go girls."

"To whom do you wish to speak?" asked a snobby executive assistant, female.

"Uh, uh — Ab — Mo — " I stammered. Tried to

remember what the Ab and/or the Mo stood for besides Abdominal Muscles and Mo' of them because The Texan lifted weights, had the body of a varsity football star. "Your boss, Mr. Abmo, please. The owner and founder of this company."

"Name, please—" She was very rigid, screening Big Boss's calls with such superior efficiency, bossiness, I wondered if she had a satin robe and towel with her name embroidered on them tucked inside one of The Texan's closets.

"Uh—" I'd called The Texan The Texan in my mind and memory for so many years, never calling him by any name when I was with him, I couldn't for the life of me remember The Texan's name, first, middle or last. "Just tell him, Mr. Abmo, please, it's his Texas *cousin* calling."

"If you are his cousin, ma'am, why don't you tell me his last name?"

"Uh—Honest, I'm his cousin. Tell him it's Jane—"

She sneered, repeated herself: "Ma'am, I repeat: if you are his cousin, tell me his name." She got snottier. A Babybooming feminist, I supposed, or a yuppie-want-it-all-now go-getter. I bet her role models were Margaret Thatcher and Martha Stewart and Material Girl Madonna. Mine had been Olive Oyl and Lois Lane and Baby Snooks.

"What's your favorite color?" I asked her.

"That's really none of your business, ma'am."

Uh, oh. Kick-butt, no nonsense-feminist.

She doesn't need no Popeye to 86 bully Blutos nor a Superman to stop speeding bullets. And Mick Jagger better never call her a Stupid Girl because she seems totally capable of getting lots of satisfaction.

"I bet it's red," I said. "Your efficient, intelligent voice seems like the voice of someone who would like red."

"Ma'am, you must be crazy. I must end this

235

conversation now. This is a very busy office, I do not have time for—"

"Wait, wait—Listen, your boss's favorite color is red. If I weren't his cousin, would I know something so personal as that about him? He's Irish, too, got green eyes, like a leprechaun's got."

"Ma'am, if you should know anything personal about the owner of this multi-million-dollar industry to whom you claim you are closely related, you should surely know his name. And for your information, my favorite color is pink." Nobody's fool, she hung up.

I knew she'd tell me. She couldn't resist. People love to tell what their favorite color is. When I was a go-go girl long ago in ancient times, to start up a conversation with a sorry cuss, sad sack or a crazy one, I'd ask what his favorite color was. Ask what someone's had for breakfast, they usually can't remember. Ask if he loves you, he doesn't know or won't tell you if he does, just to be mean. Ask what his zodiac sign is and he might say: "Familiarity breeds contempt."

So, good. The Texan's bulwark/harridan/battle-axe executive assistant's favorite color was pink. The Texan hated pink. And had she connected me with him that day, I might've told The Texan how much his gift to me our last night together in his enchanted motor home castle-on-the-roadside made me want to cry and run away and never come back. Inside that fancy box, turned out, was a t-shirt, that one so popular with Feminists at the time that had blazoned across the front a quote by Gloria Steinem:

"A Woman Needs A Man Like A Fish Needs A Bicycle." Though the t-shirt was red, it was obvious that The Texan hadn't ever known ME at all; all those years he'd never understood me. He'd thought me a Feminist, which was about the worst slur a man you thought liked you

236

could call you back then in those ancient times—especially if you weren't a Feminist.

I really didn't know what I was back then. Professional Student. Francophile. Future Careerist. Bad Mother. I was just doing the best I could while I tried to crystallize my latent knowledge—and pull myself together like my father had wanted me to do. And besides, the t-shirt fit me horribly. Made in China and saggy, it made me look detestable in my poverty, fat as a big bloody moon, and as lumpy as a huge bag full of drab and dreary necessities from the discount store: toilet paper, a ton of dog food, a year's supply of detergent, and oatmeal. When I looked at myself wearing it in the mirror I looked like a barbaric yawping barracuda trying to ride a bicycle with flat tires, so hangdog dowdy and dumb—like a rookie recruit of a ragtag regiment, perhaps one named the D.D.W.D.D., pronounced "dwodd" and standing for Dreary Desdemonas—those lewd minxes!—Who Didn't Die after a million attempts to smother her with a pillow.

But I couldn't've told him: that up until he gave me that t-shirt, I'd thought there'd been a sweet kinship and magic between us in those witty games of the mind we played for years and that he'd understood me. You can never tell someone who doesn't understand you that they don't understand you because they just don't understand—especially if you don't understand yourself either.

But for sure, I would've told The Texan the correct punch line to my ancient go-go girl joke—and he would've understood—after he ponderously asked: "How many *dead* go-go girls does it take to screw in a light bulb?"

Yes, *dead* go-go girls.

"None? Because they screw in waterbeds?"

Nope.

The answer to "How many *dead* go-go girls it takes to screw in a light bulb?" is: "None. Because us old go-go girls never die, we just fray away — "

Ha-ha-ha, I hear The Texan laugh, liking my stupid Ancient Go-Go Girl joke while he fills my chilled martini glass to the brim with clear, sparkling gin.

Then he'll splash a little gin into my bellybutton and grin, my leprechaun-eyed Clark Gable, as I lay, Lady, lay across his big waterbed, while outside his window a silver moon waxes or wanes — you know how you can never really tell if the moon is coming or going.

Go-Go Girl Reunion

Those who don't show up at Reunions either
have something to hide or think they're too good.
So since go-go girls once let it all hang out of bikinis
and can neither claim that vice nor the virtue, we all
showed up at the Playgal Club where years before
we'd slung beer and shook our tail feathers till 2 a.m.:
Jenny the most beautiful and best dancer of all was there
wearing pink shantung and a sable, the only one of us
to marry a millionaire although we all tried and Jodi
showed up, now thinner and a reborn Christian; Tiara,
too, in spite of warrants for her arrest. Barbie was still
a barmaid but now lived with a younger, better-shooting
pool hustler; Linda Lee just bought a new Mercedes, a
nose job and boob job all paid for by one of her old sugar
daddies. And Dee-Dee, wearing thick glasses, her eyes
having gone bad from too much LSD, had kicked drugs
and now drank nothing but Jack Daniels on the rocks.
Betty had given up macramé and now taught aerobics.
Suzi Q got a brokers license and was getting rich
on commercial real estate; Cher — not the real one —
just got her PhD in Psychology from Prestigious U
and said she'd seen more weirdoes and crazies
when she worked at the Playgal than she
ever saw in a Psycho ward.
The new Playgal owner, Dick Dale, told his band to
play "Night Train" and all the old go-go girls
drunk enough got up on the stage, raised their skirts
over their knees and wiggled around
while Dick Dale took Polaroids and said over the
microphone to the audience and us that us go-go girls
weren't getting older we were only getting better!
And above the whistles, hoots and applause, I

heard one of Dick Dale's 20-something
cocktail waitresses laugh and say
to a co-worker: "*Yeah, sure,*" knowing for certain
that she would never show up to any reunion of any kind.
Wizened with young, she thought she knew how
to hold back sunsets
with her tongue.

.

Chapter 11 | A Big Box of Amalgamated Bricks

"Kill me tomorrow; let me live to-night!"
--Desdemona to Othello

Same Old-Same Old Nightmare comes at me again:
The Big Black Beast In the Big Black Night: He wants to kill
her. He's said so for a year. Look at him: furious beast:
smashing his big fists, shoulders, feet, then his big black-
haired head against and through the plate glass bay window
to get at her after she slam-locked the front door to run for
her life and up the stairs to save her three children sleeping
upstairs to cover them with her body, shield them from his
bomb fire so he won't kill them too, the baby, his. How can
he be so crazy? So full of hate for her when she's done
nothing to deserve this? Or has she? She's not even sure
anymore after decades of self-introspection and dream
interpretation. It must be her fault, surely, to have made him
so damned furious he fears nothing, not even getting sliced
into pink meat by the plate glass bay window he crashes
through, every shard piercing into him or ricocheting off
him beneath his feet worth it as he defenestrates, comes on
through to the other side, dragging ripped drapes behind
him and wrapped around him, a mummy's shroud, a ragged
rugged cape covering this deadly madman coming at her, to
kill her as she runs up the staircase and he roars at her:
WHORE, WHORE, WHORE, WHORE.

See, this is her mistake, over and over, her Big
Mistake: Running up those stairs to save her children. See,
had she not been such a stupid girl and instead run out that
front door like she did the last time, she could've saved
herself. He didn't want the children, never did he want to
kill them but she couldn't be sure, see. No mother's ever

241

sure of her children's safely. So, in her uncertainty, she ran to shield them and that's when he, a black lightning bolt, got her by the hair of her head and dragged her down the stairs. If only I'd run out the front door, had not run upstairs — But no, I'm stupid, so I am going to die — We're all going to die. Death Nothing, yet Everything.

Someone trying to kill you is the strangest, weird, insane thing that can happen to you. And always, it seems like it's your own damned fault.

God, I can't stand it anymore ... I wake up slowly, thirsty, my head throbbing, bang-boom-thud, bang-boom-thud, bang-boom-thud, fourteen rock-hard stairs, my foot caught in the wrought iron banister for a moment but the yanked descent yanks it free, blood-letting spurts from my naked skin as I'm tossed and twisted into the glass and dragged by him, the Defenestrated Amalgamated Madman, down, down, down reach rock-hard stair.

I know this scene by heart. I am going to die this time. Yes, I am. NO, you're not. Just wake up, Stupid. So, I do. My heart pounding. How can my Psyche, that cruel olde bitch, keep doing this to me? Play that horrible nightmare over and over in my mind? Redundancy of the memories making my heart and soul grow weaker. I don't know how much longer I can deal with this. I can barely lift myself out of bed. Why did I have to dream that nightmare today, of all days, the day that Othello's son is coming to see me. How can I see the son of my attempted murderer today? He's coming this morning, this sunny day in May.

In fact, he's here now, at my door: The Son of Othello: Reave Gentry the Third. And my God, he looks nearly exactly like my attempted murderer, his furious father, my indefatigable bête noire, my inescapable Othello, my Evermore Nightmare that won't go away. But Reave Gentry the Third has nicknamed himself Rev. Now aged 30. Grown

12 inches taller since I last saw him at his father's funeral 15 years ago. Stands gentlemanly tall on my porch, with his hands behind his back while the women walk through the door first: His half-sister, Othello's and my daughter Maureen, Cassandra Jane, her pregnant daughter, my granddaughter and namesake and Rev's half-cousin. Then enters Rev's bride of two weeks: Kareesha, a beautiful black girl expecting a baby in six months. They sit down on the sofa as Rev sits in my Poet Husband's oxblood leather chair. I pour tea and offer a plate of oatmeal cookies I've baked from my Jane's Never Plain Good 4 You Cook Book published two years ago while Rev shows us the sonogram of his future baby son — and Othello's grandson.

"What a fine boy he'll be," I say, gazing at the long legs of this angular, sturdy but zigzagging electronically-imaged fetus provided for our awestruck inspection by modern prenatal technology. Soon, I imagine, there will be a zoom control mechanism of high-yield imaging radiation powerful enough to illuminate fetal eyelashes so we can count them on the eyes of our gestating babes.

Rev's thick black hair, just like his father's, sticks straight up out of his scalp and reaches for the sky. Rev's much handsomer than his father, lankier and four inches taller and he smiles white, good teeth like his mother Laura's, a very pretty woman, and Othello's second wife. Laura didn't know when she married Othello that he'd gone to prison for attempting to murder a wife; he told her that he'd been convicted of involuntary manslaughter after he killed a man, defending himself, in a barroom brawl. How manly, that. Maureen told Laura the truth when they met for the first time to plan Othello's funeral. How I wish Laura hadn't told Rev what his father did to me. I didn't think he needed to know this ugly thing about his father; but Laura, a feminist and single mother who raised Rev by herself and outraged like many of us were by the recent acquittal of O.J. Simpson accused of murdering his wife Nicole, wanted Rev to know The Truth. Now this Truth waddles thick and fat like a huge elephant in the room. But maybe I'm the only one who sees the elephant, feels the weight of its big black foot on my toes.

"A future NBA champ, for sure," I predict, knowing that Rev was a good basketball player in junior college; didn't play football like his father. Rev's more graceful than his father was. Yes, yes, a future NBA champ this future baby will be, everyone agrees: Rev, Kareesha, Maureen and Cassandra Jane. So: Othello, Dead Patriarch, if he were still alive, would become a grandfather and a great-grandfather in the same year, just a month apart.

I hand the sonogram back to Rev, who lovingly places it inside his wallet next to a picture I gave him of his father at age 19, Othello, posed with a football in his quarterback hands. And I feel faint. That Nightmare. Just two hours ago I watched the vivid replay of Rev's father attempting to murder me again. Right now my hands are shaking while my shook up soul wants to yell to them DO YOU KNOW WHAT I'VE JUST LIVED THROUGH AGAIN? Yet here I am asking: "More tea?" As if nothing on earth matters more than enough tea in a cup with just the right amount of milk and sugar. No thanks, they all say, just being polite by sipping the Earl Grey I made; they really want coffee, I know, and lots of it but I don't drink coffee. I push toward them the big plate of oatmeal cookies.

"Your father's favorite cookie," I say. "A recipe is in the cookbook. He liked double raisins and chopped pecans."

Kareesha thumbs through my cookbook I gave them for a wedding gift, bookmarked Othello's favorite meals I fixed when I was married to him. Rev laughs at a copy of an old photo I tucked next to Tapioca Pudding: 17-year-old Me sitting on Othello's 17-year-old shoulders, Othello staring

244

insipidly, making his Wolf Face at the camera while I, attempting humor, pretending to have a good time, poke a finger in each of his ears. "You guys look so happy and young," Rev says. "High school sweethearts, huh?" Rev laughs, not noticing at all the pissed off look on his father's young, dangerous face. I try to laugh, too, but cough instead.

"You okay?" asks Rev.

"Yes, I'm just getting over the flu," I lie. I've got to liven this up somehow though I feel pushed out of an airplane, falling through the sky. Feel unstrung from a noose, let go by the lynch mob, rope burns choking my throat—while an elephant snorts. I hadn't dreamed that nightmare in months. Thought for sure the dreams would go away after I heard the news of the babies coming this year: Kareesha's (Othello's—and Laura's—first grandson) due in October; and Cassandra Jane's (Othello's—and my—first great-grandchild) arriving in November. I was so certain that these amazing genetic facts would make the nightmare go away for good. Certain that Wherever Othello is, IF we do, in fact, GO anywhere post-mortem, Othello surely would be filled with protoplasmic-cosmic joy and pride and WANT to unite peacefully with me if not in heart and reality, then in some kind of reconciliatory spirit of DNA, make the past forgotten, share and celebrate the wonder of our unintentional family's extension, the heightening of our mutual totem, the broadening of our family tree branches— however misbegotten—into Eternity. For weeks I romanticized this notion to such an extent that I had a dream two weeks ago Othello was happy about it, too. He called me in the dream on the telephone. He's never done that in a dream before. And he whispered to me in a croaky, growling voice: "We have a nice family." Then he hung up. I woke up. And I was certain I'd never have another nightmare about him trying to kill me again. But I did,

245

dammit, reinstating him, apparently, as my irrevocable Bête Noire. That Good Dream, portending Good Omen, just a con by my subconscious, a dirty trick my damned Psyche played on me. Again. Fooled you, you Stupid Girl, she says to me while I dream on, a dreary schmuck.

"Tapioca? Rev's Dad liked tapioca pudding? So does Rev," Kareesha says, looking at the cook book. Rev bends toward the cook book to look at another bookmark picture of his father and me—a copy of our prom photo I tucked next to the Devil's Food Cake recipe I always baked Othello for his birthday. No one except me ever notices Othello's hand clenched into a fist on my waist; his hand is dark, as if he's grabbed a big slice of Devil's Food cake and squeezes it.

"Let me show you some more photos." I open the antique trunk near the sofa and remove from it my Big Box of Amalgamated Bricks: decades' worth of souvenirs and assorted junk beneath the effluvial chronological strata of My Life: 1940s Little Lulu, Superman, and Popeye comics, 1950s and '60s Seventeen magazines and Photoplays with covers of my Role Models of Exceptional Beauty: Marilyn Monroe, Elizabeth Taylor, Audrey Hepburn, Natalie Wood; old magazine covers of my Role Models of Exquisite Expertise: Jane Addams, Eleanor Roosevelt, Fanny Brice, Billie Holiday, Jackie Kennedy Onassis, Elaine May, Gloria Steinem, Rachel Carson, Janis Joplin, Cher (the real one), Tina Turner, Frida Kahlo, Alice Walker, Princess Diana, Maya Angelou, Queen Elizabeth, Oprah Winfrey, Hillary Clinton, Michelle Obama. Oh, and my best role model of all: My Beautiful Mother, on the 1997 cover of my literary magazine *Pearl,* though I could never live up to her high standards of neatness and virtue.

"You're making your bed in heaven," she said to me as she lay dying in 1986 as I cared for her every earthly need.

Then I see again *Life* magazine's commemorative

issue of the November 22, 1963, assassination of President John F. Kennedy. (My father died, too, on November 22, only three years later.) I shove all the paper faces aside to open the Big Box of Amalgamated Bricks and find right on top: a note The Texan wrote me when he sent a dozen red roses, two years ago, after he saw an article about my cookbook in the newspaper: "Sure do miss your good Texas food." Under that, the old copy of *Playgal* magazine with Big Don Maraschino's half-naked pull-out centerfold. What a good-looking guy he was. To the back of the magazine I'd taped his obituary from 10 years ago when he died of AIDS in the arms of his long-time companion, Sonny Buoy. They were both gay, of course. How stupid that none of us go-go girls didn't know. We were too busy Being Young, Doing Our Own Thing, Getting Satisfaction.

After Big Don died, Sonny Buoy sent me a little package containing, of all things, such a surprise: my ancient diamond starburst pendant Les Church had given me in 1966. That little thing, The Thing, the impetus, an accidental Iago, that had made Othello go so crazy-mad jealous, made him do what he did to me in 1966. Lost, that little thing, all those years and I never knew what happened to it, so many times had wanted it, because so many times, little things mean a lot. Sonny Buoy had found it in the bed in 1967 the morning after I slept 13 hours, soundly, with Big Don — and he'd kept it because he'd been jealous of me and Big Don, had thought we were lovers. The diamond was gone, though; came unglued and disappeared into a shag carpet. And the platinum chain was broken. "Sorry," Sonny wrote, signing his name "Sunni." So. Big Don died young. Not me, as I thought I would in 1966. I sprawl open my palm for the first time in decades to look at my life line of Right Now. It's as long as a stretch of Highway 101 on a map from L.A. to San Francisco. Some glitches, potholes in the road still ahead, so my palm shows. So I wasn't Desdemona after all. I'll die Old. Ancient.

But in the meantime, why can't I have recurring dreams about Rhett Butler-Big Don carrying me in his big arms? Or The Texan taking me for long drives in his silver Lincoln Continental while I wear red satin slippers? Or sipping champagne with Charles Bukowski while he reads me a new poem he just wrote? And, oh, here's the invitation I got 10 years ago from Linda Alura to attend the wedding of her daughter Belinda whose father turned out to be that famous Black Panther who went to prison way back in 1966 for something he didn't do; but finally got paroled 25 years later when they found the real cop killer. Linda's long lost beloved Belinda was found easy as pie on the Internet after Linda had looked for her, hired detectives, for decades. And beneath that: a letter from hippie huz T.J. DuRong, 1970 Honor Farm jail bird that begins: "Dear Janie, my sweat" instead of "my sweet." Or did T.J. misspell sweet sweat on purpose? Then beneath that my autographs from a Famous Astronaut, Joe DiMaggio, and Charles Bukowski.

And I'm reunited again with the last letter my father wrote me, dated June 23, 1966, after he found out I was a go-go girl working at La Pink Pantera: "You must stop this disgusting nonsense now and pull yourself together, get back into college now so you can make yourself a decent and respectable living and raise those children right," he demanded.

I want to show Maureen, Cassandra Jane, Kareesha and Rev all this but they are busy talking. Oh, and there, finally, near the bottom of the Big Box of Amalgamated Bricks amongst the souvenirs from my Time Travel from Young to Now: what I'd been looking for: 1957 sports page news clippings of Othello's famous high school football prowess. "What a WHIZ!" says one headline. I hand the yellowed pieces to Rev, interrupting what he's saying to Maureen.

"Wow," Rev says.

"Your father was an extraordinary athlete. I once saw him throw a 99-yard touchdown pass. He could've been greater than Joe Namath." But they've never heard of Joe Namath. So long ago, and so much happens, fame fades fast.

Then I give him Othello's kindergarten picture, his high school I.D.—and wadded-up letters from him scrawled on blue-lined notebook paper.

"Your father handed me a letter in high school every day after his one o'clock Latin class across the hall from my French class—" Maureen, Cassandra and Kareesha all lean together to read over Rev's wide shoulders the stupid stuff Othello wrote me. Mostly accusations of flirting with this boy or that boy. None of it true. They laugh at the childish stick figures Othello drew of him and me and two kids we'd have someday.

"And here's the poem I wrote him when we were 15. 'Amalgamated Bricks'—titled that because that's what he reminded me of. It's a very bad poem. A mixed metaphor— corny and melodramatic—" I shut up. I don't feel good enough to give a lecture on Bad Poetry, my young and stupid choice of objective correlative.

Maureen reads it aloud: "'Amalgamated Bricks, that's what you are ...An uninhabitable planet ...So far, far, far ...'"

They laugh. I laugh and say: "It's a very bad poem, all right. But at age 15, I really, really meant it—with all my heart." I want to tell them how hard I tried to get Othello to just go away, and leave me be, thought the poem would prove to him how we weren't meant for each other.

"Well, Mom," Maureen says, smiling at me, her blue eyes twinkling, "I don't quite understand what amalgamated bricks mean. But at least the poem rhymes."

"Yes, rhyme matters a lot," I say, intending irony.

Time to leave—they're on their way to Disneyland—when Rev stops, points to a photo on my green wall amongst an assemblage of family portraits. "That your father?" Rev asks. Yes, I say; then he says, somberly: "My mother says your father saved her life. That if your father hadn't got my father put in jail, he might've done to her what he did to you and maybe finished the job."

Ok, so now the Big Black Beast has come unleashed, Othello's elephantine dark ghost snorts at us, kicks out a big foot, readying to rampage. How I wish Rev's mother Laura hadn't told Rev what happened. Oh, God, how I wish he—and Maureen—didn't know about their father and me, the ugly stuff, until Rev says: "Your father looks like a good man." My ash blonde-haired father, stately at age 48 in his grey business suit, smokes a Lucky Strike and stares sincerely at the Polaroid camera I pointed at him decades ago, just months before he'd die of a heart attack just three months after Othello Did What He Did to Me. The Big Black Beast snorts, his dark ghost's hot breath on my face when Rev says:

"I'm really grateful your father did what he did to get my father put away." Three-to-ten, Othello got for attempting my murder. His son now near the same age Othello was when he went away to Soledad. Rev places his hand gently on my shoulder and says: "I'm sorry your father died because of my father. You're lucky to've had such a good dad."

"Yes, I am. And now it's your turn to be a good dad."

Rev puts his arm around his new wife's shoulder, touches, gently her rounding belly, and says: "I'm going to try." And suddenly the Big Black Beast turns his big dark ghost head to one side, confused, blinks one big black eye at me—and disappears into a cloud of nightmare smoke.

And suddenly, Time flying like a gone-crazy crow,

here I am, three months later in August, driving up Highway 101, Maureen behind the wheel of her black car, the sizzling California summer sun sparkling in her pale blue eyes, six-months-pregnant Cassandra Jane, sleeping in the back seat, California yellow, yellow everywhere: yellow grass on the yellow hills, yellow sky reflecting yellow high noon sun. On our merry way to Kareesha and Rev's baby shower at Rev's mother Laura's house in Cranville, 30 miles northeast of San Francisco when suddenly Maureen turns off the freeway at a fast food place to buy something to eat. She does not know that she's stopped at the small town of Soledad, a mile from Soledad State Prison we just passed by. Soledad is Spanish for Lonely and what a lonely prison, for sure, set far back into some foothills, unseen from the freeway, surrounded by tons of Keep Out amalgamated razor wire and filled with bad vibes of ruined lives.

And I've only seen Soledad twice in my life. The first time in 1970 when Othello was still incarcerated there. On my way to Monterey with T.J. DuRong, we'd just dropped mescaline an hour ago in San Luis Obispo—my first and last time doing a psychedelic drug, Credence Clearwater on a four-track tape playing over and over: "Keep on chooglin'." Me behind the wheel of the beige Volkswagen Bug when the mescaline hit, just as I saw the sign: Soledad Men's Correctional Facility and suddenly saw a huge dark shadow on the side of the road I was certain was Othello who'd just—coincidentally, incredibly—escaped from his maximum security cell, timing his Great Escape psychically, precisely at the same time he'd know I passed by. But in the rearview mirror I saw that the shadow of Othello was really a big broken down oak tree.

At the motel in Monterey, while T.J. tripped out on the old movie *Gunfight at the O.K. Corral* he watched on tv, I wallowed in hallucination-made guilt for testifying against

251

Othello, getting him sent to that god awful, lonely place. Mea culpa, mea culpa, I hallucinated, Credence Clearwater reverberations urging my psychedelicized cranial aberrations to keep on chooglin'. But today, 100 years later, I'm glad Othello went to that lonely, eerie place of amalgamated razor wire. Today he'd've got sentenced to 30 years for What He Did to Me. And it took 30 years for me to stop blaming myself for What He Did and stop believing I Deserved It—because I Was a Stupid Whore. A lewd minx.

It really changes your life when someone tries to kill you—and almost does.

For a few decades I believed I could have stopped him, adding more blame to myself because had I stopped him, he wouldn't've gone to prison. See, after he defenestrated, yanked me down from the stairs by the hair of my head and threw me across the room and I fell into the glass in the middle of the living room floor, he stopped, stood there catching his breath, looking down at me, broken and bloody on the floor. A cruel, crazy Colossus of Rhodes, a huge dark arch looming over me, his legs spread apart, his granite fists on his hips, he paused, panted, so I reached up and grabbed his—

Remembering his flaccid genitals inside his baggy khakis embarrasses me now. I'd barely touched them when he roared, then retaliated, fought back by grabbing more fistfuls of my hair and throwing me again across the room. If only I'd grabbed harder, maybe he'd've doubled up in pain, fallen down wounded and agonized into the glass shards and I could've run up the stairs, scooped my scared kids into my arms and run out the door and got into my car and sped away. There never would have been any attempted murder, and I wouldn't ever have been a Stupid Whore. Othello might've gone away for good. We'd all be okay. Nothing bad would've ever happened again. If only I'd've been more efficient in trying to save my life.

And the mescaline sure didn't help my pitiful guilt trip and agonizing memories any. The intent of taking the mescaline, T.J. had said, was to find Enlightenment, Nirvana, serenity, "a groovy time-out from the game of bullshit karma"—T.J., a flowering hippie, so groovily described the illegal substance abuse of psychedelic drugs, the Letter "R" in his Personal Alphabet standing not for "Responsible" as I'd thought when I first met him but rather for "Reprobate." In just two weeks, T.J. DuRong, doing wrong as always, will get busted for possession of marijuana and mescaline with intent to sell; in fact, tomorrow after we check out of this Monterey motel, he will sell a bunch of mescaline, unbeknownst to me, to some guys at a beer bar on Cannery Row while I shop next door for abalone shells. What a stupid girl I'd been believing T.J.'s Midnight Rambling line of rap that he was big and strong, talented and ambitious—but mostly his promise to be my Bodyguard in case Othello ever found me. God, a good man is sure hard to find.

Back in the Now: Inside the fast food place, I can't believe it when I hear Credence Clearwater singing on the intercom: "keep on chooglin'." Maureen and Cassandra order their fast food and I walk outside to the patio, no one there, because it's 105 degrees and everyone crowds inside for the air conditioning.

"Keep on chooglin'," Credence plays—a special performance just for me and the metallic audience of freeway fast traffic zooming past, bypassing Soledad, the town and prison, on their way to San Luis Obispo to the south, Salinas to the north, Monterey, Carmel and Big Sur to the west. Soledad smack dab situated in the East of Eden: John Steinbeck Country, the epicenter cornucopia of California's farmland. Fragrances of nearby broccoli, kale, garlic and onion fields fill the air, eradicate the polluting odors of motor vehicle exhaust fumes of cars, cars, cars, big cars, small cars I now know none of the names of speeding to and fro the mountain range straight ahead, made purple this time of day as it separates this hot eastside of Eden from the temperate, desirable Gardenside of Eden on the other side filled with fabled ancient oaks, pines, redwoods, eucalyptus trees, ferns, kelp, driftwood and seaweed. Fog and clouds eddying out of the northern Californian Pacific Ocean swirl their misty spindrift and try to fly up and roll smoothly over the mountain peaks, but the sun-scorched heat on this east side sucks it dry, swallows it whole in its huge hot thirsty sky throat. Proof that Monterey, Carmel and Big Sur Paradise exists on the other side of the mountaintops: rainbow remnants arc and reach over the purple pine tops and fray, droop away, dissipate into pale mist and form silver light halos over the highest August-scorched shrub shadows.

How I worried those years Othello spent in Soledad that he'd die there. That would've been my fault, too. But he lived on, married Laura, to whom he confessed being an ex-con, spent three years in Soledad — for killing a man in a barroom brawl. They had a son, divorced when he was mean to Laura, starting slapping her around, one time across the room; then Othello spent his life of extravagant encounters His Way: gambling, drinking, carousing and finally dying at age 51 of congestive heart failure.

Guiltless, I went to his funeral. Maureen, deeply mournful, wanted me there. What a sight he was, almost 300 pounds of him (bloated from gluttony), a big box of amalgamated brick man crammed into that coffin. Dead rebel, Othello's huge, dark-skinned hands, when still alive, ever-ready fists, had been rearranged in death to simulate prayer and gentility as they lay crossed neatly like a

254

kindergarten boy's upon a clean, crisp blue long-sleeved shirt. Reave Gentry Jr.'s ex-wife Laura and his grieving children 27-year-old Maureen and the 14-year-old Reave Gentry the 3rd picked out that shirt together, lovingly. Othello's thin, Cherokee-dark lips had been made to spread across his face into a shining maroon ribbon-smile of attempted benevolence designed by a sweet-intentioned mortician who'd not noticed the natural insolence of this corpse that in reality sprouted back to life out of death into a post-mortem smirk.

"Surreal," said my good husband, the poet I finally got to marry. At last a Good Man. "Everything you told me about him was true."

When I bent over my long-ago husband to look one last time at his bored malevolence, his thick hair (then iron-grey wolfish), it seemed I'd only imagined his once fit, famous-footballer body and his once-handsome face that in his teens and 20s resembled Elvis Presley's so much he attracted giggling teen girl groupies who drove past his house tossing upon his porch teasing love notes and telephone numbers. I touched Dead Othello's huge, cold hands that once caressed by the light of drive-in movies my young candy face, then 10 years later broke it to bits with his knuckles now cold as snow. I will never be sorry to say nor blame myself for saying that I was not saddened one second to see him dead. Complicated but simple: he was an uninhabitable planet and there he lay unto himself in his nether-universe. So harmless now; so very scary when he found us in 1979. But it turned out okay.

"Stop! In the Name of Love" shriek Diana Ross and the Supremes over the blasting loud speaker in the Now of this fast food place, their supreme sweet voices echoing off the traffic just as Maureen waves to me, time to go. So we,

Maureen, Cassandra and (in utero) my future great-grandson and I all together drive on up north to see Rev, Kareesha and Laura. First, stopping at San Bruno to visit my father and mother's grave. Cold and foggy there at the cemetery, I shiver, and my thoughtful granddaughter Cassandra hands me from her tote bag a jacket—my old avocado green jacket she's been wearing since her sister Clara found it in an old box stored in a closet all these years. The same Coco Chanel imitation I wore everywhere with its matching skirt in 1966. It still fits—and back in style. I wore this jacket and its matching skirt when I had lunch with the Famous Astronaut; wore the suit the night I went to audition at Whisky a Go-Go in Hollywood when Jim Morrison bumped into me, spilled beer on my shoulder. Wore it when I went to the police department, August, 1966, to file a criminal complaint against Othello for threatening to kill me two weeks before he tried to do what he did.

"A woman, a dog and a walnut tree—" said the cop when I signed my criminal complaint: "—the more you beat 'em, the better they be." And I wore this to my father's funeral November 22, 1966, and then I wore it when I was having my 19th Nervous Breakdown the day I testified in Criminal Court against Othello for trying to murder me. When the judge pronounced him Guilty, Othello flipped over the defendant's table, lunged at me, scratched my neck with his fingernail. The blood stain on the jacket collar resembles milk chocolate now. Later that day, safe in Sammy Glassman's Hollywood penthouse, I wore this jacket when I asked Linda Alura: "Will we be friends when we're old women?" and she answered: "If we live long enough to be old women." And it surely didn't seem possible in that time and place of our overburdened, lugubrious Young that we could possibly survive the tonnage of heaping Old. But we did, though that 1967 day I was feeling woeful and worn out, done to and done in. Othello reined in, at last, after much trouble. The rampaging bête noire, going, going. Gone. Away. Went.

"Sorry, Daddy," I whisper to myself as I look down at my parents' green grass grave and their shared headstone: her name on one side, his, facing north, on the other side, the big letter A's in his name gleaming white, ghostly, pointedly AVNER RAY JAMES in the fog. "So sorry I still haven't pulled myself together. But I'm trying, Daddy."

After Maureen, Cassandra and I—and Othello's and my future great-grandson—leave my father and mother's graveside, we'll go to San Francisco for clam chowder at Fisherman's Wharf, same place, I'll tell them, I ate oysters for the first time with my parents in 1944 when we lived in San Francisco till 1948. I'll show them where my mother and I stood on VJ-Day, 1945, the End of World War Two and describe to them all the kissing, shouting, weeping and laughing on the sidewalks and in the streets, how traffic came to a stop, car horns honked and the cable cars clang-clang-clanged gaily in celebration. I'll show them the corner of Powell and Bush where my father in 1947 stopped!—in the name of love—his car, a 1939 cream-colored Ford coupe, in traffic in a rainstorm to rescue a lost, soaking wet yellow dog we'd name Mugsie. When a light sky mist sprays against the window of Maureen's black car, I'll shiver again and huddle into my ancient avocado green jacket, armor to keep me warm, simple linen recently recovered from a big box of amalgamated brick cloth memories and I'll show Maureen the way to drive us over the Golden Gate Bridge, past the museum, the Presidio and tollbooths. But the Golden Gate Bridge will be covered in a fog.

So I won't be able to show them the very spot on October 24, 1966, the day I drove over the Golden Gate Bridge with my father for the very last time, where, all my objective correlatives and mixed metaphors gathered up tight, I remembered the poem I wrote at age 15 and recited it to myself: "Amalgamated bricks/that's what you are/An uninhabitable planet/so far, far, far..."

Right in the middle of the Golden Gate Bridge was where I remembered that old poem, while my father, an excellent mimic, sang, perfectly imitating Tony Bennett on the radio crooning "I Left My Heart In San Francisco."

I'd wanted so much to show them, let them hear my father's baritone voice, too. But I won't be able to point out that particular golden-orange peak of the Golden Gate Bridge to my daughter and granddaughter. Halfway across the bridge is where it was: Alcatraz Island and Oakland to the left, sunset to the right, Sausalito to the north, the aquamarine diamond-sparkle-topped waves of the restless Pacific Ocean all around, our irreducible Past behind us, our Future ahead invisible and unforeseeable, as we go, go, becoming and becoming until we are went. I won't be able to show them because all of it, the Golden Gate Bridge, the crisp blue August sky and my daughter, granddaughter and future great-grandson and I will be engulfed in a brief Eden, fever-cooled in the cold, cold San Francisco summer fog.

@ Naked Street
& Reincarnation Way

If reincarnation is really real,
I do not wish to be reincarnated,
Tossed out into this cold world
Naked again. It's taken me all my
Life to find enough clothes to keep
My soul and skin warm and
I still don't know what to wear.

Chapter 12 / "Come on Baby, Light My Fie-YARRR"

"...and our love become a funeral pyre..."
—Jim Morrison & The Doors

In another fog, a pre-summer gray-muggy June 1, 2013, Marilyn Monroe's 87th birthday, 11 years, ten months and some-odd days since the tragic titanic loss of the World Trade Center, and three months before the extinction of the Black Rhino, and five months before 35,000 walruses wash up on an Alaska shore because they can't find sea ice to rest upon in Arctic waters, I can't believe it that I'm standing in line—me, ancient me—undoubtedly the oldest person standing in line—with my Poet Husband and 200-plus adoring Doors fans in downtown Long Beach, California USA at Fingerprints Records to see, meet, and get autographed books and tapes and LPs and CDs about and by The Doors' drummer, John Densmore about whom my Poet Husband says to this old-looking guy standing in line with us: "John Densmore was undoubtedly the greatest rock drummer of them all."

"Right on. I agree," says, the old guy, leaning on a cane. He wears a baggy, tattered old t-shirt with The Doors' faces on the front.

Poet Husband goes on: "John Densmore had a perfect rapport with Jim Morrison's lyrics, Jim's singing and Jim's music. When I saw the Doors, live, in 1970—right over there at the Arena [just four blocks away from where we wait on 4th Street], it was like there was a psychic connection between the four of them: Ray Manzarak and Robby Krieger, John Densmore and Jim Morrison. They themselves called it the Magic Circle—and I saw it in person." I've never seen before my poet husband so thrilled. He really loves The

Doors, and has, since he was a teenager in the 1960s.

"Wow," says the old guy, "you're lucky. I never got to see the Doors, live. I was born in 1972, after Morrison died." So the old-looking guy isn't so old after all. I'm almost old enough to be his grandmother. I knew it: I am the most ancient one of them all standing in line. The line moves about one inch per minute — this wait will take hours! — the line circles around the block! And the sun scorching its way out of the fog is blasting the sidewalk hot enough to fry an egg on it. The not-so-old guy says: "My mom and dad fell in love to the Doors' music. I was conceived as they made love to 'Light My Fire' their last night together before my father shipped out to Vietnam. He died. I never knew him."

My Poet Husband goes on: "Jim Morrison was in the tradition of Blake and Jung. His music and his lyrics, his performance on stage created a new spirituality for our era."

"Out of sight, man. I never thought of the Doors like that. I just liked listening to them." The guy holds gently, like it's a sweet, beloved pet puppy, a cassette of Jim Morrison's poetry with The Doors music: "An American Prayer."

"They named themselves after a quote from William Blake: 'If the doors of perception were cleansed, everything would appear to man as it is, infinite,'" says my poetry-reading poet husband.

"Wow, far out, I never knew that," says the guy.

I feel like a carnivore in the vegetable department, a spy in a house of love, a beer can in the garden. I am a fraud; I shouldn't even be standing here with all these nice, adoring Doors fan. I don't even *like* The Doors. When a working-stiff go-go girl long, long ago, Summer of Love 1967, one long, hot August afternoon, I had to dance to the Doors over and over and over at Joe's Bar & Grill. Had I been a typist, the Doors' sounds were the equivalent factotum-frenzied cacophony of clackety-clack, bing-bang typewriter and adding machine office noise. A factory girl in a cannery, their music the rattle-tin-can-whirr of the assembly line. I especially hated that long-long seven-minute version of "Light My Fire" penny-pinching go-go bar owners like Joe played every ten minutes on the jukebox. Ever try dancing to that six times an hour—while trying to smile and look cute—and groovy? Wearing high heels and a fringed bikini?

Every six minutes, another seven minutes of light my fire, light my fire, as I shing-a-linged like a ding-a-ling to Manzarak's keyboards, Densmore's drums, Krieger's thrums, Morrison's existential hums till my backbone slipped, my toes cripped from the get-down profundity of the redundancy twisting me in that mirrored corner in Joe's dark bar filled with 100 reflections of Me. To amuse myself I re-wrote the lyrics in my jukebox-zapped, over-danced, burnt-out brain: parodies: "Come on baby, smite my dire— before our love becomes an electrocution wire—boy: our love couldn't get much more tired—come on baby, smite my dire, before our love gets stuck in the briar and Joe the owner of Joe's Bar & Grill desires to get me fired, boy—I can't get much more expired—" Self-absorbed-bathetic-bored like that, that hot August, 1967, afternoon, I accidentally kicked over the beers of these two guys sitting on barstools too close to the too-small dance floor just inches away from my high-heeled shoes when they reached to grab my ankle, wanting to see me fall down trapped in that corner, held captive by those beer-streaked wrap-around mirrors.

I'm *sure* they tried to make me tumble off that six-foot-high stage where a piano bar had been, Pretty Pauline at the Piano delighting bar and grill patrons with her sweet renditions of "Stardust," "As Time Goes By," up till a month ago when this silly go-go stuff became so popular, guys wanting to see goofy, young, wiggling, bellybutton-baring, fringed-bikini-clad go-go girls. But not those guys. They missed their Pretty Pauline at the Piano, wanted to see *her* reflection in those mirrors. I worked for that freelance dance agency Rich Street that Summer of Love, 1967, owned by Ricardo Estrada, who did fire me after that day when Joe told him how I'd kicked over those guys' beers — and Joe'd had to replace the beers for free.

"Those two guys tried to trip me, Rico, make me fall off the stage. I could've broken my neck or a leg!" Those two guys were electrocution wires, I wanted to add, stuck in the dire — the die-YARRR — of my briar!

"Sorry, kid — but I gotta let you go. Joe's pissed off. Joe said you were a klutz. Those guys were his pals. And Joe's a pal of mine, books a lot of my Rich Street Girls." Thus ended my brief, lucrative stroll, doing the Temptation Walk, James Brown, and Mashed Potato down the Funky Broadway of Rich Street where Rico paid me a lot of money (the equivalent today of $300) for a three-hour gig.

Turned out okay. Next week I'll luck out and go to work, making half as much money, though, at the Playgal Club where big, bad bouncers, Spike and Ernesto, protected us girls from misogynist thugs, malevolent lugs, jerks, sorry cusses and pervs, and where for nearly two years I'd dance go-go to Dick Dale's laid-back surf guitar playing "Misirlou" three times a night.

On the way around the block to the head of the line to see what's going on, why the line's moving so slowly, I pass by the many, many, amazing, adoring Doors fans, some of them kids, teenagers, wearing Goth, bright-red-dyed hair, pierced tongues, noses, eyebrows, skin-tight leggings, middle-aged "kids" in 1980s' punk rocker black, ragged jeans, gray-haired men and women bent over with osteo or in wheelchairs wearing tie-dyes and olive drab and camouflage and peace signs—some of them reading books, most of them with cell phones or doo-dads I don't know names of, Doors' sounds wafting from the thingies they hold in their hands as if the music magically pours from out beneath their fingernails, their skin, and souls: Riders on the Storm, Love Me Two Times, L.A. Woman, Don't You Love Her Madly as she walks right out that door likes she's done one hundred times before. My grandmothers didn't know how to drive a car; my mother couldn't use a typewriter; I can't tweet or twitter. What thing or thingie thing will these kids not know how to do or use when they are old and ancient?

These Doors fans are the sons and daughters, great- and great-great-grandchildren of the Non-One-Per-centers: descendants of cowboys and Indians, indigenous Mexicans, Spanish conquistadores, homesteaders, Jesse James train robbers, immigrants, railroad men, gold miners, coal miners, firemen, policemen, auto-body men, shipyard workers, construction workers, cotton-pickers, peach-pickers, school teachers, stevedores, steel workers, oil workers, Bikers, bums, plumbers, golfers, go-fers, Teamsters, sailors, tailors, blackmailers, swordfish fishermen, ice cream men, Fuller Brush men, bakery truck drivers, Willie Lomans, high school football stars, hippies, aerospace engineers, pirates, poets, paupers, hitchhiker kings of the road, World War 1 and 2 and Korean War and Vietnam and Gulf War and Iraqi-Afghanistan War vets. "All deities reside in the human breast," I recall William Blake saying and note how everyone now wears his/her role model on his/her body, their deities residing upon their human chests: Che Guevara, Barack Obama's HOPE, Charles Bukowski, Day of the Dead skulls and skeleton bones, Pussy Riot, Frida Kahlo, Hello Kitty, Malala Yousafzai—who, at age 17, will be the youngest to win a Nobel Prize. A little girl wearing a Justin Bieber t-shirt

263

holds the hand of her mother wearing a Jim Morrison t-shirt. One beautiful girl with a blue ponytail and bangs wears a foot-long tattoo of Marilyn Monroe on her buffed-out bicep.

"What a beautiful tattoo of Marilyn," I tell her.

"Thanks!" she says, her pretty, young blue eyes sparkling aquamarine the same color as her dyed hair in the scorching sunshine. She has a pierced navel; a hoop with a crucifix dangles from the squeamish hole of it.

"Today's Marilyn Monroe's 87th birthday," I tell her. And her eyes widen with happiness as she says:

"Oh, really? How cool! I love her movies. My favorite's 'The Misfits'."

"Mine, too," I say, and want to tell her how I once met Joe DiMaggio, but don't. "Remember the ending of 'The Misfits' when Marilyn says 'Life starts from now'? Except that Arthur Miller really says that. He wrote the movie."

"Oh, yes, I know. I love Arthur Miller's plays. I was a drama major but just dropped out of Cal State. Couldn't afford the tuition anymore or pay back student loans." She shrugs her shoulders. I shrug mine, too, don't tell her I can't afford to pay back my student loan either which is now quintuple of what I borrowed 40 years ago to go to law school; and still, they keep reminding me with monthly, threating bills and telephone calls.

"If you want to get a tattoo like this, too, go to my brother Jody's tattoo parlor over on Chestnut. This Marilyn's his own design. Tell him Jossie sent you. We're twins."

"I will, I will," I say, wondering if it's against the law—a health violation perhaps—to tattoo someone as old as me or an economic hardship because it would take a lot of ink to zip-zap a needle through my thousands of ancient wrinkles. Maybe tattooing someone my age might be a form of Elder Abuse, or involuntary manslaughter as I imagine the pierce of a tattoo needle and my soul shrieking like a bat out of hell out of the squeamish hole of me and I disintegrate into a pile of compost like the wicked witch in *The Wizard of Oz*. I feel flattered she thinks me young enough—and compos mentos enough to be tattooed.

Inside the record store I see John Densmore smiling at an adoring Doors fan. Except for his neat stylish hair now turned gray, Densmore looks boyishly dapper and happy just like he did that night in 1966 when I auditioned at Whisky a Go-Go for a go-go girl job. (I was trying to hide out from Othello who was stalking me, threatening to kill me.) Densmore's the reason the line's moving so slowly: he's so nice, chatting patiently to each adoring fan while he signs his/her Doors memorabilia and lets them take his picture. The woman with him right now leans on a walker. What a nice guy. I thought back then in 1966 he was a nice guy, Krieger and Manzarak, too, wondered what such nice guys were doing hanging around that raunchy-looking guy growling into the microphone.

I thought at first Jim Morrison was a hobo, or some weird hippie anti-establishmentarian who'd wandered into Whisky a Go-Go off Sunset Boulevard, drunk, and hopped onto the stage like a lot of bad drunks will rudely do in night clubs. Jim Morrison's clothes and hair and boots were filthy. But the other go-go girls said he was the lead singer. And he'd just dropped some LSD. Later, when they got so famous, I couldn't believe it. I want to tell John Densmore this when I finally get to meet him, tell him how I'd auditioned to the Doors 100 years ago, LIVE. Wonder what he'll say, I wonder, as I go for a walk around the block. Will I be the very first ancient go-go girl he's ever met? Or are there millions of ancient go-go girls just like me he's met one hundred times before?

I walk on the shady side of the street, away from the adoring Doors fans, who move another mere one inch closer in the scorching sunshine toward their King, their Guru God, their Rock Star Messiah who will soon light-their-fie-YAR: a sweet deity: John Densmore to take them to their Valhalla, Mt. Olympus, Blue Heaven, Twelfth of Never. Who'd've thought that that old 1960s-1970s rock music would live on like it has and capture so many new, younger hearts? Instead of becoming old-timey, all that music became legendary, classic-iconic, mantra-hymns of yore that so many kids today think the 1960s the Greatest Decade of the 20th Century?

"Without music, life would be a mistake," said Nietzsche in the time of Beethoven and Wagner. What would he have said about The Doors? The Stones? The Beatles?

Around the corner stands the once posh, now run-down affordable housing, Lafayette Hotel where teenage Othello, looking like a malevolent Elvis, took me to our Prom in 1957, his fist propped unforgettably, menacingly upon my waist in our prom photo. On this street back then, women wore mink stoles, but now a homeless man holding a sign that says "Homeless & Hungry Please Help" stands on the corner. I reach inside my tote bag for the extra bottle of water I always carry for some homeless person I see, with a five-dollar bill taped to it, and hand it to him.

"Thank you," he whispers, forlornly, ashamed.

"You're welcome," I whisper, too, pat his shoulder, ashamed, too, because neither of us can do anything about this. "Truly, I live in dark times!" Bertolt Brecht said in 1936. What would Brecht and those 1960s' ladies with their picket signs, those decent, disgruntled, ancient go-go girl-hating H.A.D.I.T.S. (Housewives Against Decadence In This Society) think of this, all this homelessness? Their granddaughters should be here, renamed Humanity Against Dire In This Society, with bullhorns and cell phones and palm-held cameras to show and tell the world. Make dire stop. Now.

Across the street is the building where the fanciest restaurant in town, The Victor Hugo Inn, established in 1935, served such fine French cuisine, the menus were in French. The snooty tuxedoed waiters spoke French, as did the maître d' who, officious and bossy as a French gendarme, made men wear a jacket and tie to get in. Crazy Ted wore a brown, too-short wool herringbone suit with a brown bow-tie the color of poop that scorching July heat-wave night in 1966 he took Linda Alura and me there for steak and lobster after he promised to buy us Dom Perignon. Glumly, a bit terrified, we sat there staring at the bulge in Crazy Ted's breast pocket; we'd never before sipped champagne in the presence of a loaded gun, a 45, and we hoped we never would again.

I attended Dick Dale's wedding reception held here in 1968 when he married that beautiful Hawaiian girl. A huge buffet table held silver bowls of Beluga caviar. Annette Funicello was there, sat all alone, looking sad, over there where a beautiful bougainvillea-covered patio used to be. I asked for her autograph, told her I was her biggest fan. Annette smiled; such a beautiful girl with shining, long, black hair.

The last time I dined at the Victor Hugo before it became a disco in 1975, then a punk rock hangout named Toe Jam in the 1980s, was with T.J. DuRong who wore an orange and purple necktie as wide and ugly as road-kill. Don't recall now why I was so mad at T.J. that night, no doubt just enraged by yet another of his do-wrong scofflaw secrets I'd uncovered that made me yell during dessert at him: "To think I once thought the letter A in your Personal Alphabet stood for Assiduous Achiever! Now I know it stands for Atrocious Asshole!" And when he laughed, thinking me hilarious instead of hellacious, I dumped my

267

Maraschino Cherry Charlotte Russe on top of his fuzzy-haired head. As cherries dribbled like blood clots down his face, T.J. DuRong laughed louder, stood up and took a bow, poised as a Shakespearean actor, and flapped his white napkin into the air like a surrender flag, as if we'd rehearsed this 100 times before. Everyone laughed, thinking he was merely trying to tame the shrew, even our snobby French waiter laughed, then shouted: "Vive l'amour!"

Ah, but now that posh old building is now painted purple and it's a popular gay bar. I saw Mick Jakson, my old boss in 1965 at The Fort, who'd morphed into a female impersonator in 2002 and re-named Mikki JaquSin, perform there, do his Cher, Liza, and his showstopper Marilyn Monroe routine, wiggle and jiggle a giddy "Diamonds are a girl's best friend." The Fort—which is only a five miles northwest from where I now stand—is now a greasy muffler shop; was painted pink a decade ago when it was a beauty salon for a while. Next year it'll be a nudie/karaoke/sports bar and painted black fort-like once again. I watched with Mick from The Fort's rooftop the August 12, 1965 L.A. Watts Riots. What a scary night that was listening to the gunfire in the distance, seeing the L.A. sky all lit up red-golden on-fire just like the burning of Atlanta in the old 1939 movie *Gone with the Wind*. Ah, but my old go-go girlfriend Linda Alura did the best Marilyn Monroe imitation I ever saw. Because she looked so much like, and sounded like Marilyn; one of Linda's last attempts at getting into the movies was when she auditioned for a made-for-tv Marilyn bio. They'd wanted her to chop off her long blonde hair and let them bleach it whitish and rat it into a big, stiff, hair-sprayed Doris Day bubble hair-do and she refused.

Oh, dear, my beautiful old go-go girlfriend Linda Alura. I almost forgot. She died two months ago. Linda Alura taught me how to dance in the frying pan in 1966. Just a month away from the first anniversary of the August, 1965, Los Angeles Watts Riots. When she wanted to go see this great, new, not-yet-famous black female soul singer, Aretha Franklin. In Watts. At that groovy nite club, the Maverick, where they played all the latest Soul Sounds that Linda loved to groove to. Wilson Picket's "Mustang Sally" her jukebox pick at La Pink Pantera when she'd hop up on the stage and do her "ride, Sally, ride" moves, her slo-mo Pony steps while she emulated whipping some invisible guy, bumped and humped him, female superior, wrapping her slender torso around the back of the mustang of him, pretending to "ride, ride" him, moves she'd get arrested for obscenity by a vice officer for doing if one were around on the look-out for "crimes." It was against the law—with a $1,000 fine—back then for go-go girls to make such smooth moves to the sexy-easy music like they played there at that Watts night club. For Blacks only. No sign posted on the box office at the Maverick Club said so, but ever since the ferocious fiery riots of a year ago, everyone in L.A. who wasn't stupid or wasn't a cop or wasn't black knew not to hang around this dark part of town where it was so dark at night because the locals shot out the streetlights for the privacy to do what they wanted to do—and the look on the big, strong Nubian Prince Goliath selling tickets to get in, said so. As did the nasty looks in the dark eyes of the cool black night club goers, the groovy dudes and pretty mini-skirted young black chicks who glowered: Get the hell out of Watts, you white bitches. Until Linda Alura whispered up to one of the huge black bouncers, the one a head taller than Goliath. I couldn't hear what Linda said to him, but it made him smile movie star teeth, nod, Yes, Yes, Baby, and gaze down admiringly, respectfully at Linda's beautiful naturally blonde yellow hair that swooped and swayed down to the middle of her backless yellow mini dress and made her look as luscious as a 5-foot-six-inch, 115-pound slice of lemon cream pie, and waved his hand for me to Go ahead, as the red velvet rope was dropped down for me, my freebie entrée into the In Crowd of Black L.A.

I wore a navy blue two-piece Chanel-imitation, staid 4-inch-high tan pumps more suitable for an interview for a job as a stenographer. I didn't look like a go-go girl nor did I move cool and mellow like one; when I danced to my jukebox pick at La Pink Pantera, I did a distraught, writhing motion to the Rolling Stones' "(Can't Get No) Satisfaction" with a lot of Jerks to simulate the effects of my personal excruciating misery because Mr. Amalgamated Bricks was stalking me, but most of all: I didn't like Being a Go-Go Girl the way Linda Alura and some of the other go-go girls did. I was a Square. But Linda put up with me, sang to me when I got on her nerves, affectionately, imitating Elvis Presley: "You're so square — but baby, I don't care."

At the Maverick, Wilson Pickett, James Brown, Ray Charles, Otis Redding soul music wafted from the jukebox inside as I stepped squarely and lively toward the nite club entrance along-side the dapper, cool black guys, beautiful black chicks, their curly hair straightened to pile high into French twists like Diana Ross and the Supremes wore then. In three years, 1969, when Angela Davis becomes their role model, they'll go natural, wear Afros. I dipped my brown, lightly fluffed flip hairdo a schoolteacher might wear in 1966 through the red velvet curtain, but when I looked back for Linda, she was gone. Disappeared. Vanished into the dark black moonless night in the heart of darkness of Watts, Los Angeles, California, USA, where the streetlights have been shot out and I am the only white bitch in this dark huge room where 50 or more cool, black locals sit on capacious-fat, pregnant-plump pillows on the shiny wooden dance floor. Flickering overhead amber lights ogle, and fluorescent

270

wands illuminate the whites of the eyes, the white of teeth of the cool, black people sipping drinks, and the passing joints of marijuana glowing red-golden tips in the dark—every one of the cool blacks giving me evil-eyed looks of Go to Hell. Now, Bitch. And I'm certain for the first time in my life of being a Good Girl for 26 long years, praying now and then when I believed in this or that god, never even having said the curse work Fuck yet, that I actually will go to Hell. Any minute, I will, I was certain of it, because I felt my stomach and my knees droop as if descending into a black hole. And no one ever deserved it more than I did for this pure act of officious stupidity of intermeddling.

Where on this dark, forsaken earth was my go-go girlfriend Linda Alura? Why had she brought me here? No one would allow me to sit on a pillow. So I stood there, a fugitive from a brain drain, folded my arms, diddled with the chain of my handbag, as if admiring the glistening of my self-conscious boredom, held tight to it—I might need identification when I reached the River Styx and needed a boat ride. The busy cocktail waitresses snubbed me. So did the bartender at the jam-packed bar when I asked for a plain soda with three maraschino cherries. Couldn't leave the place because the doors were closed and two big black guys leaned against them, doorstops. A young guy, obviously gay, but I didn't know that then because I didn't know anything yet about gay guys, think when they're acting nice and sweet, they just are emulating a woman to be nice and sweet. He handed me a plain soda with three maraschino cherries and asks: "Where your girlfriend? She's gor-gee-ous!" And he flipped his head around like he had a shawl of yellow blonde hair hanging down his back just like Linda's. Someone whispers to him.

"Oh? Yeah? Wow!" he says, turns back to say to me: "Well, honey, you hanging with a celebrity! Your girlfriend's partying privately with Mr. A!"

"Mr. A? Who's that?"

"Oh, come on, baby, don't play square. YOU know—You read the newspapers, don't you?"

Then: TA DA! Out of a door that looks like it's a closet door comes Aretha Franklin and some musicians. The room fills with the thunder of cheers, clapping, whistles, and Aretha Franklin wastes no time making this night—though Linda Alura nearly ruins it—one of the best nights of my life—when Aretha zaps right up to that microphone and beings singing a song I'd never head before but will become my personal anthem for the rest of my life: "Respect." After a half hour of belting out her swinging soul sounds, Aretha waved everyone to get up to dance and they all packed together on the small dance floor. Gay Guy grabbed me and strutted his stuff—best dancing man I'd ever danced with—and ever would. Gay Guy did the James Brown, slid a slick Moonwalk, the Alligator, Mashed Potato, the—I didn't even know the dance names of most of those moves.

"Come on, girl, DO it, too!"

And I tried. Like the words to the Rolling Stones' "Satisfaction"—I tried and I tried. Gay Guy yelled at me:

"Is you black, honey? You move smooth. I know you got some black blood. Just a little bit? White girls don't move smooth like you. And I see you got some fuzz hair around your neck—"

He twisted one of my curls. He's the first person to ever notice that, yes, I do have black blood. Just a little bit. My mother's father's mother's father was black—born in New Orleans, long ago. But I figured Gay Guy was just trying to treat me nice; make me feel part of the in crowd. I nodded, Yes, I got black blood, a little bit, from my great-grandmother, and he smiled big, put his hands on my hips, jiggled them a certain way, and I could do it. Dancing's not hard if someone shows you how. He pointed down at his feet, did his cool-move steps slow-motion so I could emulate. Try real hard to "get on up," be a jive machine in a land of a thousand dances. I don't know my great-grandmother's name. But I know she died beneath a pecan tree someplace in Texas. My mother inherited her same deadly illness and died in a hospital bed. I inherited that illness, too. Where will I die? Gay Guy speeds up his foot action, I try harder.

"Fine, honey, fine. But you still got some square moves. You hold your hands up in the air like you're calling time out at a football game. You gotta watch what you do if you wanna dance cool, dance smooth and fine in the frying pan. See, honey, when the beat goes fast and you can't go fast, too, you listen for the downbeat—hear it? Don't never wanna go faster than you can go fast in the frying pan, you'll look dumb—and square—and you'll get all burned up."

I never even had a priest talk to me this earnestly about do-good Life even when I was converting to Catholicism. Gay Guy showed me how to shake my tail feather, let my backbone slip, turn my body all around, put my hands on my hips, honey, and shake it like a bowl of soup.

"Good, honey, you lookin' good." I never even had a guy in love with me bend my ear with sexy grit like this. I shook all over just like Ray Charles told Aretha Franklin to tell me to do. Respect. Respect. R-E-S-P-E-C-T. And, wow, how thrilling it would've been to know that night Aretha's rendezvous with destiny in 2009 when she will sing "America" at the inauguration of the first Black President of the United States of America, Barack Obama.

After the show, two-thirty in the dark morning, outside the night club, the moon peeked just a tip of its big white hat to the west of us as it disappeared down the black alley behind some dumpsters. By now the black chicks and dudes had warmed up to me. After all, we all had much in common now. Music our common denominator, our unifier as equal listeners, enjoyers, admirers and witnesses of a perfect, harmonious absolute Ten Commandment-credo of respect, respect, respect, when we'd all shared a magnificent moment in this special time of our lives. And I bet you that still, to this very day, they remember, too, just like I do, that night of Aretha Franklin when she was brand new, not-yet famous, and how in two weeks when her "Respect" is aired on national radio, it'll be Number One of the charts for months. Respect in 1966 what we all needed while young guys were shipping out for Vietnam. Respect while everyone mourned over JFK, stiff and afraid of Tomorrow which was going to get worse and worse. Respect while everyone so tense that summer of 1966, feeling the world gearing up for some great expectation which is always a surprise, sometimes unbearably gruesome — but never what's expected. Never, never is latent knowledge ever crystallized.

When Gay Guy waves goodbye to me, so do a bunch of his friends. One black girl even smiles at me. I feel SO good, to quote James Brown. I feel so black. And almost beautiful. I smiled back, waved, and soon everyone was gone. Just me standing there. Maybe the Beatles would see me Standing There and wanna hold my hand. I found Linda's yellow Mustang easily. The only car parked on the street for blocks and blocks. Thank god she left the doors unlocked. I got inside, felt so tired, worried about my kids: What would my babysitter think? I'd never stayed out this late in my life, except when I worked the night shift at The Fort a year ago. Really. That's how square I was.

I sighed. Wondered what would become of me, there, on the River Styx, waiting for the boat. An hour went by but it felt like 20 when finally I saw the yellow glow of Linda Alura's golden aura walking out of the darkness toward me and her Mustang. A ray of twilight lit up her dark companion who was dressed in black. "Mr. A," I surmised. God, he was gorgeous. Looked like a movie star. No. He looked like that Black Panther guy I saw on the front page of the L.A. newspapers who got arrested last month accused of doing something horrible, killing a cop or something worse they send you to a bad-ass maximum security prison for doing. He's accused of being the alleged head of the L.A. Black Panthers. And I don't remember his name. Arnold? Adam? Albert? *And* he's a fugitive at large! He escaped from the L.A. County Jail just last week and there's a $10,000 reward on his head! A few feet away from the yellow Mustang, Mr. A lifted yellow-golden Linda Alura up on her feet and kissed her lusciously, gentlemanly, as he'd spoon Maraschino cherries and whipped cream from a Charlotte Russe in a snobby French restaurant. She wrapped her arms around his neck like he was the best thing she'd ever had. And she never wanted him to go away. When he walked away, she stood there watching the back of him till he'd gone, disappeared into the ash-gray twilight of a newborn August day that would bring scorching sunlight in just an hour.

"You're still here?" Linda said, astonished to see me. She wiped tears from her eyes.

"Where would I go?"

"Take a taxi? Maybe take off with some groovy guy you picked up to take you home."

She cared not one whit about me, nor what happened to me, as she sighed, thinking only of herself. She smiled that contented kitten look she always got when her lips curled in the corners. I'd never seen her so happy and never would see her that happy ever again. She lit up a joint of marijuana, inhaled, and held it deep in her chest like prayer.

"Wow," she whispered. "What a night."

I'm too tired to speak. Hurt, too, that she'd leave me like that in unchartered territory, abandon me on that desert island. I felt betrayed and someday, when we're older, are both grandmothers, been friends for 26 years and her yellow hair has turned silver-white but is even more beautiful because it looks like virgin snow in winter sunlight, drinking with her a second bottle of Dom Perignon, both of us drunk, I'll become super-pissed-off when I remember that night and say very loudly, "Fuck! You betrayed me! You left me all by myself! I could've been killed, knifed by those irate blacks! Just days before the first anniversary of the 1965 L.A. Riots, everyone in L.A. all up tight, shook up, and worried about a new uprising!"

"A riot is the voice of the unheard, said Martin Luther King, Jr.," Linda Alura will say, calmly, sagely as a saint.

"You abandoned me! Imperiled me while you cavorted and consorted and coitus'd with a known criminal! A fugitive at large! Fuck!"

"Oh, mellow out. He was innocent. Being framed for some Watts Riots conspiracy thing he didn't do. Why do you care? You got to see the great Aretha Franklin. Those black kids were some really cool cats. Besides, you were in far more danger from that brute, your ex-husband—a white man—who was going to try to kill you in just days." Yes, he finally did to me what he'd been saying he'd do to me on August 16, 1966. Whereas the Watts Riots first anniversary passed by quietly and peacefully. "You probably had one of the most fun nights of your life with Aretha and those cool kids. While I had the best night of my life, too. Ah, Mr. A— What a man." She will sigh, deeply. "What a lover. Best I ever had. He moved and grooved over me like melted butter. Made my skin feel like it glowed alabaster in the

276

moonlight as he placed his panther hand on my breast. Wow. I still feel him over me whenever I think about it. Remembering that night helps me sleep nights I can't sleep. He called me his baby, his own baby. I love to be called baby."

I asked her again, in 1990, just like I asked her in 1966: "Will be still be friends when we're old?" She didn't answer; she just rolled herself another joint of marijuana and poured us the last fizzy drops from the second bottle of Dom Perignon. And now Linda Alura's dead. And no, we weren't friends when we were old. We hadn't spoken since 2003 when we met for beer and liverwurst sandwiches on rye on my 63rd birthday at Joe Jost's pool hall three miles northeast from where I stand right now. Linda, at age 59, still so beautiful and alluring, she got away with smoking a cigarette though public smoking had been banned years ago—the young, smiling bartender even bringing her an ashtray. And, as she told me how Sammy was still hiding out from the IRS, FBI—and the Mafia—and what a fine daughter Belinda was, and how cute her granddaughter was, she blew smoke in my face—just like always—and called me Baby.

"Baby," is what Linda Alura said to me that August 16, 1966, night when she knelt at my side where I lay on the floor, semi-conscious, and naked after Othello did what he did. She helped me back into the nightgown he'd yanked off me, covering up my cuts, bruises, and bloody parts, so very careful not to hurt me more than I'd been hurt already. "Baby, everything is going to be okay," she whispered to me, gently as she would a baby, her own baby, her voice deep and husky like a Lauren Bacall.

"Baby, baby—" sweet beautiful Linda Alura cooed, as she lifted me to my feet, the police not helping, not caring, just glowering at me disgustedly, wondering what rotten

277

stuff I'd done to that guy to make me deserve this, cause him to do what he did. Linda's presence was redeeming sustenance, my Golden Chalice in that Asunderland, her resonant, reassuring deep voice the voice you want to hear, need to hear, to bring you back from the brink, dancing in the frying pan, standing in line at the River Styx, and Linda did.

Back at the record store, the June First late afternoon fog rolling back in, at last the end of the line is near the entrance door. The almost-old guy and my Poet Husband, my Good Husband, are silent now, each adoring Doors fan deep into the songs and music of their own personal reverie about The Doors. Good Husband—and I thank god one more time for this Good Husband—doesn't even seem to notice that I've been gone, busy with reveries of my own.

Now Densmore's just feet away. Now inches. And *TA DA!* We're next! And when we meet him, he smiles glad-to-see-ya at us, shakes our hands, signs my poet husband's Doors stuff: Densmore's memoir, *The Doors: Unhinged,* an old Doors LP, two CDs, and finally I get to tell John Densmore my little gleeful Tale of The Doors:

"I once danced live to you guys back in 1966, June, when you guys played at Whisky a Go-Go and I auditioned for a job as a go-go girl."

I wait for him to be amazed by the fact that here I am, me, this ancient thing, yes, ancient me, I was once a real, live go-go girl. And here I am after waiting in line for two hours. Here I am, at last beside him, smiling at him, 46 years later, on Marilyn Monroe's 87th birthday!

"And I got hired for the go-go girl job!" I add.

Then I place my hand on John Densmore's shoulder and wait, wait breathlessly, for him to speak. But John Densmore, Rock Star Messiah, drummer for The Doors of yore, doesn't say anything to me.

All John Densmore does is look at me, and then give me a great, big, sweet, silent smile.

Turned out okay. A year and threesome weeks from then, I'll luck out and get an invite to a CD launch party for the L.A. jazz poet Michael C Ford in Venice, California, just two blocks from the apartment building where Jim Morrison lived up on the rooftop in 1965, at Hen House Studios where the remaining Doors, John Densmore and guitarist Robby Krieger will play back up to Michael C's jazz poetry reading and I'll get a chance to actually talk to Densmore again and this time, maybe, get a response. Ah, but Densmore won't be there that night because he'll be in the hospital that night after an emergency appendicitis. So I plan on telling my Ancient Go-Go Girl Tale to Robby Krieger.

What cool cats are there: young and old adoring Doors' fans, friends, and family. And for sure, I'm the most ancient of them all, old enough to be their grandmother, some of them. Drinks are on the house, Hen House Studios, that is. A taco wagon. Night comes, and at last Michael C reads his cool-fine jazz poetry, Robby Krieger and some other cool musicians, including a saxophone, backing him up. After Michael C's provocative-poetic, show-stopping epiphanies, Krieger steps forward for a solo, then he and the guys in the band work it on out together, and blast out some groovy new compositions intertwining shadowy refrains of old Doors' tunes. I'm sure I hear Come on baby, light my fie-yarrr several times, but maybe I only imagine it. All the cool people there who can dance, dance, especially the beautiful young women, wearing black, some black leather, their shapely bottoms, brimming bosoms shaking and quaking, moving groovy, smiting all their dire as they get higher to the modern rock sounds as unrecognizable to me now as the Doors were to me in 1967's Summer of Love. This Summer of Un-Love, 2014, will be a scary one of much dire, drudge, drought, Drones, and dread: more so than ever before, each year bad stuff kicking up tons of new ugly dust, as the world becomes too, too much with us and sticks like tar in our craw. Bloody wars rage world-wide dynamite, race riots after an innocent black boy is shot six times by racist white police. Homelessness. Hunger. Ebola, AIDS, Malaria, Cholera. Pandemic Madness. And terrifying Global Warming.

But this groovy, cool and smooth night, 26 days after Marilyn Monroe's 88th birthday, will be THE best time I will ever have in my life when I dance for the first time in decades, and let my backbone slip one more time, get on up, get down, shake my bowl of soup, in the loop, loosey-goosey, letting it all hang out with these beautiful, loving-it-madly L.A. Women, these young babes, these Doors groupies like suddenly I've become, too! A Doors Groupie: Yes! Factotum: No! I dance tonight because I want to dance.

My, how times keep on a-changin' as about 50 or more of us guests stand side-by-side on the wooden floor around the small stage, a Magic Circle of Doors adorers, some of us hip-shaking Mamas, merrymaking Maenads, enthralled by the deity of gaiety, turning it loose, be-bop-a-lula jive crazy rock 'n' rolling soul sisters crossing the Grand Canyon-wide Generation Gap from Then to Now and Always to walk down Groupieville's Funky Broadway. A beautiful blonde hands me a joint of marijuana. I pretend to take a big suck, pretend to inhale deeply. I don't want her to know I'm a square. Not that she'd care.

"Jim! Jim!" another beautiful blonde cries out. "Jim LIVES! Feel Jim?" she asks me, and I smile at her, nod, and she smiles at me, and we dance together, butt-boogie-bump hips, her black leather against my ankle-length strapless summer dress. I feel myself forgive Jim Morrison for that long, long version of "Light My Fire" I had to dance to, dance to, and dance to that dreary 1967 August afternoon I almost fell off the stage. Jim Morrison's ghost has finally smited my dire, lit my fire! And maybe Morrison's ghost really does dance with us. After all, Jim once lived on a rooftop just blocks from this Hen House Studio.

The music's great! And then it ends. Krieger and his bandmates and jazz poet Michael C take bows, smile big, truly appreciating the crowd's wows and applause, as I come to the end, one more time, of another chapter of my surreal, terpsichoreal life. My Glotessey of simple, emblematic, idiosyncratic, but true life tales which, if published in about 50 percent of the world where women are required by law to veil their faces, cover their heads, cloak their bodies so as not to offend angry misogynist gods and arouse the lust of men, would get me sentenced to 1,000 lashes or death by stoning or beheading.

We all crowd around Robby Krieger and Michael C Ford when they hop off the stage to sign CDs. I wait my turn, inch forward toward Michael C and Krieger, practice a sweet smile, rehearse in my head what I'm going to say to Robby Krieger when I tell him my Ancient Go-Go Girl Tale. I decide not to wallow in the mire and tell him how I'd thought Jim Morrison was a stoned hippie who'd wandered off Sunset Boulevard into Whisky's and hopped onto the stage that night I danced to The Doors so long ago. Nor will I mention how hard it was to dance to Jim that night he mumbled into the microphone, nearly incoherently. Self-righteous convert, I'll tell Krieger how much I'd *loved* dancing to The Doors that night, how they'd lit my fire, how I couldn't've ever gotten so much higher, and how I've been a big fan all these years, not just of Jim's, but of John Densmore's drums, and him and his fine guitar.

Ah! Only one fan's ahead of me now. And at last it's my turn next, when Good Poet Husband taps my shoulder and says:

"Jane, Jane, let's go. I'm tired. It's a long drive home."

"But—"I mutter to him.

But he looks so tired. I feel silly making him wait while I, being a silly groupie, wait to tell Robby Krieger something stupid. It's always a long trip back home in the dark. Good Poet Husband's nearly ancient now, too. He works long hours standing on concrete as a machinist, bending and carving steel with his bare hands.

"Please, Jane. I'm really tired. Please, let's go."

So I turn away from the rock star messiah, take my benevolent husband's hand, and we go.

What work it is being young, crystallizing latent knowledge, trying to pull ourselves together while stepping lively to step and fetch it, hopping on and off that fateful

282

chronological train taking you to places to dance in the frying pan you know not where, nor know how long it will take you to get there.

What work it is being old, packing up all that baggage over and over again to go-go and go-go to the next stop ahead, far out, far out, and out of sight.

At least the ticket to ride is free.

Lucky us.

JOAN JOBE SMITH, pronounced Dead Before Birth, due to a difficult 37-hour labor, was born alive—and laughing—three weeks early, feet first in Paris, Texas, January 25, 1940, during a Norther, four months and two weeks before the Nazi invasion of Paris, France. After working seven years during the 1960s-1970s as a go-go girl/freelance dancer/barmaid/bartender in various Southern California go-go night clubs, she went back to college in 1972 for the knowledge, receiving an Associate of Arts Degree from Golden West College, Bachelor of Arts from California State University Long Beach, spent one year in law school, and in 1979 was awarded her Master of Fine Arts in Fiction Writing from the University of California Irvine. Founding editor in 1974 of *Pearl* magazine (named for her mother Margaret and Janis Joplin) and in 2001 *The Bukowski Review*, her award-winning poetry, prose, art, cooking columns, have been published internationally in more than 1000 anthologies, literary journals, newspapers, billboards, and collected in 25 books. Bloomsday, 1990, she married poet Fred Voss and lives in Long Beach, California, USA. She is the mother of three, grandmother of eight, and great-grandmother of four great-grandsons and two great-granddaughters.

The original 1974 draft of her *Tales of An Ancient Go-Go Girl*, a 40-page chapbook of narrative poems and episodic prose, was read and lauded by her then-mentor and friend, Charles Bukowski, who told her to retitle it *The Crotchwatchers* because she wasn't ancient—yet. Rejected as her proposed thesis at UCI, *Tales* were abandoned until 2003 when they were restyled and extended as narrative memoir—a "Glotessey"—completed in 2004—until 2014 when Chapter 12 was composed for inclusion, and concluded 40 years later, September 14, at 1:37 pm when Joan Jobe Smith had become—irrefutably—Ancient—with more so to come.

Joan Jobe Smith @ Skylight Books,
Hollywood, California, 2013.
Photo by Elaine King.

The events depicted upon these
pages are all true. Only names
have been changed
of some of the real people and places—sometimes
for the fun of it, sometimes to soothe
the stun of it.

—JJS

The **"Flying Morrison"**— a mural created from the July 15, 1967,
photo by Jim Coke (www.JimCoke.com) of The Doors' Jim
Morrison @ L.A.'s first rock festival, the Fantasy Faire, Devonshire
Downs, Northridge, California—2 weeks before The Doors' "Light
My Fire" became #1 hit. On July 8, 2014, 48 years after dancing
live, June, 1966, to The Doors @ Whisky a Go-Go, Joan Jobe Smith
recalls slow-mo shadow memories as she leans against the west-
facing wall display of the "Flying Morrison" @ 425 East 4th Street,
Long Beach, California, 90802, USA.

Made in the USA
Charleston, SC
23 January 2015